PASSION FOR DISTANCE

the story of my 100 marathons

Julia Thorn

M
MELBOURNE BOOKS

Published by Melbourne Books
Level 9, 100 Collins Street,
Melbourne, VIC, 3000
Australia

www.melbournebooks.com.au
info@melbournebooks.com.au

National Library of Australia
Cataloguing-in-Publication entry:

Author: Thorn, Julia.

Title: Passion for Distance:
The Story of My 100 Marathons

ISBN: 9781877096587 (pbk.)

Subjects: Thorn, Julia.
Marathon running.
Runners (Sports)—Australia—Biography.
Women runners—Australia—Biography.
Marathon running—Records.
Dewey Number: 796.4252092

Printed in Singapore by KHL Printing Co. Pte Ltd

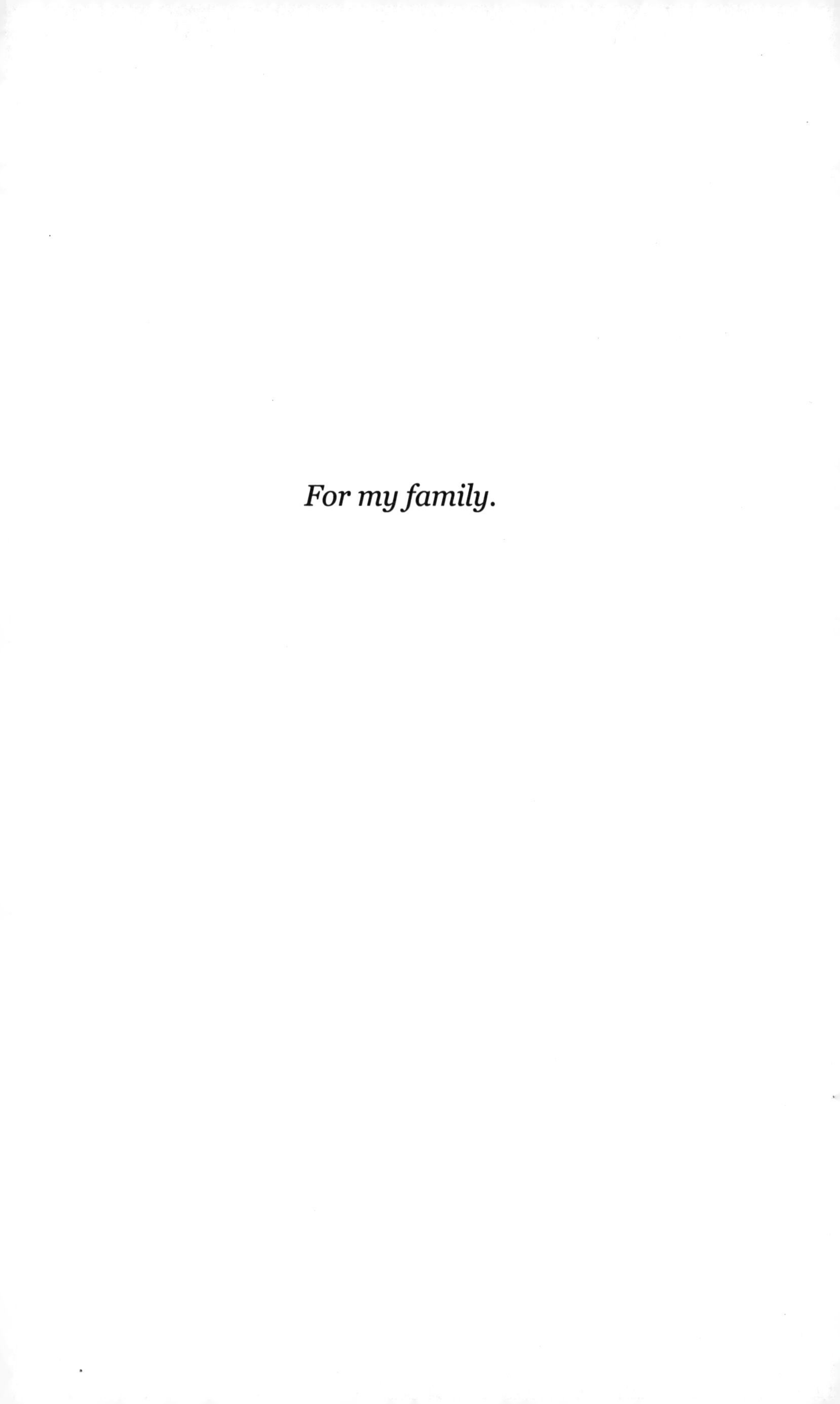

For my family.

Introduction

A marathon is a 42.195-kilometre running race, a hard physical feat of endurance. Just hearing the word conjures up challenge and difficulty. Many people dream of having a go. Thousands have already tried it. Few people have run a hundred.

One day, like many folk seeking a personal challenge, I decided to try to run a marathon — just to see if I could do it. I never thought beyond running that one. I certainly never set out to run a hundred of them. What a joke! All I set myself to do was to complete this one marathon, and then I would have done something I could be proud of all my life.

My day at the Rotorua Marathon in New Zealand — 3 May 1997 — was a success. Over the next few years I ran other marathons. It didn't take me long to work out that I treasure everything about the 42.2-kilometre marathon experience. I enjoy the intense planning and preparation I know I have to go through every time I attempt this demanding task. I love the carnival atmosphere that envelops the larger events and I appreciate the beauty of the scenery at the smaller races. I earn memories that will last forever. And I cherish the sensation of being completely spent after achieving the day's goal of finishing the marathon.

The marathon presents a conundrum that keeps me enthralled: the race is painfully hard, but the whole process of preparation, execution and recovery gives me the greatest satisfaction. I have never lost the thrill of turning up and facing the challenge. I have never failed to get caught up in the excitement that precedes all running races, but especially the longer ones: that mixture of expectation, hope and fear. Every finish is as gratifying as the very first; it is never, ever, just another marathon finish. Even after so many successful finishes I have never lost the day-before nerves, and continue to worry that I might have forgotten how to run or that I might disappoint myself.

Running a marathon is one thing, but the pattern I have eventually settled for — running a great many of these 42.2-kilometre races each year — is quite another matter. Where one marathon per year felt good, five — or 15 — a year felt even better. I had discovered a secret: the more marathons I ran, the happier I became. On 1 May 2010 I ran my hundredth marathon. It took me nine years to reach my 50th marathon and only four more to reach the hundredth. I am the first and only Australian female to have run a hundred marathons.

I hadn't been running marathons for long when I observed that my intention to run marathon after marathon went against the grain. I understood from reading about marathon running that, just occasionally, it would be okay to run two marathons with only a month off in between, but you need 13 weeks for a marathon build-up and to spend less time preparing is foolhardy. Luckily for me, I started to meet other runners who were running marathons frequently and I hung on to their words instead. I gained the confidence to run and participate my way. I set my own goals. I listened to my own body. I learnt from my own experiences.

My quest to run marathons has taken me to far-flung places and given me sensational experiences. I have run along rural roads in Thailand lit by candles on a humid evening. I have been able to run across the Auckland Harbour Bridge on the only day in the year it was open to pedestrians. I have run through the marathon tunnel into the Olympic stadium in both Sydney and Stockholm. I have run through Hollywood and through Tokyo's Ginza. I have paused during a marathon in outback South Australia for a steam train to cross my path. I have run with only two other competitors on Christmas Island, and with a crowd of 40,000 competitors in New York. I have run in a Chicago heatwave and in a hailstorm in Norway.

I have had good marathons and bad marathons. It is always easier to sign up for the next marathon after a good one. When I am running several marathons in quick succession I always make sure the first one has the best possible chance of going well on the day. But if there is one thing I have gathered from doing so many, it is that no marathon has to be really unpleasant; it is what you make of it. Sure, there is that awful thing that marathoners call 'The Wall', but you don't have to find it. And if you do find it — well, cheer up because there will always be a better day. I told a marathoner friend the other day that my 60th marathon was my worst. His response was, 'By that time you had run so many you should have had it all sorted out.' I learnt some lessons from that race but I am sure there are still mistakes waiting for me.

The price I have paid in running so many marathons has been a loss of speed. Speed and volume do not sit well together in the long term. I will never run as fast as I used to and it has taken me a while to come to terms with this. I always try as hard as I can at every marathon, because part of the appeal is that I am running against the clock, but I have become a slower runner. I console myself that my times can't always live up to people's expectations. When I tell a non-runner that I have run a marathon, they often latch onto the one aspect of the event they feel comfortable to enquire about, and ask: 'What was your time?' I am happy to tell anyone my race times. The problem is that when the only marathon your companion has heard of took place at the Olympics, their perception of how long it takes to run a marathon is going to be skewed to the faster end of the spectrum. From their TV viewing, many people know that a marathon takes around two hours to complete. So my four hours and change is not going to sound too flashy, even when in many overseas races it puts me in the top half of the field.

Basically, I have swapped one skill for another: I can no longer run fast but I can run frequently without injury or loss of motivation. I can pace myself to finish what I have started, and finish in reasonable comfort. I finish in such comfort that I can already be contemplating the next marathon as I leave, and in sufficiently good repair that friends who see me afterwards cannot believe I have just run that distance.

I have been asked lots of questions over the years. My knees have elicited many enquiries. My knees have never troubled me. But every runner succumbs to injury eventually. With a mixture of good fortune and looking after myself, I have avoided too much of this. Nevertheless, I have twice had breaks from running with foot problems. The first, a neuroma which caused constant burning sensations on the sole of my foot, was resolved with surgery and three months' recovery time in 1998, when I was able to ride my bike instead of running. The second, a stress fracture in 2007, was resolved with rest and ten weeks of water exercise in place of running. I also get minor muscle aches and pains — niggles, as runners choose to call them — but I regard these as the price I pay for being a runner and I expect to bounce back within a few days.

Another question is to name my favourite marathon. It would have to be the New York City Marathon. The original 'people's marathon' is still the best to this day. The hype and hoopla surrounding the event, both before the race and during it, have to be seen to be believed. On top of this I had a magic race day there when everything went well.

I am also often asked how long my next marathon is going to be. I laugh inwardly at this question. Recently a friend introduced me to her neighbour, saying, 'Julia runs marathons.' 'And how long, approximately, would those runs be?' enquired the neighbour. To me one of the special things about the marathon is that it is a very specific beast. In this aspect it is unique in the sporting world. It is 42.195 kilometres long and always will be. But I never say that; I just say 'Oh, about 42 kilometres' and wait for the reaction.

All the marathons in my hundred have been the specific standard marathon distance as laid down by the International Amateur Athletic Federation in May 1921, at 26 miles, 385 yards — known metrically as 42.195 kilometres. In the vernacular we abbreviate this to '42.2' or '26.2'. (You'll notice that in my descriptions of marathons I have talked in kilometres where the course was set in kilometres and I have talked in miles where the course was set in miles, as in the US and the UK.) They have all been official races. This means they were open to the public and featured — as a minimum — a timekeeper, a measured course, an entry fee and precise registration procedures, a mass start at a specified time, aid stations on the course, published results, and the intention to be an annual event. I emphasise all these aspects of an official marathon since it is a very different proposition to run a marathon as a race, as opposed to going for a 42.2-kilometre jog with a group of mates.

I have also run several races that were called 'marathons' but which were of a different distance, usually longer. These do not form part of my hundred.

But the question I like best is more fundamental. I like to be asked how I started running. I was not always a runner. I come from a family with no interest in sports. We never attended matches, never watched sports on the TV and, apart from listening to a Wimbledon final on someone's car radio while hitch-hiking one summer, I have no recollection of any exposure to competitive sports in my early life. I am safe in saying that I would never have come across the notion of a marathon until I was in my 20s. I did not deliberately avoid sports; I simply didn't come across any. I used to go for walks from time to time and that was about it.

Growing up, I saw myself as one of the people least likely to achieve anything in the athletic sphere. I have never regarded myself as having any natural athletic ability. At my high school in England we had a challenge in Physical Education one summer to run a mile on the sports fields, which meant running five laps around the edge. After I had finished my fourth lap I knew beyond all shadow of doubt that I could not run another inch, so I lied to the teacher that I had run five laps. Thank goodness we did not have electronic lap scoring, so my lie was never exposed.

Then in my final term at university I decided to go for a jog early one morning around a sports oval where I knew there was a measured mile course; I just wanted to see if I could do it. I couldn't make it. I was so exhausted I had to give up after a few hundred yards and was just glad that nobody I knew had seen me in that state. By that stage I had joined the university badminton club so I was playing one sport regularly.

As things transpired, it was bike riding that led me to running. On a whim I went out and bought a bike when I started working in London. I intended to use it on weekends, but I soon found that commuting to work by bike was quicker than taking public transport. I discovered it was far more fun than taking the train and my riding became a talking point among my peers.

So I got fit on my bike. I don't think I appreciated at the time just how fit I had become compared to my younger years. I brought this fitness with me to Australia, when I immigrated to Sydney with my husband Denis in 1983. I maintained a high level of fitness through long-distance bike riding, usually spending weekends riding in the New South Wales Southern Highlands or in the Blue Mountains. Looking back, I can see that this is when I last came to realise I was motivated to exercise by the possibility of the endurance feats I could attempt.

In 1988, at the age of 30, I packed in my job as an accountant. Not only was I unhappy with my career; I also harboured a deep-seated desire to try a really long bike ride, and I would never have been able to get enough leave from work to manage this. With Denis's blessing I cycled from Lands End to John O'Groats in the UK, then from Oslo to North Cape in Norway and back down through Finland. I planned and executed this trip alone. This took me the best part of three months and I thoroughly enjoyed it.

While I was away Denis started running and completed the iconic City to Surf race in Sydney. When I came home I demanded to see some proof that he was now a runner so he took me for a jog in Centennial Park. It was ten years since I had last tried running and I never imagined it could be for me, but as I was already fit I found that I could run without great discomfort. I didn't have the disasters I had experienced before. I fell in love with the simplicity of running. No equipment; just me and the road, or trail, or beach. I can't explain the attraction any other way. I don't find running any easier than the next person — I have been told I have poor biomechanics and should have settled for a different pastime. But I have persevered, and my life will be poorer the moment I cease doing this.

The two of us did a few ten-kilometre races, and then it wasn't long before we attempted a half marathon together: in Sydney on Anzac Day 1989. It went well so we tried another one soon after, this time in Canberra.

I gradually became less interested in bike riding, but not before I went on one last long road ride across Australia, from Townsville to Broome via Darwin and Kakadu National Park, over a six-week period. I had only been running for a year at that stage so I didn't miss not doing any while I was away. When I came home I put my cycling behind me and concentrated on running. We moved to Brisbane not long afterwards and started a family. I always intended to resume running when the children were older, but marathon running was not yet on my radar.

I never went back to accounting. Instead I tried my hand at writing, first working at a cycling magazine, also writing several bike-touring guidebooks, and then freelancing on running, swimming and bike riding for various publications. This turned out to be a convenient career switch when we started our family, as I could work from home and could adapt easily when we moved cities several times. I intended to be a full-time mum for my kids, and I never envisaged the amount of travelling I would be doing once they were older.

In recent years I have been back to England and I sometimes visit the city where I went to university. I always make a point of going for a run there, just to savour the feeling. I like to run the mile of trail that I had been unable to complete back in my university days. Sometimes I remember earlier times and I have daydreams about bumping into my school sports teachers and telling them that I have become a marathon runner, just to see the shock on their faces.

I do not see myself as an athlete. I don't train rigorously. I don't compete for prize money. I am merely undertaking personal challenges to enrich my life. I am enjoying myself.

Let me show you how priceless these marathons have been.

Initiation

Why get into this in the first place? Marathons are gruelling. You don't actually have to run to know this. You hear about 40,000 people entering the New York City Marathon or 35,000 people running the London Marathon and it sounds as though there can't be many folk who do not run marathons. Was this something that I too could try?

It was a challenge. But unlike contemplating a hike up Mount Everest, I saw it as a challenge I would very likely be able to complete. In hindsight I was quite naïve. I didn't realise how often marathon runners get injured, or the importance of good hydration, or that the advice in training manuals does not apply to everybody. I went into this with my eyes half-closed.

We — being myself, Denis and two children aged six months and three years — had moved to Auckland, New Zealand, from Brisbane at the beginning of 1994 in connection with Denis's work. We knew nobody in Auckland and I worked hard at making acquaintances through my children's playgroups, but it was a lonely and frustrating time.

I used to jog a little, maybe half an hour two or three times a week. It was important to me to have this physical outlet, giving me the so-called 'me time' that new mothers often speak of. I always came home invigorated, with my head cleared of the fog caused by all those sleepless nights. I dreamed of getting back to running bigger distances but knew it would not happen for a while, with the constraints of young children and perpetual tiredness. At this time in my life even a half marathon sounded like an insurmountable challenge.

Then one day in February 1994 Denis said to me, 'I've found something for you to do,' and showed me a flyer for the upcoming 25th Rotorua Marathon that April. I have to admit that for about five seconds I contemplated running this marathon, but quickly came back to reality with a thud and indeed failed to believe that anyone could ever run that far. By that stage I knew how long a marathon was, since I had run half the distance a couple of times, but I had not yet met anyone who had run a whole 42.2. Nevertheless, the seed had been sown.

Time passed and in 1995 my third child was born. Our family was complete and I turned my thoughts to taking my running more seriously. In early 1996 the idea of tackling the Rotorua Marathon briefly crossed my mind, but my plans and hopes were dashed when I pulled a calf muscle at the gym where I occasionally worked out. A week later I had another accident, probably brought on by my limping with a sore leg: I tripped while carrying both my baby and my toddler at the same time. I pulled a muscle in my back and was banned from any sporting activity for three months.

I used to have a babysitter come to the house once a week to help with my baby, and towards the end of the three months I did sneak out and go for a half-hour run on a few occasions. I found that this helped me feel looser so I judged it to be a good thing despite the doctor's orders to rest. Also, it was extremely enjoyable. At this point I committed myself, in my own mind, to running the Rotorua Marathon the following year. I was soon able to start preparing.

Most of the time I ran alone because I had to be so flexible about when I could fit the run in with childcare, but I sometimes ran with a small group from the gym, which had a crèche. We ran a route near the gym that went in the bush and was mostly on dirt tracks. In October 1996 our group ran the Auckland Half Marathon, and I remember watching some of the runners who had run the full marathon (taking place at the same time) arrive at the finish line. What I noticed the most was the sense of achievement on their faces. I thought I would like to feel that.

I continued after that race to train for the marathon in Rotorua, the only one of our group with this goal. I didn't follow a training program, but I had a rough idea how much running I needed to do in the lead-up. I used to drop off my four-year-old at kindergarten, and if things worked out I could leave my 18-month-old at a crèche at the same time and hit the road for an hour or so. I would run along the waterfront from St Heliers to Mission Bay in Auckland, and this has to be one of the loveliest places in the world to run: views across the water to Rangitoto Island, several big sandy beaches, huge pohutukawa trees along the path and no roads to cross. This used to happen about twice a week, and then I would run on the weekend. I ran about 40 kilometres a week.

I had a loop of 18 kilometres with a few hills which I was able to run several times in my training, but I knew that I had to do more. While we were on a family holiday north of Auckland I decided to tackle a 30-kilometre run on the open road and I ran from our holiday accommodation to the town of Kaitaia. My husband clocked the distance in the car. It seemed an extraordinarily long way to run, and I was not in a hurry to do it again.

Looking back, my training was not really adequate, but ignorance is bliss and I arrived on the start line feeling confident. That unjustified confidence served me well on the day since I had no idea what I was in for. This was just before the days of online running chatter, where newbie runners can glean useful knowledge from more experienced athletes. I had read a few magazine articles, and I had by now watched the marathon at the Olympics and Commonwealth Games on the TV. I also had a friend who had run a few marathons, but she had run at an elite level and trained seriously so her experience was very different from mine.

The Rotorua Marathon, which started with only 12 runners in 1965, is the best attended marathon in the country. If you live in New Zealand and you're looking for a first marathon to run, the chances are that Rotorua will be the one. The marathon course makes one circuit of Lake Rotorua. It's so simple. It's handy that the lake is the size it is, but it's even handier that someone realised this size would translate into a marathon. That was a great moment for New Zealand sport. The route is beside the water for a long way. The roads are closed to traffic, and while this is a big race by New Zealand standards the course is never crowded.

This part of New Zealand's North Island has been a hotbed of volcanic activity, with much of the landscape, including many lakes and mountains, being of volcanic origin. Rotorua's lake is in the sunken crater of a volcano that erupted a while back — an estimated 240,000 years ago. Mokoia Island in the centre of this lake, which is apparently not very deep, enhances the overall prettiness.

There are many Maori legends associated with Rotorua. If there's one Kiwi song you recognise it's probably the mournful lament *Pokarekare ana*, whose first line translates as 'Troubled are the waters of Rotorua'. The current words of the song are based on the legend of Hinemoa and Tutanekai: Tutanekai lived on Mokoia Island, and the couple fulfilled their destiny when Hinemoa swam across Lake Rotorua to the island so that they could wed.

You find lots of geothermal activity around town, with naturally heated hot pools, boiling mud pools, geysers and the smell of sulphur which is very noticeable, especially as you arrive in town. I recall driving into town late on the Friday night before the marathon and the smell suddenly hitting. I didn't notice it much while running. That was a good thing because, as with most people, I didn't like it. But while the sulphurous odour hanging in the air may be hated by many, the thermal pools are one of Rotorua's drawcards — especially to tired legs after running a marathon. Most runners would be heading straight for a soak in the hot pools after crossing the finish line, either at their hotel or in one of the public bathing places such as the Blue Baths or the Polynesian Spa (both in the Government Gardens). The race director issued a warning to us not to stay too long in the hot water; once I sat down in the hot pool I realised why such a warning was necessary. It's hard to pull yourself out, and if you don't you can quickly become dehydrated and overheated.

Back in 1997 there was only one distance on race day. You ran a full marathon or you didn't run. No half measures. You could pick an uninformed runner if they asked you whether you were doing the full or the half. If you chose to bail out halfway around the lake you were in for a long swim home. This was one of the attractions of the event — everyone was in it together for the long haul.

The marathon course heads out of town towards the satellite settlement of Ngongotaha, passing the hillside that has become popular for luge riding — you can see the gondola that takes you to the top and there is also a restaurant up there. The road leading to Ngongotaha has a rural feel, green paddocks and a few rustic farmhouses. It's a nice introduction to the course, with nothing too strenuous to work at along there apart from a few light undulations.

You eventually end up at the lake edge. It is this next stage of the marathon that gives the route its reputation as a scenic one. It's delightful

— little beaches, willows, views of the town across the lake. I wanted to go and paddle, but instead I muttered a few words to other runners and thought about the hills ahead.

The marathon is renowned for its hills: two nasty climbs near the halfway mark. It's on these hills that inexperienced runners can lose the plot. I took the first hill nice and easy because I was hearing warning sounds about the next one from the more experienced runners around me. Running hills during a marathon you need to feel positively relaxed, especially when the hills are a long way from the finish. Heartbreak Hill, aptly named by the thousands of runners who have conquered it, comes in the second half after the 25-kilometre point; it is indeed long and heartbreaking.

There is little in the way of enticing scenery after that hill. Actually, it's downright boring, but by this time you are facing your own internal issues and these can demand more attention than the scenery. This is the point in the race where your legs have had enough and you are worried that you will never reach that finish line. Runners joke about the Rotorua airport along here, which seems like a very big airport when it takes so long to run past it. The light industrial area that follows is a dull slog and if you can get your tired legs to work as if functioning on autopilot, so much the better.

I have very vivid memories from that first marathon. Most prominent are the final ten kilometres when I played cat-and-mouse with a portly runner wearing a T-shirt with a slogan on the back: *Don't let the old trout get you down.* I think I took on the role of old trout, especially when I passed him, and it was with much relief that I passed him one final time a few kilometres before the finish. I was tired of reading and rereading that slogan and mentally pulling up the football socks that he wore slumped around his ankles.

Returning to town again was a big thrill. All of a sudden lots of spectators appeared. As a first-time runner I started to understand the enormity of this achievement. I remember promising myself at the 40-kilometre mark that if I got through this I would never have to do it again. I felt empty and exhilarated at the same time. There is no feeling that compares with the endorphin rush you get as you approach the finish of a marathon. My finishing time was 3 hours, 51 minutes, and I thought that was quite fantastic. It was an Olympic medal to me, and while I had felt I could break four hours, really doing so was another thing altogether.

First marathons give moments to treasure. The first marathon experience is like no other run, whatever happens. In some ways my first marathon was unremarkable. I did not end up in hospital having outrun my limits, and I did not win the prize for fastest debut performance; I was somewhere in between. But the marathon was remarkable to me. I took home the pride of succeeding at the challenge I had set myself, while also knowing it was a challenge I would not have contemplated a couple of years earlier.

Within an hour of finishing I was sure I would like to have another go one day. That day came around ten months later, when I took the bus from Auckland to New Plymouth for my second marathon.

By the time I got to the start line of the New Plymouth Marathon in early 1998 I really thought I had this marathon lark sorted out. Fuelled with everyone else's expectations as well as my own, I fully expected to run a far faster time than I had in Rotorua. I had even planned an enthusiastic phone call home to the family to tell them about my fantastic result many days before the event took place. Sadly, I was to find out that there is no certainty about a marathon until it is over. Nice as it may be to dream about fast times and personal bests when you are out on a long and difficult training run, don't count such chickens before they are hatched. After years of marathon experience I have come to see that fast times do happen and personal bests are there for the taking, but only after some real hard work has been done and if absolutely everything goes perfectly on the race day.

The New Plymouth Marathon is described as a downhill run, so it can sound like a doddle if that's how you want to interpret a slight elevation loss while running 42 kilometres. Maybe it was this that led me to have a rather casual approach to my training. Although almost a year had passed since my run at Rotorua, for some reason I did not see a need to run a lot of big distances before this second marathon. My longest training run was 25 kilometres, done once only — something I can get away with now having run so many marathons, but not recommended if you want to get through your major race of the year in a degree of comfort.

The night before the race I simply could not sleep, partly due to nervous anticipation. I realise now this is quite normal. You'd be hard pressed to find a runner who gets a proper night's sleep before a marathon. I lay in bed tossing and turning in panic. I would have been a great deal less panicky if I had planned the details of this trip better. The marathon is held over a point-to-point course. It starts halfway up Mount Taranaki and finishes on the coast at Waitara. The best option is to stay at Bell Block near Waitara and take the runners' bus from Bell Block to the race start on the mountain. When I booked my trip to New Plymouth the most convenient hotels were already full. I had to arrange a taxi from central New Plymouth to Bell Block, where the better organised runners were staying, so I could take the bus with them.

I spent the night worrying. Firstly, I worried whether I would wake up in time for the taxi I had booked; secondly, whether the taxi would come; and thirdly, whether it would take me to the right place. The fridge was noisy, the street beneath my window well-lit, and directly below my room seemed to be a gathering point for late-night revellers. Finally, I drifted into a fitful two-hour slumber before being woken by my alarm for the taxi.

I survived the night and eventually learnt that it doesn't matter too much if you don't sleep well before a marathon. There is so much adrenaline that you aren't exactly going to doze off on the run or even notice a slightly thick head. You feel grotty standing on the start line but the feeling lifts once the starting gun has gone off. But I would definitely prefer to have a good night's sleep before a race.

In the years since I ran at New Plymouth I have become something of an expert at identifying noisy hotel rooms. I especially dislike those little fridges. When I go into a hotel room I make an examination of the fridge before I do anything else. I have disconnected them, stuffed them with towels and requested a different room on the basis of the noises emanating from the fridge (in French, in the middle of the night). Don't get me started on air-conditioners.

The first four kilometres of the marathon were downhill in the cool dawn on the slopes of Mount Taranaki. I think I set out too fast, which is liable to happen with a downhill start. I soon ran out of steam. I ran with a pair of runners from Rotorua for the first half of the race, but they were going slightly too fast for me and at Inglewood I pulled back. By this time I realised I was in for a hard day at the office, and the novice's boundless enthusiasm, which had helped me conquer my weaknesses at the Rotorua Marathon, was not there to help me. I felt sluggish. I found the long, straight roads tedious. And I could see my dreams of a faster time than before for what they were: pure fantasy.

I managed to reach the finish line in a few seconds under four hours. I was dismayed by this because in those days I never expected to run over four hours. I assumed that your second marathon was faster than your first and that this progression continued for some while. When I look back now at the results for this marathon I see that I finished third in my age group and did not do too badly at all, but I didn't feel that successful at the time.

Having had a disappointing performance here, I decided when I arrived home that I would have a second shot at the Rotorua Marathon in seven weeks' time. Was I still a novice at all this?

Seven weeks was just the right length of time for a foot problem to flare up — and it was so severe that I could not run at all during the week before the marathon. Like many injured runners I went straight into denial. I went to see a sports physiotherapist daily and kidded myself that everything would be fine. Later on I accepted that if my foot hurt so badly two days before the race and I could not finish a four-kilometre run, then I should probably not be thinking about running a full marathon that weekend.

The pain of not being able to participate in a race goes beyond the physical pain that caused you to drop out. There's the pain on race day of knowing the race is in progress and that you are not running; there's the pain of seeing your buddies in the finisher's T-shirt afterwards; and there's the final indignity of being sent a full results book in the mail several weeks later when you are starting to forget that you did not run.

I had a big break after this marathon, and my next few experiences were mixed. It was a full 18 months before I ran the Auckland Marathon in October 1999. The break was too long and I put a lot of pressure on myself to run a fast time. But I did not do enough training. I thought I could run a good marathon on willpower and you can't.

The marathon route in those days involved a double out-and-back from the city to St Heliers: a pleasant waterfront course marred only by a hill at the 12-kilometre mark and, worse, the same hill at the 32-kilometre mark. Geology works in mysterious ways, because we all found that the hill, which had been 50,000 years in the making, steepened more during the duration of the marathon.

I started out far too fast with a couple of friends from the Waiheke Island Harriers, the running club I belonged to, and by the ten-kilometre mark I could not keep up with them. Since I had expected to complete the marathon considerably faster than them, and my race history suggested I would be able to, I was disappointed. By the second turnaround in St Heliers I was suffering and I made the return back to the city slowly, knowing I was about to finish the marathon in over four hours. I believed, then, that only a snail would rejoice over such a result.

My weekday running partner, Ray, who had completed the half marathon, met me with two kilometres to go and accompanied me to the finish. I could barely keep up with him, and he may have been walking. But what amazed Ray was the speed of my recovery. By the next week I was back running our usual route at our usual pace, showing no signs of the fatigue I had suffered in the closing stages of the marathon.

Six months later I made my first overseas trip to run a marathon. I went to Sydney in April 2000 for the Host City Marathon, a trial of the marathon course to be used in the Olympic Games later that year. I was really excited about doing this one, and it was a big deal in those days for me to be away from the family for several days. The marathon field was large by Australian or New Zealand standards, with almost 5000 runners, and with a good proportion of visitors this meant I was bumping into runners everywhere I went during the two days before the marathon.

The marathon course took us over the Harbour Bridge, through central Sydney, into Centennial Park and out to the new Olympic stadium at Homebush. It was fantastic to run through this city on roads closed to traffic, and also to know that we were part of an important mission to see if the marathon route was going to be satisfactory for the world's best runners. The highlight was our entry into the stadium via the marathon tunnel, an honour which is usually only bestowed on runners in the real Olympic Games. I was tired by that stage and anxious to be finished, but I still managed to be thrilled to be there.

The main problem for me in these early years of my marathon running career was managing to get my training done. I already realised that I was training as little as possible, but even to do what I deemed essential I had to be creative in squeezing my running in among my child-rearing duties. Once my second child went to school things became much easier. Before that I often had difficulty coordinating kindergarten and crèche for the younger two in such a way that I could get out for a run. I was still having many broken nights so running in the very early morning was not a palatable option. My husband travelled a lot and worked late, so evening running was often out of the question. I snatched runs in the daytime where I could and ran at weekends.

A friend told me that when her kids were little she used to take one of them in the stroller to an oval, park it in the centre, and run around the edge while keeping an eye on the child. It had never occurred to me to do this, and I had missed my chance as the kids were now too old to be tied down. I lamented missed opportunities. Then, one morning, when I was at school with one daughter for netball practice and the younger one was playing on the swings, I had a bright idea and sneaked away while neither was looking. All the other mothers were watching their progeny so I figured my absence would be okay. I went for a ten-minute run consisting of repeated loops of the school perimeter. It was the dullest run I had ever done. After ten minutes a very distraught child, my own younger daughter, called out to me as she approached me in a remote corner of the school grounds. She had spent enough time on the swings. I never tried this again.

I had enjoyed the marathon in Sydney, and when I came home I decided to enter the Auckland Marathon again that year.

The 2000 Auckland Marathon took runners over the Harbour Bridge on a course that the race had not been able to use since 1993. Auckland's Harbour Bridge is an awesome sight in a beautiful city, but it's usually off-limits to non-motorised transport. There is no walkway or bikeway along the bridge. Normally there is no time when pedestrians are allowed to cross the bridge, so this was to be a one-off opportunity.

Numbers in the races were strictly limited. While the bridge is able to carry heavy tonnage daily in terms of cars and trucks, it seemed that thousands of runners posed a threat to its stability. The race was filled to capacity months before the starting gun was fired, to the great disappointment of many. My running partner fabricated his own race number and completed the half marathon, while my life partner was not so bold and missed out on running. For some reason he has never forgiven me for this and it is only with great trepidation that I would ever speak about this race at home.

The marathon has remained significant for me because I was carrying an injury but elected not to pull out of the race. I had been running sprints on the beach with my kids five days before the race when I became too enthusiastic and pulled my hamstring. It was one of those dramatic moments when you come to an abrupt halt in full flight because you feel someone has fired a bullet into the back of your leg.

I limped off to the physiotherapist and asked her to get me in shape to run a marathon at the weekend. Like many runners I am probably a physio's nightmare when I require to be healed immediately. (A doctor once said to me that we runners always want to be mended yesterday, and while that may be true I didn't go back to him.) With a dedicated regime of walking and slow jogging, a trial three-kilometre run the day before the marathon and a lot of stubborn willpower — okay, I believe there was daily ultrasound, massage and acupuncture involved as well — I got to the start line. This was against the advice of my more experienced running cronies who said I would live to regret my decision. But I felt I had no real choice — I was shortly to leave Auckland for good and I may not get another chance at this marathon, especially to run over the bridge.

Since I was injured, I ran the marathon really slowly to halfway. I hadn't done that before, usually going out too fast and paying the price later. At halfway I felt pretty secure and picked up the pace. By the time we reached St Heliers, my home ground, I felt I was onto something good and I cruised to the finish. I was passing people all along and not all of them spectators either. At the 40-kilometre sign it was a case of *Already!* and at 42 kilometres I thought, *Wow, almost done.*

I took home two messages from this marathon. Firstly, that some advice is best left on the shelf; you have to trust your own intuition about whether or not it is safe to run. Secondly, I learnt that a slow first half can make for a fast second half, and this will leave you with such good feelings that it is easy to fill in the next entry form.

At the end of the year we moved back to Australia, and a whole new chapter in my marathon running was about to begin.

A tour around Australia

After we returned to Australia in 2001 I searched for a new running goal, and the challenge of completing a marathon in every state appealed to me. I was already on the way, having run the Host City Marathon in Sydney in 2000. At first I wanted to do a marathon in every capital city, but there was no marathon in Darwin. So I settled for running in every capital city plus Alice Springs, giving myself two years to finish the seven remaining marathons.

This challenge meant running marathons more frequently than I had in the past. I had run two in 2000 and that had felt good. I was in Melbourne for the first time, where I didn't know anyone (runners or otherwise), and nobody was going to tell me not to run so many marathons. In those days I was still very receptive to advice from others and would take what they said onboard without considering whether it was relevant to me. The worst of it was that I would listen to advice from plenty of people who had no idea whatsoever about marathon running. They warned me about damage to my body and about arthritis and about dropping dead while out on a run. For reasons I have not been able to fathom, people would sometimes try quite seriously to turn me against running.

While I marathoned my way around Australia I developed a lot more confidence in both the manner and the frequency of my running.

Not one of the marathons that made up this series of eight (Sydney, Canberra, Brisbane, Adelaide, Melbourne, Hobart, Perth and Alice Springs) would appear in the list of my all-time top ten marathons. None were outstandingly beautiful or atmospheric (or tough). This was a surprise to me, because I would tend to expect big cities to put on the best marathons; they have resources, sponsors and a large pool of runners. They were all pleasant enough, but I can recommend other marathons around Australia and the rest of the world more highly. They were city marathons but not in the best parts of those cities. None of them had crowds of spectators or any kind of hype. There was no interest in these marathons from anyone other than the runners and their immediate supporters. A few of the courses were pretty, but there was nothing really sensational.

The courses were flat compared to the marathons I had run in New Zealand and this took some getting used to. Runners tend to talk more favourably about flat marathons as they make for faster race times, forgetting that there's always a view at the top of the hill. I find a bit of variety helps both my muscles and my mind.

Having said all that, on a personal level those eight marathons have been a microcosm of my marathon experiences over the past 13 years, and for that I cannot value them highly enough. They provided me with every sensation that marathon running has given me in the years since I completed this series. They taught me invaluable lessons about coping and triumphing over the difficult physical demands of completing a marathon. I learnt also how to deal with the emotional elements, and how to play mind games.

I sampled various different course layouts — a point-to-point course in Melbourne, a loop course in Adelaide, an out-and-back marathon in Perth, a repeated lap course in Hobart. The shape of the course can have a big impact on the way you react to the marathon.

There were good days and bad days. When I ran my fastest marathon to date in Canberra I had the sensation of an effortless race, a feeling I have now had after a handful of my faster marathons.

In Brisbane I had a struggle with dehydration and a tedious route. But I finished the race. I could always look back and remember how inner strength had pulled me through.

When I reflect on the Perth Marathon and see the disappointment I felt on finishing in a slower time than expected, I feel something I was to feel repeatedly until I ceased being concerned about my finishing time. I had trained and my body had let me down. Or was it my mind that had let me down? Or maybe I just could not run as fast as I thought I could. In those days my finishing time really mattered to me.

My lonely run in Alice Springs showed me that small marathons can be rather special.

But I learnt my biggest lesson during the Adelaide Marathon. The weather was foul, wet and wild, and after ten kilometres I was slopping past small factories wondering how I was supposed to deal with this. It suddenly dawned on me that I had a flight booked to take me home that afternoon, so I would definitely be finished by then. As a direct result of this seemingly minor thought on a back street in South Australia I now carry the conviction that however bad I may be feeling during a marathon, it will at some point be over.

I trained through a very long and warm summer for the Canberra Marathon in April 2001. Even with much more time available to train, as all three children were now at school all day, I did not follow a proper training program. It's time to confess that I have never been good at using a training program. They make me feel restricted and then I'm not running because I want to; I'm running because I have to. At the beginning of each week I would have a vague plan of what I was going to do, and sometimes I even wrote this down. My aim would be to run about five hours a week, swim two or three times and ride my bike two or three times.

I ran in the heat of the day because that was when I had free time, and I boosted my training with several triathlons in the southern suburbs of Melbourne. These triathlons were probably very helpful to my running. I've never been one to do any fast running, like speed work or intervals. I just like to run. But when I'm running during a triathlon I know that I am in a race and I will go as fast as I can. Since the run is the last part of the triathlon, this means I am running as hard as I can on already tired legs — and that would have to be of some training value.

I found that there were generally few women in my age group (40–45) so I could try to get on the podium. The best you can do at these local triathlons is to win your age group; there is often no overall ranking. I had previously had no experience of winning anything sporting in my life so this was a great opportunity, and if I could clinch the deal on the run I loved it.

My run in Canberra was a surprising success. The route involved a loop around the parliamentary triangle followed by a long out-and-back along the south side of Lake Burley Griffin. It was a cool, clear day, and the lake was like a mill pond. I can even look back and call this race the most picturesque of the year, which I would never have expected of Canberra. Of the four occasions that I have now run the Canberra Marathon, this was the time I liked the best. My training paid off and I felt I was cruising much of the way. I liked the quiet roads; I was not sure if they were closed to traffic or if these were normal conditions for a Sunday morning in Canberra. The spectators — family members of the runners — are always friendly in Canberra, and I appreciated being called out to by name by the marshals, who all had a list of the runners' names for this very purpose. (The course had changed by the next time

I ran here and it was far less visually rewarding as it involved running on a road north of the lake without many lake views.)

I had hoped all along that I could run a marathon faster than I had so far managed. But I was losing faith and I did not expect to beat my time from Rotorua, which back then was still my fastest marathon, by as much as 15 minutes.

As I ran back towards the finish line along the lake I realised that I was all set to run a personal best, and I could achieve that even if I walked to the finish. I was also going to run a Boston qualifying time for the first time by finishing in under 3 hours, 45 minutes. In those days I had no plans to run the Boston Marathon but it was nice to know I would have the option to do so. For many runners, qualifying for Boston is the pinnacle of marathon achievement. Boston is the only marathon in the world with a strict qualifying requirement. The possibility of running there had not crossed my mind before.

This experience of completing a marathon in a faster time than I had believed myself to be capable of was unusual. It was a big shock. In 100 marathons I have only had this happen twice. I ran 84 more marathons before this was to occur again.

Three weeks later I went to Brisbane for their marathon. I had been on an emotional high after my run in Canberra but the Brisbane Marathon had a severely deflating effect on me. I joke about that marathon now because the route was very boring, but at the time my performance left me disappointed, tired and questioning whether I wanted to run any more marathons.

Among the things I learnt was that for me personally, the choice of course is paramount — good scenery makes up for any amount of discomfort, tiredness and bad weather. Over the years I have had numerous internal debates about whether I should deliberately seek out scenic marathons, or whether I should be putting more effort into making my training runs scenic and not worry too much about what will be in store for my eyes on race day. Every time, I come down in favour of saving the best for race day. The race is so hard that every little bit of reward you can give yourself helps.

In 2001 the Brisbane Marathon did not use its traditional course along the Brisbane River. I'm not sure if I had realised this before the race. I had lived in Brisbane for four years in the 1990s and this city was where my post-childbirth running — my comeback, so to speak — got started. I used to do short runs along the river while my first child was at crèche. In short, I had a fondness for the riverside paths which made me keen to return to Brisbane for the marathon. Living in Melbourne, I did not know that a new busway had just been created in southern Brisbane and it was due to be unveiled (or inaugurated, or whatever the term is for buses using a bus lane for the first time) the day after the marathon. The race organisers had what seemed to them a brilliant idea: that the marathon should follow the new busway the day before its official opening. Pedestrians would never again have this opportunity to use it and to sample its splendour.

I would have been more than happy to miss out on this opportunity. The busway was long, straight and punctuated only by — wait for it — bus stops. There was a wall along one side to block out the views of natural vegetation. The chance for spectators to stand around to cheer us on was nil. The bus lane was parallel to the main road connecting Brisbane with the Gold Coast so we heard cars rushing by and had fleeting glimpses of them.

I didn't sleep well the night before the marathon. Silly thing, really — I was worried because I had omitted to pick up any safety pins at the race registration and I didn't know how I would attach my race number to my singlet. I tried to reassure myself that either there would be safety pins at the race start (there were, as it turned out), or as a last resort I could carry my race number in my hand. But the night before a marathon is not the time to have unresolved issues and my active mind saw to it that I barely slept.

So here was a dull race to be run in warm weather on very little sleep. The marathon started at South Bank. The first ten kilometres were very pleasant as we ran along the Brisbane River through West End, mostly in parkland. There was hardly anybody around and this looked like a promising event. We returned to South Bank and headed out on the busway.

The remainder of the marathon is a touch foggy in my head, but I know that for most of the distance I just wanted it to be over. I was moving slower and slower, feeling warmer and warmer. I couldn't quite understand what was happening since in my previous marathon, only three weeks earlier, I had run my fastest time to date and had felt fine for most of the way. It happened to be a humid day and there was no shade; in fact, the wall beside the bus lane reflected a substantial amount of heat, making our journey warmer than it need have been. It's not unusual for the weather to still be summery in Brisbane at this time of year (late April), but the normal riverside course would have had the benefit of the sight of the river with its cooling effect. As I ran I became increasingly hot and uncomfortable.

Runners sometimes talk about hitting 'The Wall', meaning that you completely run out of steam and are unable to proceed forwards as if a wall were blocking your path. This is disastrous for your race aspirations and totally debilitating. I do not think I have ever fully clunked headlong into a wall such as this during a marathon, but in this Brisbane race I came pretty close. I was truly having difficulty moving forward and had to continually coax myself along. At some points I was unable to imagine myself finishing the marathon.

Concurrently with the marathon there was a double marathon in progress. These runners also used the busway in their race and separate drinks tables were laid out for them. The key difference was that these guys had sports drinks as well as water, and I had not previously considered the role of sports drink in my drinking during a marathon. I guess that in my past six marathons I had been lucky and had been drinking both water and sports drink without thinking about why I was doing this; I merely drank what was on offer. Here, on the busway, I realised that to get through the run I wanted more than water, as the water was neither slaking my thirst nor easing my fatigue at all. In hindsight, and with a bit of swotting up on the science, I can see that I needed carbohydrates to give me more energy and I needed electrolytes to enable the water I was drinking to hydrate me. This was the first time I really experienced dehydration during a marathon, but it was a problem I would come to know well.

In desperation, at the 32-kilometre drinks table for the double marathon runners I grabbed a cup of sports drink. I was told the drinks were not for the marathon runners. Did I care? I flagrantly disobeyed the rules. As I swiped a cup that was not rightfully mine for the taking, I could see the marshal at that drinks table reflecting, *Those runners are a bad lot, stealing each other's drinks. Who do they think they are? It's only a fun run.* I was feeling proud of myself for having taken assertive action. Although, truth to tell, I have harboured guilt about this for many years. The sports drink was some help although I had let my dehydration get the better of me for too long and I wasn't able to make up for lost time. With absolute delight I finally returned to South Bank. By now it was busy, and the last kilometre meant dodging families with strollers and dogs. This was almost the last straw. I felt overly stressed, having to manoeuvre past people who had no idea of the effort it was taking me.

I didn't want to do another marathon after that. I don't mean I never wanted to do another one *ever*; I just wasn't quite ready for the next one.

But it was winter in Melbourne. Gradually, I started running again along the coast path near my home on those lovely crisp mornings and my mind became receptive to more marathons.

In August I resumed my tour of the Australian states, running the Adelaide Marathon. The marathon was good. The weather was bad. Snow was forecast for the Mount Lofty Ranges, which I am advised only happens about once every seven years, and in Adelaide we had hail. This was the worst weather I have ever had for a marathon. And worse, I had an interrupted night when the members of a rock band, returning from a gig, decided to have a jam session in their room next door to mine at around 2am. (Though, admittedly, this gave me a chance to listen to the rain during the breaks in their music.)

I was wet and cold for the whole marathon. But it was an entirely positive experience. Running in bad weather can be fantastic and, when you think about it, what else could you do on a wet Sunday as a visitor in town? The early part took us through a light industrial area and we paid a visit to the airport, but the bulk of the route was along the Torrens River. I managed to run a very even pace from start to finish. I enjoyed the tranquillity of the bike trails around the river, and the course was sufficiently undulating to be interesting, without being hilly. When I arrived at the finish line at the old Adelaide gaol — read into that what you will — I found that I had finished in sixth place among the women. Not only this, but I had accurately predicted my finishing time before leaving home, for the first and only time ever. Running in these conditions was a valuable experience; it taught me that I can run well in bad weather and I should not panic when the forecast for race day is poor.

In October 2001 I lined up for the Melbourne Marathon. The route in those days was one way from Frankston to Albert Park, and susceptible to either a headwind or a tailwind. We had a tailwind that year. I had clear intentions of running a fast time, but like many other runners I headed out too fast and staged a collapse in the second half. The marathon was reminiscent of the Auckland Marathon for me in that I had to cover my regular training grounds during the race. I was not quite sure whether I liked this, especially when I ran close to my house and could not pop in for a break.

Early in January 2002 I ran the Hobart Marathon. This one started at the Cadbury chocolate factory, and comprised two loops through suburbs close to the Derwent Entertainment Centre, on roads which became too busy by mid-morning. I stayed at a motel that was on the marathon route; I had a lot of difficulty in finding it when I arrived in town. The silver lining was that the roads used for the marathon seemed very familiar to me by race day as I had been driving up and down them looking for the motel.

I believe the course could have been more interesting if it had been based in another part of Hobart, because Hobart is a beautiful city. We got glimpses of the river but it was by no means a focus of the run. Many of the interstate participants do this marathon because there is no other one available at this time of year in Australia, and that is fiercely in its favour. The other factor in its favour is the thought of chocolate at the finish line. Never underestimate the power of chocolate. I was there asking a marshal for mine before I could find my way out of the finishing chute.

I was delighted to finish third overall, but I was embarrassed to be on the podium with what I regarded as a relatively slow finishing time of 3 hours, 54 minutes. Fortunately, when the results were reported in the local newspaper the reporter mistakenly gave my personal best time as the time I ran at the Hobart Marathon, and my pride was salvaged.

I drove up Mount Wellington after the race and it was snowing. January, remember?

Perth was next on the list; it was July 2002. It rained. I was told that the weather is often bad for this marathon, but in reality it has been good almost every year on marathon day since my initial visit.

The marathon uses bike/pedestrian paths the whole way so is completely off-road, which is very nice. That's the good part. But plenty of bikes use the path even while the marathon is in progress and some riders appear hell-bent on terrorising the runners or are totally oblivious to them. That's not so good. I saw numerous instances of bikes overtaking each other at high speed while passing runners, right in the face of oncoming bikes. Early on in the marathon we runners are likely to be vigilant and take care of ourselves, keeping to the edge of the path or even going onto the grass when necessary. But in the later stages runners become tired and are liable to weave around on the path and be less agile at skipping deftly out of the way of an oncoming bike.

Bike dangers aside, this is a lovely course for a marathon. It's an out-and-back route that takes place fairly centrally without being smack in the city centre. The bike paths, which are all sealed save a few hundred metres, follow the edge of the Swan River from the Burswood water sports centre to the suburb of Attadale and back. There's just a slight variation at the start and finish of the route so that the turnaround is at 23.5 kilometres rather than halfway. Psychologically this is a good thing as it makes the run seem quicker on your return, or at least it should.

On the outward trip we ran across the Windan Bridge and on through East Perth before recrossing the river on the Causeway Bridge. As we went over the bridge above Heirisson Island I looked out for the kangaroos that live in the sanctuary on the island but I didn't see them. Never mind — I had seen them on the previous day when I went for a short run around the island. I still find it amazing, speaking as a person who grew up in England, that there really is a city in Australia with kangaroos in the city centre. We then followed the river through South

Perth, glanced over at the old Swan Brewery and passed the flashy architecture of Applecross mansions. After the turnaround at Troy Park we had a nasty headwind all the way back to Burswood, and I arrived at the finish cold and soaked through.

I was frustrated with my Perth race, but looking back I cannot see why, other than having anticipated a faster run and having struggled with the wind. I put my disappointment down to having too long a break between marathons — this was fast becoming a handy excuse for any sub-par performance.

Finally it was time for the last stop on this tour of Australia, with the Alice Springs Marathon in August 2002. I looked forward to this one with the gusto that I more recently applied to my hundredth marathon. It would signify achieving a major goal.

The field at the Alice Springs Marathon was unusually small in 2002: a mere 17 runners. It is usually a boutique event, an intimate marathon, but on this occasion a group of German runners, who come over every year for the race, made their arrangements for the wrong weekend. They were to arrive to run the marathon a week late and we ran without them. The field was halved. To the credit of the Alice Springs running club, they held the marathon again a week later for the visitors, and many years after this I met someone from Melbourne who had run this second marathon, having found himself in Alice that weekend.

This was a different sort of marathon. I had never been so alone for a full marathon; much of the time I could not even see any other runners. I was pleased to find out that this did not matter one bit. If anything, it meant I felt more of a bond with my fellow runners that day because we were part of an exclusive group.

The marathon started at the Araluen Arts Centre on the edge of town, and my motel owner was intrigued when I asked him to order me a taxi to take me there at 6am. 'I don't think it will be open at that time,' he said and called out to his wife to make sure before I could explain. The owner had already marked me down as an unusual customer when I complained about a buzzing sound from the ceiling the minute I stepped into my room. But I was always on the lookout for problems with motel rooms that might keep me awake.

We set out on our marathon in the dark and I wore long pants as it was quite chilly. By the end of the marathon, when I had long since discarded my pants, I was to have sunburnt legs. We spread out down the road immediately, and I next saw my fellow runners when I passed a bunch of them at halfway. Our route was alongside the McDonnell Ranges, so we could watch the rocks turn pink with the rising sun and then red for the day. There was scrubby bush all around. The sky deepened to dark blue and there we had it: vivid red, blue and green. I kept my eyes peeled for dingoes and, yes, snakes but saw neither.

The most impressive feature of the course was the Heavitree Gap, where huge rocks forced the road to narrow. Some runners paused for photos.

The course was out-and-back that year. Some years it is a loop, but to complete the loop you have to cross the railway line and there has been negative feedback on occasion when runners had to wait up to half an hour for a freight train to pass.

I felt rather emotional as I approached the arts centre on my return trip. I knew that I had completed my challenge, and in good shape. I probably shed a few tears as I ran past the timing clock. Then I had a massage which I will not forget in a hurry. Post-race massage is always painful, but here I had two masseurs working on me and I cannot recommend this: I could not use my usual powers of keeping my mind off the pain when I had two pains coming at the same time from two places.

The awards ceremony was very pleasant, in a way that was only possible because of the small number of participants. We got together at a local deluxe hotel for a buffet lunch. I sneaked a swim in the pool while we were waiting to sit down. When the awards were handed out every runner received a trophy, a red stone carving in the shape of the Northern Territory. I placed third female, and this time I felt I deserved to.

By the end of my tour around the country I could well and truly consider myself a marathon runner. I knew that marathon running was something I loved doing. There was no stopping now. I decided I had to go for one of the truly prestigious marathons, and I signed up to run the London Marathon.

London's marathon

In 2001 I had run a marathon outside of Australasia for the first time. I tagged the San Francisco Marathon onto a family holiday to California, where the best part for all the younger members was the time spent at Disneyland. They could not understand why we had to leave Disneyland a day early and fly from Los Angeles to San Francisco just for a marathon, but they came along anyway. Afterwards, the kids all told their friends that they had been able to go to Disneyland because their mother wanted to run a marathon in San Francisco. Likewise, my husband tells everyone the reason for this holiday, to this day. If I'm there I protest that the marathon was slotted in by pure fluke. I assert with complete sincerity that I had booked the trip before I found out about the marathon. This is gospel truth. But really there is nothing I can say that will get me off the hook.

Being in Disneyland for a week before running a marathon does not necessarily set the groundwork for a successful marathon; walking around the theme park all day long then settling in for a hefty dose of junk food to revitalise in the evening. In other words, tiring out my body and then failing to nourish it well. And before starting the marathon I was able to indulge my perennial pre-race worry: that I have got the date of the race wrong.

We flew into San Francisco and I wanted to go immediately to the race expo and registration. On our way to the appointed place we could see no sign whatsoever of an impending marathon. That's probably not too surprising because so much goes on in San Francisco and this is a relatively small marathon. We walked along from Fisherman's Wharf to the supposed expo site while I chattered nervously. The others were trying to enjoy what is one of the world's top foreshore strolls while enduring Mother's panic attack that we had all come to San Francisco on the wrong day. Suddenly I saw several people carrying identical plastic bags bearing a sports logo. They must have been to the race registration. The black cloud above me lifted. I may even have cracked a smile.

We dined in our room on McDonald's the night before the race — junk food had by now become the normal way of life on this holiday and was keeping the rest of the family happy — and I crept out at dawn to catch the bus to the marathon start. Why we had to go so early I will never know. But this seems to be a feature of marathons. It's a way of making the event more painful than it has to be, or a test of character, because if you can't get up three hours earlier than usual to run a marathon you might not be able to run a marathon at all.

I remember sitting next to a guy on the bus who was running his 18th marathon and that seemed nothing short of phenomenal to me, about to run my eighth. In those early days I would pay close attention to anyone who had run more than a few marathons and ask lots of questions. I hung on their every word and hoped I could become a prolific marathon runner by absorbing their aura.

The Golden Gate Bridge is the symbol of San Francisco, but from 1999 to 2001 (when I went there) the marathon didn't cross it. That was bad planning on my part. We did, however, run close to the bridge and many runners stopped to take a photo of it as we passed. I'm not sure they were going to take a very special souvenir home since the bridge was shrouded in mist, and to be quite honest we didn't even see it. One runner moving along just in front of me will remember it well: he tripped over another runner (who had stopped dead in his tracks to take a photo) and needed medical attention as a result.

San Francisco is a beautiful city and the marathon course did it justice. From Golden Gate Park we took in the touristy waterfront, then the financial district, Chinatown and downtown. We had a big climb through Haight Ashbury, the hippie and gay area, and ran for miles along the Pacific shoreline before returning to Golden Gate Park.

I can't remember too much about the race because I was just so overawed with the fact that I was running a marathon in San Francisco. This was my first marathon outside Australia or New Zealand, and thus was a big occasion for me — yet it was only a small race by US standards, with 2500 or so runners. On my previous visits to the city I had never imagined I would one day run a marathon there. Actually, the last time I had been there, as part of a long-distance cycling trip, I hadn't even imagined that I would one day run a marathon. I can go further than that: I had never even run, full stop.

It was a cold day. Even at the finish it was cold, as we stood in line to collect copious amounts of free foodstuffs. There was so much food on offer that you wouldn't have needed to cook for a week, had it been the sort of food you'd want to eat. There were boxes of breakfast cereal, cookies, instant noodles, pouches of sports drink and then many varieties of headache and flu tablets. The problem was that with so much up for grabs the line moved very slowly — nobody wanted to miss out. So we stood there with our foil blankets around our shoulders waiting for handouts that would likely end up in the rubbish bin, when really we should have been collecting our warm clothing and heading back to base camp.

Overall I liked this experience of marathon running overseas. Such a stroke of luck that I had been able to go there!

In April 2003 I ran the London Marathon. This was my 15th marathon and I felt like an old-timer. But I had never done a marathon on this scale: 30,000 runners and a route through the centre of a huge city.

I was born and grew up in England so it was inevitable that one day I would want to run the London Marathon. The London event was first held in 1981, two years before we left England for a new life in Australia, had over 7000 runners (20,000 applied to run) and was modelled on the New York City Marathon. It was an instant success and has not looked back since. For the 1982 race there were 90,000 applicants, with 18,000 receiving a starter's bib. Along with New York it has the highest profile in the world of any marathon. You don't have to be a runner, or even know a runner, to know of the London Marathon.

During the night after my arrival in London, and only two nights before the marathon, I had an excruciating cramp in my left calf. It woke me with a jolt and I walked around my hotel room trying to straighten out my leg, while wondering if this would stop me from running. Actually, it is an exaggeration to say that I walked around my room because I was on a budget and the room was so tiny I could hardly fit in it when standing still, but I stretched my calf as best I could. In the morning some pain was still there, but only a shadow of the pain I had felt in the night. I forced myself to go for a short jog around Russell Square Gardens, still sore, but at least I satisfied myself that running was possible. Anyway, I saw some Kenyan runners in tracksuits so that made it all worthwhile. I was careful what I did with my legs for the rest of the day; in other words, I sat down a lot.

The start of the London Marathon is pretty special. As with other big city races, you get to the start line hours before anything happens. You hang around wondering what to do while the organisers say over and over again, 'Welcome to the London Marathon. This is the red (or blue or green) start.' While waiting I killed time queuing for the toilet, using the toilet, then queuing for the toilet again, and chatting to people in the queue. Some of the folk I met have already tried a marathon; for some this was a new venture. Here, as with everywhere, first-timers are full of curiosity. Maybe a bit scared. This is a step into the unknown.

I love finding out the reasons why people have decided to enter a marathon. I have heard so many heart-warming stories about decisions to make dramatic lifestyle changes; about taking on a challenge; about using the marathon to help cope with personal issues: illness, work stress, marriage breakdown and bereavement. I spoke to a woman who had turned to running when she lost her job. With all the extra free time she needed a new interest and the running improved her health, too. I spoke to a runner who had been very overweight and had started running one day after seeing himself in the mirror; he realised he had a choice between remaining completely sedentary and unhealthy or picking up the reins of his life again. Sometimes the reason is quite mundane, but the impact the marathon will have on that runner's life is just as important. For every runner there is a tale that has brought them to this start line.

Charity runners have a high profile at the London Marathon. Some run for well-known aid organisations while others run for local causes or in support of charities that have benefited someone they know. Some take on the challenge to honour a loved one who may be ill or have passed away. The 26-mile run is seen as a fitting tribute because to complete it requires considerable dedication and time. Tied up in the marathon endeavour are hundreds of tales of personal loss or hardship, and this helps makes the marathon day an emotionally charged one.

Other marathons encourage runners to participate and raise money for a cause, but not on the same scale as in London. The race earns more for a whole host of charities than any other marathon. Runners can even enter the race via a charity portal (bypassing the ballot to secure a race bib) whereby they guarantee a base level of donation to their chosen charity.

Whatever the reason, this race is always packed. I had run in a few races with a sizeable field, but shorter in distance than this one, and I always believed that the road reaches a saturation point when a run has over 3000 participants. After that number the runners around you can't get any closer; it's just that the tail ahead and behind is longer. What I had not anticipated was the level of spectator support that came with this race. There were people everywhere, not just along both sides of the roads, but on the roofs of pubs, on lampposts and on car roofs. They generated a volume of noise that was so loud and so unceasing that when we entered a tunnel near the end of the course for a few minutes we runners breathed a collective sigh of relief at the respite from the din.

This amount of support doesn't just happen by chance. The race organisers see to it that the spectators have as much fun as the runners. They publicise the race all over the city for many weeks and encourage public involvement. You might think the bands and amusements are solely for the runners, but actually they are providing ceaseless entertainment for the spectators too — the guys who are stuck in one place for hours on end, and have had their city disrupted by the race. And, what's more, today's audience will make up a proportion of next year's runners.

The course of the London Marathon is probably as good as it can be — which is not to bag it but to point out the challenges the organising committee would be up against. It is hard for a major city to offer runners its best parts when 30,000 folk take to the roads on foot. You need to use wide roads with easy access all along for emergency vehicles and helpers. You need to keep traffic disruption to a minimum. You need a start area and finishing point which can both accommodate thousands of people at the same time and have good access for vehicles. While considering all this you need to throw in as many major landmarks as you can so the runners have a day they will never forget. Both London and New York do a grand job despite the challenges. In both marathons there are fantastic bits and less interesting bits.

There have been few changes since 1981. The race starts in Blackheath, with three groups of runners who converge after three miles. For most of the early miles I just marvelled at the volume of runners. The major sight of the first part is the Cutty Sark sailing ship, which was built in 1869 to help with the tea trade. In 2003 it was still a few years away from being damaged by fire so we were able to admire the vessel in its original glory. Twelve miles into the race we concluded our tour of the south side of the River Thames and the Docklands, crossing the river on Tower Bridge, and this is the most memorable part of the first half. It's an unusual-looking bridge, and good to get a chance for a proper look.

This was the first bridge to be built over the Thames in the East End of London and it was completed in 1894. The style is Victorian Gothic. It's a suspension bridge in three sections, with two stone pillars of traditional design flanking the middle section. The central part of the bridge can open, and it still opens daily. The design allowed for a high level walkway across the middle section, unaffected by the bridge opening, and this walkway gives the bridge its unorthodox appearance. Very early on in the bridge's life it became clear that pedestrians did not like climbing to this walkway and it was rarely used.

Straight after crossing the river the route had a stretch on cobblestones near the Tower of London, some of which was covered with carpet for our comfort. Two years later the route was altered so runners could avoid the cobbles — too many people had been tripping over. I think it was because the carpet became slippery, not because of the cobblestones, which added a romantic touch to the race.

In the second half we spent ten miles looping around the Isle of Dogs, jogging through the docks on this side of the river and passing the financial district of Canary Wharf. With plenty of pubs filled with vocal supporters and bands playing, there was never a dull moment. The Thames has a dramatic bend here but it's not a part of London that tourists would usually frequent.

The familiar London landmarks all come towards the end of the race. We got a second look at Tower Bridge, then passed St Paul's Cathedral, Trafalgar Square with Nelson's column, the Houses of Parliament and Westminster Abbey, and we could see the London Eye across the river. There was a long stretch along the Embankment, which I loved, and the trip underground into the Blackfriars Underpass for a few moments of quiet. I was also hoping to catch a glimpse of my in-laws along the route here, but frankly you would have no chance of picking anyone out unless you knew exactly where they were going to be. They had told me beforehand that they were going to watch the race from the Embankment but that was the only clue I had. By the time I rounded the bend to run towards Buckingham Palace and the finish in the Mall, I was dead tired. But it's a great venue for a marathon finish — the grand wide road lined by St James's Palace and ornate public buildings.

The most draining part of the day was shuffling through the finishing chute. Everyone had ground to a very slow walk and I was finding it almost unbearable to remain upright. I had to stand and wait at the clothes retrieval area for my warm-up clothes and this was painful. My back was cramping. Someone in the queue suggested that I go and have a sit-down, and come back later. But I was cold; I wanted my clothes so that I could leave and get on with recovering from the run. They didn't seem to have organised the storage well and several people were hunting desperately for our things, never seeming to find anything among the random piles of bags strewn about. As a result of this ordeal, I have developed an aversion to leaving clothes with the race organisers to be collected later, and I vowed to not do this at the larger marathons I go to. And even at the smaller ones I never wanted to leave anything that I couldn't abandon for good if I had to.

I was pleased with my finishing time because I realised that this was not a race held under optimal conditions. There were too many runners to allow anyone except the elites at the front to run at their own pace. Not only the throngs of runners, but the slippery orange peels, the empty Lucozade tubes underfoot at the aid stations, and the bottlenecks caused by the aid tables made many parts of the race slower going than usual.

Yet the real highlight of the 2003 London Marathon was nothing to do with my participation. This was where Paula Radcliffe ran a female world's best marathon time of 2:15:25, beating the previous best time (also hers) by almost two minutes and setting a record which is likely to stand for a long time. News of this achievement reached us while we were out on the course and it was hard to digest — someone in one of the pubs along the way must have had a radio and they called out to us: 'Come on, you slackers. Paula has just finished in 2-hours-15!', or words to that effect.

Radcliffe's achievement has been variously treated in the record books. Some purists refuse to acknowledge it as a world's fastest for women because she was paced by a couple of guys while running a women's race. They guys didn't pass over the finish line — and, gee, it would have really upset the apple cart if they had — but their presence in the women's marathon turned the raced into a mixed competition.

For some reason this matters when you're after a female world record. Regardless of this controversy, I have enjoyed telling people that I ran in the race where the female world record was set. I was only just behind the lady ... give or take an hour and a half.

After the glamour of London I remained in Victoria for the rest of the year's marathons. In August I ran (and won) the Shepparton Marathon, running the whole way in drizzle but very pleased with a personal best of 3 hours, 31 minutes. The course was all on bike trails and this marathon had a very small field, so it was in complete contrast with my previous one. At last I felt that my time goal of beating three and a half hours was within reach.

I had been to a sports scientist at Victoria University in Melbourne two months before the Shepparton Marathon and he had run a maximal stress test on me. I was wired up to machinery, with electrodes stuck all over my body, and then told to run on a treadmill with the incline being raised every few minutes. At a certain point the scientist decided I was about to drop dead and this was his moment to make scientific conclusions about my athletic ability. It's a painful process running to exhaustion but worth it to find out what your body is capable of. The results of the tests, whose meaning I only partially understood, included data for my anaerobic threshold, maximum oxygen uptake and maximum heart rate.

I was pronounced to be in very good shape, with a big heart. I liked that bit. It's quite common for endurance runners to have an enlarged heart — this is the body's adaptation to the large amounts of blood flowing to and from the heart during prolonged exercise. Since you asked, I was aged 45 and my VO_2 max, which measures oxygen uptake while exercising, was 64.2 millilitres per kilogram per minute. My anaerobic threshold was determined from capillary blood lactate samples, and was calculated to be 13 kilometres per hour. My maximum heart rate was 182 beats per minute. In those days my resting heart rate was 46 beats per minute; I had measured it to be 39 beats per minute when I did my earlier long-distance cycle touring. The scientist felt that I was running my marathons below my true potential.

Three weeks after this year's Melbourne Marathon, I went to Portland in Victoria's west for their Three Bays Marathon. I look back very fondly on this marathon. There were only a handful of women in the race and the race organiser had told me I would have to get my skates on to make it to the podium. I assumed this was because he did not know me, while the other women, including the previous year's winner, Robyn, had all done the marathon before.

I wasn't expecting a special performance from myself, and when I sat in second place behind Robyn for three hours I thought nothing of it. I had passed her in the early kilometres, then been passed in return very soon after. As we ran back into Portland after our sightseeing around the three bays — named Bridgewater, Discovery and Portland — I saw in the distance that Robyn had stopped at a drinks station for about half a minute. Then I saw her start walking. We were two kilometres from the finish. I caught up to her and had no option but to pass her. After this I had a taste of a marathon win and I became determined she would not pass me.

I made for the finish line as if powered by a new engine. The finish was on the town oval and a compere was announcing names as runners entered a gate to the oval. I was so thrilled to hear 'First female' and then my name. As icing on the cake, this was a rare occasion when my family had been able to come to the marathon and they were at the finish line. They had seen me earlier on during the race while I was out on the course but they had gone by car to the oval and would not have known, until my name was announced, that I was in the lead.

It was great to come home in first place — even though I did not have the number of runners chasing me that Paula Radcliffe had contended with in London. I ought to disclose that both in Shepparton and at Portland there were not many women runners. In Shepparton there were two of us and in Portland I was first of four.

Speeding up

I wanted to run my marathons faster. I knew I could. But here's the problem: running a marathon at any pace is hard, and even when you have the ability to go faster you might do one little thing wrong before or during the race and the race is blown. Fortunately, by the end of 2003 I had managed to run several marathons consistently faster than previously. 2004 was looking to be my year.

I ran several 'ultra marathons' (more than marathon distance) in early 2004 and right from the start this was going to be a high-volume year. When I went to the United States to run the Big Sur Marathon in April I had already run five ultras since January.

Over the years I have read a lot of reviews of marathons. There was one event that stood out from all the rest whenever I saw it mentioned: the marathon at Big Sur in northern California. In 2004 I had the opportunity to run it, as part of a holiday with my husband. Denis has always supported my running ambitions but family needs have meant that he has rarely been able to accompany me to races.

I had high hopes after reading all the hype about the spectacular views. The marathon route follows Highway 1 from the small settlement of Big Sur up to Carmel, one of the world's truly magical coast roads, and it is a real privilege to be allowed to run along it with no traffic. Steep hills cascade down to sea level, groves of redwoods tower over the road, elegant bridges frame deep canyons, and there are tiny sandy beaches that can only be reached from the sea.

More than this nice stuff for the eyes, quite a lot of entertainment is laid on for the runners — which has really taken off in recent years but in 2004 was still not common. The entertainment includes taiko drumming bands (a Japanese style of drumming), fire-eaters, belly dancers and one pianist. This pianist, dressed in a tuxedo playing his grand piano on the Bixby Bridge, is not a permanent fixture; he only does this on marathon day. Photos of this pianist on the bridge appear in lots of magazines and people have asked me if he is real.

The so-called highway is just a two-lane road, not wide by North American standards. Building the road presented a challenge — it was built as part of President Roosevelt's New Deal program in the 1930s — as there just isn't much space for it between the mountains inland and the rocky coastline. (Until the road was built this was one of the more isolated parts of California, and the only access was by sea or on very rough inland tracks. Loggers and gold miners had settled the area in the 1850s but it had fallen into decline.) Road building apart, the real drama came with the construction of the many bridges needed to span the dozens of creeks flowing into the ocean. There are numerous tales of half-completed bridges being blown into the ocean or pushed in by landslides overnight during construction, thanks to storms and wild seas. To this day, there is still only a tiny amount of development between Carmel and Big Sur village, mainly restricted to enormously expensive boutique hotels.

The marathon route crosses 14 bridges, each one an engineering marvel. The bridges save an enormous amount of effort that would otherwise be spent trekking all the way down to sea level and back up again an additional 14 times. The course is undulating enough as it is. These bridges are elegant, simple and blend in well with the scenery.

Two of the bridges are photographed more than the others: Rocky Creek and Bixby. For my money Bixby Bridge is the gem, its concrete arch spanning a deep canyon. If you drove along here you couldn't help but stop to take in the view and peer down at the little beaches far below. And that's on the days the pianist isn't even there.

The road was completely closed for five hours for our run. This means that there can't be any spectators on the course, as only the aid station staff have access to the road. I think they pick the aid station helpers by the strength of their lungs, as they well and truly made up for the lack of other onlookers.

Most out-of-town runners stay the night before in Monterey, four kilometres from Carmel. A fleet of buses are laid on to take runners on a pre-dawn journey to the start line. I did not like the 4.30am departure, but before boarding I managed to squeeze in time for a coffee from Starbucks (conveniently, there was a takeaway outlet right in the lobby of the hotel) and a short interview with a local TV station. I'm not sure what they were expecting by interviewing a sleepy runner whose nerves were all that kept her awake.

The drive to the start was exciting. The fire-eaters were having a practice as we passed their haunt on the route. Their act looked great in the dark, even better than in daylight. One of the buses broke down on the way, but our driver, who owned the fleet but had never driven this route — fancy telling that to a bunch of nervous marathon runners on their way to a race — was able to come to the rescue. When the buses finally reached the Big Sur start line for the race they had to continue on for a few kilometres because there was no space to turn around for the return trip. This made some of the runners jumpy; as if running 26 miles wasn't enough, now there might be extra! (There wasn't.)

The weather on this coast is notoriously fickle, and for some people the possibility of a foggy day is ample reason to keep away from the marathon. As I had been warned, you can run the entire marathon and see nothing on a bad day. The winds blowing off the sea can be wild, making for a hard run. But on 25 April 2004 the weather on Highway 1 was perfect: no fog and no wind. The sun shone in a clear, blue sky. There was a sliver of fog around the Point Sur lighthouse, so it looked as if it sat up in the clouds like a fairy tale castle, but that was the only fog about.

We started with a long downhill through redwood forest, trying to warm up but at the same time not head out too fast. I did not want to burn out and wreck my whole race. I used these early miles to get my rhythm so that I could run effortlessly once the coastal stretch began.

When we left the forest and reached the coast we had mouth-watering vistas of promontories and beaches all the way to San Francisco. At roughly the same time as the views started, the climbing began too. I had been warned of the long climbs, firstly to the Big Sur lighthouse and then to Hurricane Point. Both are several kilometres long so they can take a lot out of you. The payoff is the two-mile descent to the Bixby Bridge. The Hurricane Point climb is considered so hard that you can join the Hurricane Point Survivors Club after the marathon and wear a special club T-shirt. Corny or not, this was a big hill.

Bixby marks the halfway point of the marathon. There, in the car park, was the pianist playing away: it could have been Gershwin. He had his back to the fabulous view, having chosen to face the runners instead, and luckily for him he did not have to compete with a noisy sea. The tones of the piano and the gentle surf on the beach below — did I dream this? So, yes, my friends, the pianist really does sit there and play his tunes, adding to the magic of this marathon.

The second half of the route was constantly hilly, but the hills were shorter than before. They came relentlessly, one after another. Lots of participants were walking by now.

Between Bixby and Carmel the road is close to the ocean so we got to see plenty more of the cliffs, promontories and beaches. Some runners seemed a bit blasé about the scenery but I gathered they were locals; others were stopping to take photos and gasp. The 2004 race T-shirt summed it up as the *ragged edge of the Western world.*

As Highway 1 comes into Carmel it is accessible to a lot more people, and all of a sudden there were spectators along the way. They were calling out our numbers and endlessly saying, 'Good job!' It was like coming into another world, a world with more in it than footfalls and heavy breathing. The hills don't stop, though, until the very end.

I was tiring fast, and had to play that trick of telling myself I just had to make it to the next lamppost, until a bit of friendly competition with another female gave me the spurt to get to the finish line. She would pull me along, then I would pull her along, until she managed to finish about six seconds ahead of me. I did better than I had expected here, considering the hills.

I still can't state with complete authority that this marathon is the best in the world because there are too many I have not yet done, but it is a truly remarkable event.

In June I headed to Christchurch, New Zealand, hoping to run a personal best.

I was taking my training seriously. People often ask me, 'What training do you do?' and then follow this up with, 'If you run so many marathons I guess you don't have to do any training.' To some extent it is true that each marathon can be regarded as training for the next one, and the accumulated marathons I have run should prepare me well for future ones.

At the time I was running for about six hours a week, with one long run of two hours, often on hills on the outskirts of Melbourne. I did half-hour runs where I tried to keep the pace up around five-minute kilometres or faster. I did one circuit class a week at the gym, and would also run for half an hour on the treadmill afterwards. I found this a hard workout, especially when I did a hill program on the machine. Then I was swimming once or twice a week, and I even found time for the weekly bike ride of an hour or so. I was just trying to keep fit, but I was busy.

One of the major factors in my preparation, to which I gave little credit at the time, was a weekend event I participated in not long before going to Christchurch. The event was called the Pentath Run and was held in Warwick, Queensland. It comprised a set of five races adding up to 42.2 kilometres in total. I wonder where they found that figure.

On the first day we ran a half marathon, a 4.6-kilometre cross-country run through horse paddocks, and a five-kilometre flat road race. On the second day we ran ten kilometres up a long hill and 1500 metres in the centre of town. I had trained carefully for this weekend, making myself run up to three times a day to prepare for the first day of racing. This was harder training than usual and it paid off. I had run this quasi-marathon in 3 hours, 24 minutes.

That winter I also participated in the Athletics Victoria cross-country series. They hold a series of races in Melbourne and country Victoria over several distances. I was only a journeyman, but these races attract the cream of the state's runners and it spurs you on to run in such exalted company. I always ran at the back of the field but I posted some of my fastest times over distances between four and 15 kilometres. Races like these must have been invaluable in helping me build some speed.

I went to Christchurch to break three and a half hours. I don't ever like to put this kind of pressure on myself but for this one race I made an exception. The Christchurch course is flat and many marathon records have been set here. Wind is rarely a problem and the cold seems to help generate fast times.

One of Christchurch's showpieces is the Avon River. It's a pretty little river, with banks of willows and lots of ducks. On other occasions I have followed the river on foot from the city centre to its estuary, where suburban streets give way to forest which in turn gives way to large expanses of sand and the beach at New Brighton. In the opposite direction, the Port Hills (so called because they overlook the city's port of Lyttelton) are fantastic for running, so long as the weather is clear, since these hills are all about the views. I've been there in thick fog, in howling winds and also in clear sunshine, where the views over the harbour are magic and you feel as though you are running on top of the world.

The route of the Christchurch Marathon is a meander around the city, following the Avon in the first segment and then taking a little out-and-back trip to the airport for the remainder.

The morning of the race I woke up to see a line of snow-capped peaks in the distant west. It had snowed overnight. The sight was spectacular and I could have happily stayed in my room looking at it. But there was a race to run. It promised to be a cold one. The thing about running in the cold is that I never look forward to it — I dread that business of shivering on the start line waiting for the gun. But at the same time I know that the cold helps my running and I will have a better result than I would have on a warm day.

I was staying close to the start area so I ventured out of the hotel as late as possible and noticed immediately that the majority of runners were dressed to run in thermals and beanies. I hadn't even brought this gear with me, but I did have gloves.

For the first half of the course we followed the river through a residential area. We ran along as the river twisted and turned, passing parkland of muted hues, and then came back into downtown Christchurch. Everything was quiet, until the half marathoners (who started after us) appeared on the far bank of the river. It was exciting to see this stampede of runners who far outnumbered us.

The route crossed Hagley Park, an open space that is popular for running and very pretty with poplar groves, cherry trees, oaks and more. There are small lakes, duck ponds and sports facilities. In one corner are the city's Botanic Gardens. The park is certainly one of the key features of the marathon. On a winter's morning the park takes on a hazy appearance and it's easy to see why people say the place is reminiscent of England. I had run here many times, mainly because it is so accessible when you are in central Christchurch. But at this point in the marathon I went through a low patch and felt despondent about meeting my marathon time target. I started talking to a runner from Dunedin who had survived liver cancer and had turned to running as part of his rehab. He was achieving significantly with his running and I was impressed — so impressed that my own current despair faded.

The second sector took us out towards the airport, at first along a major thoroughfare, passing shopping malls, and then into a more rural scene. Those snow-clad mountains were clearly visible. Kids were out playing sports, there were horses in the paddocks, and the sun shone weakly. I got my second wind, and as I passed the 30-kilometre mark I knew that if I really wanted to I could run the remaining 12 kilometres in under five minutes each which would give me my personal best. I felt very positive.

I had a number of problems with traffic during this race. I would always have assumed that runners would be protected from cars and other road users while running a marathon, and that part of the entry fee goes towards ensuring this. We had a lane in which to run but there were drivers who envied us and wanted to be in our lane too. It seemed as though there were plenty of drivers who saw the coning off of part of their road as either a challenge or an irritation. The problem was that once they got into our lane they could not get out again except by endangering us, squeezing us with nowhere to go to avoid getting hit.

And then we had to cross lots of roads, where there were marshals to hold up either us or the traffic so that both didn't meet in the middle of the road. The system didn't always work for me. At one junction a marshal was holding up her hand to stop an advancing car but I heard her mutter: 'I wonder if he's going to stop ...' I wasn't sure either, but the car jerked to a sudden halt just in time.

As I reached the last straight I was fully into my finishing sprint. A policeman was having little success in holding back an oncoming car that had ignored diversion signs. I had worked hard for my personal best and I wasn't prepared to miss my target time by having to slow down for a car that should not have been there in the first place. It was a moment to throw caution to the wind. I presume the car stopped, since I was still alive at the line, with a finishing time of 3 hours, 28 minutes. I had run my desired time.

I have very happy memories of this marathon. I won my age group decisively. The personal best I managed there will always be my best time, and it was highly satisfying to go to Christchurch with a goal and achieve it.

A week later I ran only 90 seconds slower at the Traralgon Marathon, in western Victoria, on another cold day. I did not quite break three and a half hours again. Funnily, I had a tussle in the last few hundred metres with another runner who managed to break three and a half hours for the first time.

The marathon in Christchurch was a watershed for me. Although I still cared how fast I completed each marathon, I did not care as much after that day. I continued to run well over the winter, but by the end of the year I was slowing down. 2004 was both a quantity and quality year for me, and by the end of it I had decided that high volume was what I thrived on. It had not yet occurred to me to contemplate running a hundred marathons, but I knew that I wanted to run this distance often.

In a holiday mood

You can sneak away to Queensland in the middle of winter for either the Gold Coast Marathon in early July or the Townsville Marathon in early August. Or, as I did in 2004, both of the above. It was too good an opportunity to escape the Melbourne cold.

I took my kids, aged eight, eleven and thirteen, up to the Gold Coast and promised them that once I had run my marathon we would be able to visit the theme parks. I was not sure if I would feel like going on the roller-coaster and down the water slides straight after a hard run, but I was going to be doing so anyway.

At this time the Gold Coast Marathon was the largest in Australia. This marathon has always had a high profile in this country, and it started out with an admirable aim. In 1978 a running club was founded on the Gold Coast as an enticement to help the local population become fit, with special training being given to those members who wanted to prepare to run a marathon. Within a year the first Gold Coast Marathon was being planned. The inaugural event in 1979 had 121 runners in the full marathon. If you think this sounds like a tiny field for a race, remember that this was still prior to the worldwide marathon boom of the 1980s.

With a field of almost 2000 entrants in the 2004 marathon, plus many thousands more in the shorter races, the event was substantial enough to have some of the features you find at larger races overseas. One such feature was a race expo with a multitude of stalls promoting marathons around the world, clothing vendors, and salespeople with foodstuffs to make your race more pleasurable (gels, electrolyte drinks, nutrition bars).

The marathon course is flat and takes runners on a trip south down the holiday strip from Southport to Mermaid Beach. Some of the route — the best part — is right by the beach, from Main Beach through Surfers Paradise to Broadbeach. It was a warm day, but early on we enjoyed the cooling sea breezes and the support of spectators out eating breakfast on their balconies. Later on we went north, passing our eventual finish line, heading for Runaway Bay. At times here we ran alongside the Broadwater with views across to the Spit and SeaWorld, where I was soon feeling seasick on the pirate ship and getting soaked on the log flume.

I like marathons with a large field of competitors. I like to run in this mixed company of all types of runners. Young girls, old men and everything in between. Some are on home ground, others are visitors. Some have done this before, others have not. Some will do it again and some will not. It's a huge party on the move, and we are going to continue inexorably forward until the end.

Our day had arrived. No wonder we feel nervous after waiting so long for the curtain to rise. First-timer or veteran, rich or poor, the race is not going to distinguish. It is going to chew us all up and spit us out. We'll be okay or not, depending on how we react to what is thrown at us.

From where I run in the field I do not see the truly competitive runners. The serious guys are all up at the front fighting to the death for money and glory. We are fighting our own smaller battles further back in the field, battles which are important to us but do not get us public recognition. The recognition we seek is within ourselves. The medal and name in the results list in the newspaper, if they happen, are a bonus.

There goes a girl running her first marathon. She has followed a training guide and is ready. The marathon is going to be tougher than she expected but she'll get through. She started running to get in shape, but soon the running became a part of her life and she no longer had to have a reason to go out and run; the desire to run came naturally. She tried shorter races, and then the marathon beckoned. At the end of it she will have new status. She will be more than a runner; she will be a *marathon* runner. And the best part, to her mind, is that she only has to run one marathon to be a marathon runner.

There go the group of students, laughing as they run. They're so comfortable they can barely understand why people say the marathon is hard. But maybe after 30 kilometres we will come across them again, walking this time and saving energy by being silent. Now they see what the marathon is all about.

There runs the middle-aged woman, head down and concentrating on her steps. She knows what's in store for her after halfway: the long kilometres that have to be run when she is tired and has had enough of this. But she's grateful to be able to run. Many of her friends don't even run when they're late for the train.

Now there's the chattering couple, taking this completely in their stride — no pun intended — knocking out the kilometres smoothly and evenly. They have a plan and are running it. They appear at ease, but that's only thanks to their dedicated training. They do this regularly and it's a significant part of their lives.

A group of club runners comes by. They are proudly wearing club colours and looking out for other members so they can share a fleeting greeting. The younger ones are feeling competitive while the older ones are ruminating on past glories.

Others are not so comfortable. You can hear it in their breathing or see it in their wildly alternating speed — fast bursts followed by a walk. They would rather it was otherwise, but they are going to make the best of a bad situation. By the time they get to work on Monday morning they will have great stories about the harshness of this race, and they will describe their distress in elaborate detail.

There is the poor runner who has had to stop with cramp, leaning on a fence by the roadside trying to stretch it out. That's an awful place to be during a marathon. His pain is our pain.

Yes, we all share a common bond. We know why we are here.

To complete this marathon we plan to run 42.195 kilometres along a designated route. A gun was fired at the start to indicate our departure. There will be some form of marker to indicate the finish line, and a timing mat because the race is timed using an electronic chip. Some competitors will finish in little over two hours; others will take five or six hours to reach that line. Along the route we are likely to be provided minimal sustenance in the form of small cups of water or a drink we may or may not like every three to five kilometres. Apart from this, we are at the mercy of our own legs.

We have set out in a spirit of keen anticipation. We have trained for this for up to a year. We have thought about every aspect of the ordeal ahead. We are in peak physical form. Our friends and family are all thinking about us. We want to do well.

We will finish in exhaustion. We will be so sore in the legs that we doubt we will ever run, or even walk, again. A lingering tiredness will persist for several days. We will be so hungry that we cannot stop eating. We will be happy. Above all, we will swear that we are never going to do this thing again.

And then a month later I am off to Townsville to run more of a boutique marathon with only 70 runners.

Most of the other participants were worried at the prospect of having to run in the heat. I gave this little thought. My main fear with this marathon was the frighteningly early start. I have great difficulty getting up really early to run. This fact alone makes me different from the vast majority of runners I have met in my life. Running, you would think after chatting to hundreds of runners, is best done before dawn. I prefer to be properly awake to run. I must be soft.

On top of this, I have recurring dreams several nights before any marathon that I have somehow missed the start, or that I have cut my travel arrangements so fine that I cannot possibly get there on time. I have had dreams about being on a bus to the race start and the bus is mysteriously in the wrong city, or that I am waiting on the platform for a train which does not arrive, or that I am at the race start and there is nobody else there because I am too late. (I have twice arrived at a race start to find nobody else there. On the first occasion I realised after a good ten minutes that I was in the wrong place, and I ended up starting the race late. On the second occasion the race start line had been shifted and within a minute of my arrival a marshal appeared to give me this news and direct me to the new start line. These real-world experiences give the anxiety left by my recurring dreams even more weight.)

My perpetual fear of not getting to the race start on time is compounded when the race starts early. I might oversleep. This explains my concern at the prospect of a 5.30am start in Townsville. The idea of toeing the line of a full marathon well before daybreak filled me with a sense of dread. This, of course, was before I even considered getting up two hours before the start to have breakfast. This is what you are supposed to do, so that your meal is digested and will not cause problems in your gut as you run. You're then allowed, according to any serious marathon training guide, to return to bed and complete your night's slumber. *Who does this?* you may well ask. Well, I don't; I eat and run. But I have spoken to elite runners who do as advised.

I have, however, made some changes to my eating habits during my time running marathons. Some people think that running gives you a licence to eat what you please. Non-runners suggest this to me with an almost wistful envy: I must be so lucky that I can pack in whatever I feel like regardless of its kilojoule content and danger to my waistline. Just this afternoon I took a break from writing and went to the shops. I was placing three doughnuts in a bag (for the kids, honestly) when a friend sidled up to me and said: 'So that's the secret of successful marathon running.' Others believe that I must live in complete austerity, never indulging in any food that could be construed as enjoyable. I've been caught eating a biscuit and someone has said: 'Oh, I'm surprised to see *you* doing that.' The truth is that I eat a normal diet. I do not binge on junk food but I do eat cake and chocolate several times a week. I pay attention to my fruit and vegetable intake, eat some meat, and aim to have fish more than once a week. I don't eat huge meals.

When I run early in the morning I have to decide if I am going to have breakfast first. I used to do all my morning running on an empty stomach, and even did half marathons without eating beforehand, but this has changed. I have found that for any run that is going to last longer than an hour I will feel better in the later stages of the run if I *do* eat a light breakfast and have a cup of coffee before setting out. If the run is shorter than that I will generally just have a cup of coffee. I find the run a little bit easier after a cup of coffee, and I don't know if this is the stimulant effect or a more scientific reason.

For years I did my own modified version of carbo-loading the day before the race, which involved eating as much as I possibly could. I especially liked to eat coffee scrolls, muffins, Chinese takeaway and hot chips. I ate so much I found it embarrassing to disclose the full details to others. This was not pure greed. I had been through some miserable races where I had not eaten properly beforehand. If you try to run a morning race without having eaten enough the day before, you are in for a bad time. You feel weak and woozy and it becomes impossible to summon up any energy at all. I knew that a mistake like this before a marathon would be totally unpleasant. I developed a fear of not eating adequately before a marathon, and I became reluctant to ease off my bulk-eating strategy.

I never felt any adverse effects on race day from this over-eating but eventually it dawned on me that this might not be the best way to go about my race preparation. In late 2003 I made changes. I stopped eating myself silly the day before the race and specifically tried to avoid unhealthy foods. For a while my marathon results improved and I deduced that making an all-out effort to get fat the day before the marathon was not the best plan.

By the time I got to Townsville I was no longer gorging myself before marathons. I ate filled rolls the night before this one, and had two bananas for breakfast while walking to the start.

On the way to the start I came across many groups of revellers still out from the previous evening and enjoying making what they thought were very clever comments about the runners filling the footpath. The city was experimenting with a 2am to 5am lock-in at all pubs and clubs, so we runners were out and about just as the doors were being unlocked.

Even I had to admit this time was perfect for running. The air temperature was perfectly poised between warm and cold, with no chill and no heat in the stillness of the night. Yes, it was still night as far as I was concerned.

When it comes to holidaying, Townsville ranks a poor second in travellers' minds to Cairns, 300 kilometres further north. But Townsville, although away from the Great Barrier Reef, has plenty to offer. It has the same balmy winter climate as Cairns, and its own offshore island, as well as beaches and nature reserves.

I had been to Townsville once before in 1989, when I cycled from there to Broome on my major transcontinental ride. Most people who cycle across Australia take the southern route from Sydney to Perth or vice versa, but I decided to take the northern route as I had never been to this part of the country. Townsville did not feel familiar when I arrived this time, but I had arrived on the overnight bus from Sydney on my last visit and I did not linger long in town, except to pick up food supplies. I had broken my thumb skiing only just before this ride started and I still had my hand in plaster, which made the chores of buying food and generally getting around on a bike a touch harder than usual. I could have waited for my thumb to heal before setting out on this trip, but, hey, I just wanted to get going and a little extra challenge was not going to stop me. Once out of Townsville I never managed to get to a medical centre to have the plaster removed, and in the end I had a local farmer cut it off with his tin snips at the pub in Richmond, beyond Hughenden. Good times.

While in Townsville I had cycled around the beachfront strip and been out to Pallarenda and the Townsville Town Common to get to know the local flora and fauna. The beachfront in 2004 would not be as I saw it in 1989. Townsville's beachfront used to be nothing to write home about — in fact, visitors would have a good sneer about it on their return home — with enough mangroves to prevent you being able to paddle and a few patches of sand that regularly disappeared after a storm. The wind and rain can be fierce up here. Then in the late 1990s the much maligned beaches and also the sea wall were totally and irrevocably destroyed by cyclones, and the entire area was redeveloped by 2000. Nowadays there is an appealing beachside strip of parkland with trails and picnic areas, as well as a water theme park, fountains and cafes. The day before the marathon I hired a kayak and paddled along the string of beaches. I was truly in a holiday mood.

Runners and walkers all congregate on the Strand beachfront area. In one direction you can run towards the casino and marina, and in the other direction you have several kilometres of beachside trails, passing rock pools, and with a spectacular view across Cleveland Bay to Magnetic Island, eight kilometres away. This hilly island is Townsville's treasure: largely national park with pristine white sand beaches and rugged bushwalks, not to mention a colony of koalas. I had a day of bushwalking on the island after the marathon, pausing for a swim at several of the beaches and enjoying a beer at a beachside cafe on Horseshoe Bay.

Apart from the beachfront area, Townsville has another drawcard: Castle Hill. This 300-metre-high rock monolith just begs to be climbed, which is why you won't be alone walking or running there at daybreak. I found this out the day before the marathon as I ran to the top along the main access road. On my way up I fell in step with a local runner and he chided me for doing this the day before the marathon. It was a steady climb with improving views over the Townsville region the higher I came. I descended on the Goat Track, a rougher trail with steep pinches.

The marathon starts at the Tobruk Pool, an outdoor swimming complex where many icons of Australian swimming have trained. In particular, it was a favourite place for team training prior to Olympic Games and world championships in the 1960s and 1970s. From here runners head for the casino and the marina, where the boats moored in the moonlight make an attractive sight. I especially enjoyed running in the dark and this was something new to me since in those days I never got up early enough to do this. My experience here has actually encouraged me to get up earlier and run before dawn from time to time.

The remainder of this first ten-kilometre loop took us along the Strand, passing another swimming pool, the Rock Pool. This one is carved into the red rocks of the foreshore. We continued alongside mangroves, where the shoreline has not been redeveloped. All the while there were views over to Magnetic Island but all we could make out across the water was the silhouette of the island's bulk and a few lights around the area of the ferry wharf.

The second loop was identical except that by then it was daylight so everything looked slightly different. Castle Hill was there but we did not have to climb it. Magnetic Island was fully revealed to us. The participants for the shorter events were hanging around waiting for their start and it was lovely to have them cheer us on.

For the third and longest loop of 21 kilometres, our route took us away from the Strand and out to the suburb of Pallarenda. Here, the running is through parkland once again. In fact this marathon route makes good use of Townsville's parks and seems to have found a way to link all the places with the city's best scenery. Pallarenda features a long beach of uninterrupted golden sand. It is backed at the northern end by the Townsville Town Common, a region of wetland where many species of waterbird are protected. From the roadside all you can see are tall grasses and sparse clumps of gum trees. This third loop also forms the entire route of the accompanying half marathon, which gets underway later than the marathon. The half marathoners miss out on the excitement of running in the dark but they get a lie-in. The quarter marathon, held even later in the morning, follows the route of the first loop. The idea is that all runners should be finishing at roughly the same time.

As for the heat, it wasn't too much of an issue during that year's marathon. We could feel the air warming up as we progressed around our third loop, but the sun's rays were not truly blazing down until I was nearly finished. I found the last couple of kilometres a bit too hot but, to take a philosophical approach, we were all suffering by that stage in a marathon anyway.

When I was done with running I went for a paddle in the sea. I did something else, too: I went to one of the lovely cafes along the Strand with tables under a curtain fig tree and drank a large iced chocolate. Then I drank a second one, and I didn't tell anybody.

Running with the crabs

At 3pm one Saturday afternoon in September 2004, I found myself on the start line of a marathon on Christmas Island. This was to have the least number of participants of any marathon I have done, with three runners and four walkers, although the walkers had set out separately four hours before the runners. I was the sole female runner so I only had to finish the race to earn the winner's trophy. My moment of glory was coming.

Everything surrounding this marathon had a somewhat surreal tinge.

I had heard about the marathon but I knew nobody who had experienced it first-hand. At that time I had a goal to run every Australian marathon, so I had to run the Christmas Island Marathon. Getting there was going to be tricky and expensive, so I asked the organisers, quite half-heartedly, if they might be able to provide some assistance with getting me over there. I had no idea that the race only attracted a handful of runners. In return I would write an article about the race and hope to have it published in a running magazine. They acknowledged my request but were doubtful if they could help. I put the idea on the backburner.

So I was amazed when I heard, quite out of the blue, that a ticket to fly from Perth to Christmas Island, and back, was waiting for me at Perth airport, if I could get myself across the country to collect it. I would be met by the race organiser at Christmas Island airport and he had my accommodation worked out at no cost to me. Is it appropriate to say that all my Christmases came at once? I traded in my frequent flyer points and I was ready to go to Perth.

The day before I left home I got cold feet about this. Why would there be a marathon on Christmas Island? This was surely a hoax to lure me to the den of an axe murderer. I took my life into my hands and phoned the Christmas Island tourism office to ask if there was a marathon in the offing. And, yes, there was. The lady I spoke to not only knew about the approaching marathon but had run it herself. Twice. So I thanked her, went over there, and had one of the best marathon trips I can remember.

The island had been in the news not long before I went over, with new revelations about the allegations of asylum seekers throwing their children overboard the ship *Tampa* in 2001, just off the island. If you knew one thing about Christmas Island it was that it has an immigrant detention centre. But there is far more to the island than that. Various resorts have come and gone, there have been attempts to get a casino licence, and the island is a multicultural success story. The snorkelling is good, there are coral beaches, and there are a multitude of rainforest drives and walks. It's warm all year. You can dine on all sorts of ethnic cuisines or go to the pub or take in an outdoor movie.

As a tiny speck in the Indian Ocean, 2600 kilometres from Perth, it is hardly surprising that little attention is paid to this island unless immigration is in the headlines. It is close to the equator and close to Jakarta, but there is a lot of ocean between the island and Australia proper.

The small plane that flew us from Perth via Learmonth to Christmas Island was filled with island expatriates returning to work after holidays or business in mainland Australia. The guy I sat next to knew the race organiser, John, although he did not know John was organising a marathon. When we disembarked on the island my companion led me up to John standing in the terminal and said, 'Here's your runner.'

John looked at me and said, 'Are you really? Are you Julia Thorn?'

I assured him that I was the real thing. I am not at all clear what it was about me that did not match his expectations.

Aircraft arrivals and departures are times for partying and celebration outside the terminal. That was a pleasant welcome. Then, having set foot on the island, I was invited to go for a run with the Hash House Harriers. It happened to be the afternoon for their weekly outing into the jungle surrounding Settlement, the place that is downtown Christmas Island. I knew about Hash runners and their slogan proclaiming them to be *Drinkers with a running problem*, but I had never run with a Hash club. And as they were organising the marathon I thought it would be fun to meet them.

Before this run I went for a short stroll near my motel and at that point I noticed I was in a warm and humid place. I found walking around not as easy as I expected. The run was not too easy either, along overgrown trails, but there was plenty of compulsory beer drinking at the end to replace lost fluids.

Christmas Island is famous for the annual crab migration each September, when thousands of red crabs that live in the jungle make the trip from their inland homes to the water's edge to have their young and then return to the jungle. All the major roads have crab grids, designed to help the crabs get under the road and avoid being squashed by vehicles during the migration. But you can see lots of crabs here any day of the year. Make any foray into the rainforest and you will hear a scuffling noise — crabs scouring the ground for food. They eat the floor of the forest until it is clear, and the forest floor is not only bare but also pockmarked with the holes these crabs live in. They're friendly crabs — they like to come into your house.

Apart from the red crabs there are large robber crabs, and I generally saw these by the roadsides.

Up above is pretty special, too. The birdlife on the island is amazing. The golden bosun is one of the endemic species; it has wonderful golden colouring and long, graceful tail feathers. Along the coastline you'll see hovering frigate birds, diving into the water for fish or trying to steal a feed from a bird that has already caught something. Brown boobies perch on the rocks, taking in the scene.

I had looked forward to the race — despite the temperature being above 25 degrees, the air thick with humidity and the prospect of many hills. I hadn't run with crabs before and I hadn't run an afternoon marathon, where presumably the air would cool as I heated up. Now the time had come and I was at the start line at the airport. Actually, I had been at the airport for hours, watching the other participants head off on their adventures. I saw the marathon relay get underway, and the half marathon and the marathon walkers. Part of the reason I was there for so long before the start of my own run was the slightly lower temperature up on the plateau.

We started out on a wide gravel road lined by rainforest and quiet apart from the rustling sounds of small birds. Since we started on a plateau we might reasonably have expected the marathon route to be all downhill. Instead, the whole course has hills. But hills give views, and there are fabulous views of the coast, especially at the southern end of the island. Ironically, the worst climb is to the LB4 lookout at the 23-kilometre mark, where we passed the lookout without being able to see the view.

As I ran I was looking out for crabs but it was several hours before my first robber crab made an appearance. It was sitting on the roadside verge, oblivious to having made my day. I don't know how I would have coped if I had run an entire marathon here without setting sight on a crab.

We covered most of the island's few roads in the course of our journey. The roads are here because of the phosphate mines, the industry that first opened up the island. This began in the 1890s and labour was brought in from peninsular Malaya. The mining operations and barren-mined land dominate the island landscape, but in recent times the jungle is encouraged to reclaim the mined areas and the scenery will improve.

In the early afternoon I noticed that the roads reflected a lot of heat, but fortunately there was ample roadside shade. The local firemen had come out to help us with hoses every ten kilometres. There were few supporters and it was lonely running. The runners from the other events were nowhere to be seen; I passed one of the marathon walkers and then saw no other race participants until the finish.

The race might have had a small field but it was nothing if not well-organised. With so few runners you could hardly expect aid stations and kilometre markers. But there were cheerfully manned aid stations — always a welcome sight. At one of them the helpers had dressed as French waiters with red check aprons, bow ties and berets, and had a table laid out with bottles of wine and candles. I grabbed water. I was carrying some lollies that I bought in the morning, but as soon as I got them into my hand they melted and looked revolting. As for the kilometre markers, these are here all year round, having been set up permanently, and I had already noticed them in my few days driving around the island.

I started my descent to the inhabited parts of the island, towards the townships of Drumsite, Poon San and Settlement, as dusk fell. It was by then cooler, with no wind. And after dusk everything was black. Blacker than black. There were only intermittent streetlights and nothing in the spaces between the townships. This was a little worrying for me as I couldn't see where I was treading. I didn't want to upset a crab by stepping on it and I didn't want to trip over. But I was running out of energy and I hadn't much strength to think about where I was placing my feet.

A course marshal arrived in his four-wheel-drive to guide me with his headlights. This was great, except that the final two kilometres are a steep downhill and I fretted that this driver may roll straight into me if I slowed down without warning. I hoped his car had good brakes. At the same time, I was thinking to myself, *What a weird way to be spending the evening, running down a hill in the dark on an island out in the Indian Ocean!*

I've run in big cities and along deserted roads but nowhere has been quite like Christmas Island. This was a marathon experience a cut above the rest.

Marathon runners everywhere will identify with this feeling: you can be so tired and yet so happy. When I reach the late stages of a marathon I am virtually running as if this is just an automatic process and expecting my legs to keep moving regardless of the discomfort. I know in my heart of hearts that this run will at some not too distant time be over, and I will have conquered another challenge. I am enjoying the dying moments despite the pain. In fact, if there were no pain I might not see this as such a worthwhile endeavour, and that, I suppose, is what makes me a marathon runner rather than a stamp collector.

When I reached the finish line I was delighted to find a party in progress. It had been in progress for some while because races had been finishing all afternoon. Whatever the stated rationale for an afternoon race, I think the true reason was to allow the island to hold a party afterwards at a party time of day rather than see all the runners and supporters go home to rest in the midday heat, as they would after an early morning race.

The small island community of barely one thousand people had got behind this race with enthusiasm. The four marathon walkers were already there and we full marathon runners were the last to arrive, just in time for the presentations. Little stalls were selling Malay and Chinese foods — curries, satays and rice — and as it was dinner time I tucked straight into a plate of something spicy, with a beer to wash it down.

This had been an amazing day — the strange setting for a marathon, the hard run in tropical conditions, and the realisation at the end that this whole running event was really an excuse for a fabulous giant party. When I had partied my fill I went across the road to my motel and phoned the family to tell them about my day. They weren't all that pleased to hear from me — I had forgotten the three-hour time difference; I had forgotten that I ran in the late afternoon rather than in the early morning; I managed to wake them up in the middle of their night. But I told them about my day anyway.

We flew back to Perth with a stop on the Cocos Keeling Islands, 900 kilometres from Christmas Island, the alternative route to flying between Perth and Christmas Island via Learmonth. The islands are a collection of atolls where the land is so close to sea level that it is barely visible until you are right above it, and on a sunny day there could be no more beautiful place in the world: the azure sea, fringing coral reef around the atolls, palm trees and white sand. The total population is under 600. Passengers who were disembarking there all carried a loaf or two of bread. The island bakery was only open three days a week, and flight arrival day was not one of the three. I walked around for ten minutes while the plane refuelled, and checked out a perfect beach. A group of passengers got on the plane here; they said that it had rained constantly for the past week and they had not had one day of sunshine. So much for paradise.

The excitement of this marathon was not over yet. Although I had the female winner's trophy and a souvenir cap and singlet, I did not have a certificate or a list of the results so I had nothing to stick in my file of race results. This didn't bother me for a while — in fact, for a long time — until I ran my hundredth marathon and decided I needed to have a complete set of records in case anyone should ask for proof of my accomplishment. There were gaps in my records but one by one I managed to plug them all, except for Christmas Island. I had the magazine article I had written about the marathon, but I shouldn't be certifying my own achievement.

I sent emails to anyone whom I knew had been involved with that marathon. Nobody had a list of results. I left the matter alone. I found my plane ticket, so at least I had proof I had been over there on marathon weekend. Then I tried once more to get written results, this time casting a wider net. But time had passed, and by 2010 there was no longer a marathon being held at all. I had this exchange with the proprietor of the motel where I had stayed, learning also that the motel had changed hands since 2004:

> *Me:* In September 2004 I came to Christmas Island to run the marathon and you very kindly accommodated me at your resort. I am trying to find someone who can provide me with a results list from that marathon as I am trying to keep records of all my marathons. Do you think you might be able to help? The race was organised by the Hash House Harriers, and I know that the guy who owned the pub at the time was involved with the event.
>
> *Motel owner:* The pub has been sold and the owner has left the island.
>
> *Me:* I remember there was a photographer named Phil who took photos at the marathon.

Motel owner: He has also left.

Me: I am not having much success so far.

Motel owner: I will forward your email to a person I know of who is involved with the Hash. Good luck!

This was sadly the end of that road. The 'person I know of' had no records from the marathon of 2004. I found that the marathon was organised by the local cricket club, not the Hash, from 2005 until 2009, at which point it was abandoned. So I contacted the cricket club. They were unable to give me any assistance, informing me that they had not been the organisers when I ran the marathon and knew nothing about the 2004 race. I tried other avenues and learnt during this time all about how the marathon began and how the course was designed. I discovered that participants from an earlier year's marathon had received laminated certificates. But I couldn't get one.

I was stumped.

I tracked down and phoned the male winner from 2004, whose name I had fortunately remembered, and confirmed with him his finishing time. He was not sure that he had received results. He agreed that I had run the marathon that year and he believed I finished in just under four hours. So it wasn't all a dream.

I conjured up in my mind all sorts of scenarios as to why the island could not provide me with a list of marathon finishers. Had they forgotten to record the details? Had the results list been sabotaged? Was this a part of an elaborate international scandal? Then I did what any self-respecting marathon runner who could not access a list of marathon results would do. I made my own.

Pace the race

The Stockholm Marathon fell into my lap — although my running friends did not see it that way.

In late 2004 I decided to enter the Comrades Marathon in South Africa the following June. This is called a 'marathon', but at 89 kilometres it is actually longer than a double marathon. To ultra marathon runners this is one of those must-do races. Having decided to travel to South Africa, I thought I may as well go to England on the way to visit my family, as I had not been over for two years. And having decided to travel to Europe to visit my family, I thought I might as well run a marathon over there. This was the point at which my fellow runners told me I was losing it.

'Running Comrades should be the pinnacle of your running career,' said one South African runner whom I ran with weekly. He had run Comrades six times. 'You do not want to run Comrades straight after running a marathon. You can't possibly be prepared.'

'Well, I'm not going to go all the way to Europe and not do one single race,' was my standard answer, for him and for anyone else who challenged me. 'Comrades is on a Thursday so I can run a marathon beforehand and have ten days to recover. I'll fit in the family visits around the running.'

By that time I was running a lot of marathons, and not always waiting very long between each one before moving on to the next. Physically, I seemed to be handling this okay. I had no injuries, and I always made sure to resume running after a marathon only when I was ready. This was generally by the Thursday after a Sunday race. Mentally, I succeeded because I had my year mapped out. Once I had run one race I could focus on the next one.

It was a big thing for me to be going away on my own for several weeks. This was the first time I was leaving the family for more than a few days. I never doubted that my husband could look after the kids in my absence, but I still felt I was making a major decision in taking this trip. I had to be sure it was going to be worthwhile.

I looked at a marathon calendar and the Stockholm Marathon was there on exactly the right day, large as life, billed as the best marathon in Europe. That was good enough for me. Stockholm, via London, here I come.

I expected great things from this event, and it delivered. It was half the size of the New York or London marathons, but it scrubbed up well in terms of scenery, atmosphere and organisation. The city offered water views, wide avenues, buildings with extravagant 19th-century facades and lush green parkland. Stockholm is built on 14 islands, and the marathon course has been designed to give runners a real taste of this special aspect of the city.

The opening kilometres were a little disappointing — we were in the heart of suburbia. There were so many of us (nowadays the race is full five months before the day itself, with a limit of 18,000 entries) and it was hard not to trip over the other runners' feet. And there were big puddles, though I can't really blame the organisers for that.

The weather had not been good so far that day. When I woke up at 3am the sky was blue with little puffy clouds. It never got truly dark there in midsummer, being so close to the North Pole. But by 7am it was raining and the promise of a fine day was gone. Then the wind came up, and by the time we lined up for the race start at 2pm it was not comfortable at all. Many runners were clad in thermals and — help! — I hadn't even brought a pair of gloves.

We had to assemble in a large open space behind the Olympic stadium, Ostermalms IP, and it was all flooded. Fortunately, the rain stopped around the time the race got underway, even though it still remained rather cold. The streets also turned out to be flooded in places.

The Kaknes TV tower was the first landmark on the route. It was shrouded in mist, so we couldn't see the radio antennae that make the tower one of the tallest structures in northern Europe. The drinks station here was a welcome sight, but I had to step into a flooded gutter to reach a drink, and this wasn't a day for me to be running with wet feet.

After the TV tower we headed for more central areas, and suddenly we were in the midst of an enchanting city. I hadn't known what to expect here as I had only arrived in Sweden the previous evening. We ran past a series of large buildings — now museums — and came to Strandvagen. This is one of the city's loveliest waterside avenues, lined by imposing 19th-century buildings on one side and moored boats on the other. We were running at the water's edge for the first time in this race. This set the tone for many more kilometres.

On the other side of the water is Djurgarden, an island which is given over to parkland and the Skansen and Vasa museums. The Skansen museum contains replica miniature Swedish farmhouses, while the Vasa museum holds the original Vasa warship that sank on its maiden voyage in 1628. The Vasa had been pulled out of the waters just outside Stockholm in the 1960s. The only other time I had been to Sweden, as a child, the ship was undergoing processes to dry out the timber; it was in a makeshift dry dock and very smelly. You couldn't tour its many decks then, but you can these days.

The marathon course took us around the outside of the old city of Gamla Stan. This is a delightful part of Stockholm but was off-limits to us marathon runners. The quaint streets are narrow and twisting, and it would have been far more enjoyable to stroll gently along on another day, taking a photo of the colourful buildings at every turn. There's an island right beside the old city, with the very old Riddarholms church, burial place for the Swedish rulers.

We passed the royal palace, which is vast and calls for a whole day of sightseeing. (I went to watch the changing of the guard here the day after the marathon and got chatting to a guy from Adelaide. Imagining everyone was in Stockholm for the marathon, I started asking him if he had run the Adelaide Marathon — then realised he wasn't a runner at all and found this an odd question.) We then crossed to Sodermalm Island. Sodermalm is basically a waterside strip of moorings backed by a residential hill, and the residents are very lucky because there is a lift, built in the 1930s, to take them up to their homes from the quayside. We were lucky, too, as we didn't have to run up there.

The only real hill of the marathon followed soon after. We had run onto yet another island, Langholmen, and climbed the Vasterbron, a high bridge. This is one of the largest bridges in Sweden and is magnificent, but presents a sharp climb. From the top we had great views of parkland directly beneath us, an area where cyclists and runners are usually to be seen. Then all too soon we were down again and running along Nord Malarstrand, with more moored boats. We came to a canal-side path on the island of Kangsholmen. Here, the running was congested as our route suddenly narrows, and we miss the spaciousness of the Vasterbron.

The remaining four kilometres to the end of this first loop were along wide shopping streets. The shops were closed, as this was Saturday afternoon, but the pavement cafes were doing great trade. It all had that wonderful European ambience of leisure time being spent in luxurious idleness.

Most of the runners around me were Swedish or Finnish. It was exciting to have people all around talking in a different language and I'd also been curious to see what other things will be different in this marathon. People had teased me about the pickled herrings the locals delight in eating for breakfast — or any meal, for that matter — and I was secretly expecting to see some herrings being gobbled during the run. So I wasn't disappointed when I came across a sign pointing to the pickled gherkins aid station. Shortly after this I saw two girls standing with a large bowl each. Inside these bowls were gherkins, and runners were helping themselves to handfuls.

I turned to a runner next to me and commented that I wasn't yet game to try this unusual marathon treat; this guy, by chance an Englishman, was having trouble even with the local sports drink so he wasn't sampling the pickled offerings either. I resolved to try the gherkins on the next lap, since this would be near the end of the marathon and I could cope with any digestive unease for a kilometre or so. Sadly, by then the gherkin girls had sold out, and I had to make do with taking a photo of the sign that shows where the girls were standing.

Flash-forward to the morning after the marathon. I was comparing notes with Don from San Francisco about the race. 'I was surprised they were savoury pickles,' he said. 'I expected them to be sweet.' Good on him for trying them. I needed to be more adventurous. Later on I noticed other unusual foods. People were handing out slivers of what looked like sugar but had a grape flavour. There were lollies which looked like marshmallows but had a stale taste and texture.

Back to the race. There was a slight difference to the course on lap two; we crossed the centre of the park with the radio tower, on what was only a dirt track, and then did a big loop around Djurgarden. This was lovely and green, and the road was drying out so it was enjoyable running. From here the second loop repeated the first one. The main difference was that the day had warmed up a little. The sun came out intermittently. I was glad I settled for a singlet and did not wear long sleeves or tights.

I was quite surprised at the number of spectators. (Don's wife explained to me afterwards that she found the course very spectator-friendly, and she had been able to catch up with Don several times without having to walk too far. Maybe I was seeing the same people over and over again.) Whatever the reason, the crowds were supportive, calling out to us. I didn't know what they were saying but it sounded encouraging.

The final stages of the marathon were special. We had a two-kilometre uphill, gradual but solid, providing a glimpse of the clock tower of the Olympic stadium which seemed to take forever to reach. The marathon finished inside the stadium, built for the 1912 Olympic Games and largely unchanged since then. This red brick stadium is only small and no longer has a running track as it is used these days for soccer matches.

We entered the stadium and ran about 200 metres to the finish line. It is always an emotional experience finishing a marathon, but entering this historic place, with the wording 'Välkommen till Stockholms stadion' on the walls, was a big buzz. The stands were not all that busy. It was nice to linger there for a while.

Meanwhile, the outside area of Ostermalms IP, where we headed to receive our finishers' T-shirts and post-race goodies, was still waterlogged. The organisers had set up an elaborate system of ramps to keep us out of the flooding but nobody cared too much about wet feet by then.

I spent a couple more days in Stockholm touring the sights, which for the most part involved taking trains and buses to see places we had passed on the marathon route. I never tried eating herrings for breakfast, but I found a stall at a covered market which sold the most beautiful fish soup I have ever tasted. Just before I left I went for a short run along a canal close to my hotel. I felt pretty good, and I was not worried I would have any problems running Comrades.

The online results for the Stockholm Marathon were comprehensive, showing the speed I had run each five-kilometre section of the course. I'd had access to this kind of information before but for some reason this time I took it in. I noticed that I had run fairly even five-kilometre splits. This showed that I had learnt something in my 33 marathons to date. In the early days I would run faster for the opening kilometres and pay dearly for this later on, even when I intended to run at the same speed all the way. I struggled to find a way to get over this hurdle. In *Lore of Running* Tim Noakes stresses the importance of keeping a consistent pace through the race and guarding against doing the early part at a speed you cannot maintain until the finish. Known as a 'positive split', running the first half of a marathon faster than the second half is a classic fault in marathon running. This is not so much a refusal to take advice from those in the know, but rather an instinctive desire to run faster when you are feeling fresh at the start. As you tire it takes more effort to maintain your earlier pace and you are likely to slow down. And later on you always feel as though you are moving faster than you actually are.

Noakes regards avoiding a positive split as a crucial piece of advice an experienced runner can pass on to a novice. I can safely agree that if you run the opposite, a 'negative split', you will either have had a most enjoyable race — by setting out so slowly that you are left with too much energy for the second half and it becomes a breeze — or you will achieve a fantastic result. My best results have all been from races where

I managed negative splits. So I had Noakes's book by my side at this time as he has good advice not only for marathon running but also for Comrades runners.

The Comrades Marathon I ran in June 2005 is not included in my hundred marathons but it was a fabulous experience nevertheless. And the way I tackled this ultra marathon has had a marked impact on my subsequent marathon running. This race affected my confidence levels going into future races. It also emphasised the important matter of planning how I would run — my race pace — and sticking to this plan on race day.

I had prepared for Comrades in a slightly unorthodox way. I knew I had to do some long runs so I set myself a number of marathons and ultras as practice before race day in June. You are really not supposed to train for a race by racing frequently. The remainder of my training had been easy jogs of half an hour to an hour and a half, sometimes twice a day for the shorter ones. Constantly running marathons and ultras meant that I was always tapering or recovering. I didn't run any of the marathons flat out, and if I was disappointed at my results, my relative slowness at least had the side effect of allowing quick recovery.

When I got to South Africa I found that I was undertrained. Two days before the race we were taken on a bus tour of the course. 'You absolutely must not miss this,' friends who had already run the race told me. 'You will be glad to be prepared.' But I have always had a problem staying awake on these pre-race tours on a warm bus, and this time was no exception. So the Comrades course, when I ran it, was quite a surprise to me.

Our tour guide had 15 Comrades finishes under his belt out of

20 starts. He said, while I was still awake, that he aimed to do 3000 kilometres in training prior to the race. In my mind I could not dredge up more than 1500 kilometres of training and even *that* required me to mentally lengthen lots of my runs.

Two days before the race was not the time to be catching up on training or even to be questioning whether I had done enough. In hindsight I think it was a mistake for this guide to be trying to scare us. At the time he certainly scared me. But this was nothing more than my lack of confidence coming to the surface. Here was a guy who had *failed* to finish Comrades on no fewer than five occasions, and I had never failed to finish a race in my life.

I had run several ultra marathons by the time I went to South Africa, but none had been as prestigious as this one. I had run trail ultras in Australia and New Zealand but they had all been niche events of between 50 to a few hundred runners. Comrades has a field of around 15,000 runners and applies qualifying standards to keep the ill-suited away. You have to have run a standard-length marathon in less than five and a half hours to be allowed to enter.

In South Africa, Comrades is the real deal. Anyone who has any association with Durban and the surrounding area has heard of it. They have either run it, had a relative run it, stood along the course to cheer on the runners, or watched it on TV. It was traditionally held on a public holiday, expressly it seems so that everyone could pay attention to it. During the Apartheid years it was held on Republic Day, 31 May, and when that holiday was abolished the race moved to Youth Day, 16 June (regardless of which day of the week this was), which is when it was held in 2005. The race date now fluctuates among Sundays in late May or early June.

The race is run in alternate directions, one year from Durban to Pietermaritzburg and the next year from Pietermaritzburg to Durban.

The distance varies very slightly from year to year. I did the so-called 'down run' from Pietermaritzburg to Durban, the direction with a net elevation loss but the harshest uphill in either race direction.

The race expo in Durban was huge and was worth more than the usual fleeting visit to collect race bib and souvenir T-shirt. I went to several little talks during the expo. These were given by past runners and self-styled Comrades experts. I sat through these talks coughing away — a memento from my trip to London where my throat had been irritated by the traffic pollution — and I was constantly having runners edge away from me as they were worried about catching a bug that would wreck their race. I was not unwell, but runners on high alert before a race were not about to believe me. I saw a funny side to this but nobody else was laughing.

It was late to be assimilating serious advice on how to run the race. I took to heart the messages about pacing yourself well on race day. *Start out slow,* they say; *start out slow and stay with it.* One of the helpful things about the Comrades course is that every kilometre is clearly marked, so you can aim for a pace and see that you stick to it. (The unfortunate part is that the course is marked in distance still to go rather than in elapsed kilometres, the latter being the normal way of marking a course. I wasn't used to this and I found it increasingly irritating. I like to know what I have done rather than what is still to come. Seeing a marker with '88 km' when you have only just left the start line is heart-breaking, while seeing the same sign when you have been running for nine hours is heaven.)

As I've said, in the past I would have an idea of how fast I was going to run and this was usually a pace that I knew I could maintain for a long time. But I had historically been hopeless at sticking to my plan, often setting out much faster and ending up running much slower. With my recent Stockholm experience in mind I decided to make a real effort to stick to a pacing plan.

According to Comrades experts, men have more of a problem than women with setting out too fast. Men rush off from the gun and burn out. I was going to carry the flag for the females and pace myself well.

I stuck to my game plan to the end. It felt great. At least, it felt great by the time I was past halfway and I could reap the main benefit: running past all those sad folk who had gone out too fast. In the early kilometres it felt as though the whole field were pouring past me. But once I reached the final 17-kilometre downhill into Durban I was often the only person I could see who was running. Spectators were calling out to me and I knew it was me they were calling to because they referred to me as *the runner*. It made me feel I was moving fast, and this is exactly how you want to feel after running for seven or eight or nine hours.

Only a short way out of Pietermaritzburg I fell in with a group of runners who lived in Westville, a town along the route we were running, and we chatted for a few kilometres. Frankie was on her ninth Comrades — she knew what she was doing, I assumed. She runs one standard marathon a year to qualify for Comrades, then trains for this race for five months. This year she hoped to run around nine and a half hours. I let her go on ahead after a while as her pace was slightly faster than mine. And guess who I saw just ahead of me as I approached the finishing chute? I couldn't believe it. There were 15,000 runners there tackling this race, and bang in front of me was Frankie, whom I had last seen eight hours earlier.

I don't have to report that this was a hard run. Any run of 89 kilometres on hilly terrain is going to be a real challenge. We started out in the dark, coped with icy temperatures as we left Pietermaritzburg, and were far too hot after hours of running in the ensuing autumn sunshine. The hills were relentless, but offered fantastic views to lift our spirits. Notably, the Valley of a Thousand Hills was a great sight, and we ran along a ridge looking at endless hills — the rumour is that there's a thousand of them. We almost had time to count them.

A hard run was made more tolerable by the frequent aid stations. These were well-stocked with water, sugary drinks, lollies, fruit and even boiled potatoes. Potatoes ingested on the run are not to my taste but some runners say there is nothing better than a salty boiled potato when you're tiring on a long run. I did not like the plastic water sachets. Cups are fine by me, but here we had to use sachets where you are supposed to bite off the corner and suck down the water. I failed to master the technique and was forever letting the water gush down my singlet or have it spurt into my eyes.

But any discomfort became trivial when we were confronted by the kindness of spirit shown by the aid station helpers. They went out of their way to see that we got what we wanted each time (spare set of legs, anyone?) and were always so polite.

I enjoyed chatting to other runners, and there was plenty of time for this. I was amazed at the number of runners who had done this race so many times before — maybe ten, 20 or 30 times. When I asked why they kept coming back I got a whole variety of answers about chasing a better time, keeping up with their friends or keeping healthy. But I already knew the real answer: they loved it. It's a very long way to run but there is a special camaraderie out on these hills. That's why a large contingent of South African-born Australians make the trek back to Durban every June.

As I ran I ticked off the towns along the route. Drummond, Hillcrest, Pinetown — these had all been names to me but now they were real places, places I had succeeded in getting through (with the help of the spectators, of course). The Comrades spectators are a breed apart. They have a whole day to devote to watching the race, and it's an excuse for a barbecue and a lot of beer. They sit by the route's edge all day long and are unwaveringly supportive of the thousands of foot soldiers coming by. If you were to ask an onlooker for a slice of bread or a glass of wine they would certainly be happy to serve you your heart's desire.

This race has a 12-hour cut-off that is rigorously enforced. Precisely 12 hours after the starting cannon has been fired up in Pietermaritzburg, the race director steps into the finish chute in Durban and fires a handgun. Nobody can officially cross the finish line after this. To make doubly sure, a group of officials hold hands in a human cordon across the finish chute. It's actually very emotional to watch this, and everyone's heart goes out to the first person who fails to make the cut-off. To make this cut-off idea a bit more runner-friendly, however, there are timing mats at seven positions along the course so you can gauge your progress and see if you are going to make it in time. In fact, there are cut-offs to obey at each of these timing mats, on the basis that if you cannot get to a mat by a certain time you will be unable to get to the finish line in time for the 12-hour shooting.

I took a lot of comfort from my progress over these mats. I had come to the race with a vague goal of getting to the end in under ten hours. This was based on chats with previous Comrades runners whom I had met around Melbourne. I was relieved when I reached the Pinetown mat and realised I could walk to the finish and be within the 12-hour cut-off. Twenty kilometres later my mood moved up two notches to elation when I knew I could walk to the finish and be done in ten hours. From then on it was a matter of persuading tired legs to work even harder and get me home in a time that would be faster than my dream time. But I had a familiar sensation of movement being out of my control, that my legs were already functioning without any conscious input, and that there was little I could do to speed up.

The last kilometres into Durban seemed very long. We went past the bridge at Tollgate, heralding the start of the city, then past the market and down Durban's main street. The street was lined six deep in spectators behind barricades — and I had thought the whole of KwaZulu-Natal was out on the hills cheering. Finally we turned for Sahara Stadium. It was a moving moment to cross that finish line. I had paced the race into almost equal halves of 4 hours, 42 minutes; and 4 hours, 45 minutes.

Afterwards, the overseas runners were given special treatment. We had a marquee in which to recover, with lovely hot food, including local curries, and beer. I was so anxious to reach it that I collapsed with cramp on the walk over. We sat around for hours as our friends came in. I chatted with an English runner whom I had sat next to on the flight from Johannesburg to Durban — he had run his first marathon in order to qualify for this race — and with other people I had met at the Comrades expo over the past few days. This was the sort of day you never want to end.

At the finish of the Adelaide Marathon, 2001.

Courtesy of SARRC

Canberra Marathon by the lake.

Courtesy of www.marathon-photos.com

top:
Taiko drummers at Big Sur Marathon
Courtesy of Bill Burleigh

bottom:
The pianist on the Bixby Bridge, Big Sur Marathon.
Courtesy of Cath Tendler Valencia

top:

The start of the Gold Coast Marathon, 2004.

Courtesy of www.marathon-photos.com

left:

Sign advertising pickled gherkins at the Stockholm Marathon.

Running the Singapore Marathon, 2005.

Courtesy of www.marathon-photos.com

Approaching the finish line of the Auckland Marathon, 2005.

Courtesy of www.marathon-photos.com

The finish of the Stockholm Marathon
at Olympic stadium.

left:

Runners pass a temple during the Thailand Temple Run.

Courtesy of www.gothailandtours.com

bottom:

The finish of the Singapore Marathon.

Hot work

Running a marathon in a hot and humid place is a whole new ball game. The first time I tried this was at the Thailand Temple Run in early 2005, in the Samut Songkram province, 50 kilometres from Bangkok. The region is liberally sprinkled with temples, hence the name of the race.

I was worried about the heat from the moment I stepped off the plane at Bangkok airport. It was midnight and 29 degrees. Warning bells started to ring, and they became louder the following day when the race organisers took us on a minivan ride along the race route. I was fine sitting inside the air-conditioned van, but as soon as we stepped outside the heat was stifling. It seemed unlikely that anyone could run in this.

I had read up about hot-climate running. The impression I got was that it is impossible to acclimatise in a day or two, which was all I had. You really need about a year to acclimatise, and to do a crash course would require running for an hour daily in the heat over a two-week period. But the chances of heat stress could be minimised if I drank frequently and ensured I got enough electrolytes in that fluid. And ran slower than usual.

I was soon introduced to the race doctor. This was the first time I had come across the concept of a doctor being on-hand before and during a race (other than the presence of a medical tent at some larger races) but it did not take long to find out the reason. He was expecting all sorts of heat-related traumas to affect the runners.

Some of the visiting runners I spoke to had already been in Thailand for a while and had been training in the local conditions. Glenden from Albuquerque, USA, had been running in Lumpini Park in Bangkok in the middle of the day. 'I'm more worried about the effect of the pollution than the heat,' he told me. Greg from Seattle was here to run his 124th marathon and he was blasé about the heat; 'I'll just go a bit slower,' he said.

This was the fourth time the event was held and we were 2100 runners spread over the three distances of ten kilometres, half and full marathon. We came, the race director told us, from 29 different countries.

For visitors this was a wonderful chance to see Thai village life at close quarters, as the race route passed through a succession of small villages. To us foreigners the simple houses, village stores and rustic bridges were all exciting — just as much as the extravagantly decorated temples — and this all added up to an exotic encounter. We were also not used to running through groves of coconut palms, or to passing tropical fruit orchards, or to seeing the farmers tending to their rice paddies.

Nor were we used to seeing waves of heat rising from the road.

This was an afternoon marathon, with a 4.30pm kick-off. While I was still in Melbourne I was very taken by the idea of running through a tropical Asian night. It sounded so romantic.

We were taken by bus to the race start, at Wat (temple) Phumrinkudeethong on a riverbank. There was a funeral in progress at the temple, but nobody seemed to mind that hundreds of runners had descended here to use the toilets and jog around the gardens.

Children were playing in the river — really the only sensible place to be on a sweltering afternoon. The air was still and the river was shrouded in a heat haze.

There was an elaborate opening ceremony before the race got underway. The monks from Wat Phumrinkudeethong were to receive merit from the race organisers in appreciation of allowing us to use their temple as race headquarters. The monks were all lined up and each in turn was handed a first-aid kit by one of the race officials — we couldn't see that these were first-aid kits but I was told this afterwards. Two Thai girls in full traditional costume looked on.

Moments before the starting gun the monks flicked holy water from a special bowl at the runners assembled at the front of the field. This was to wish us all a good race. But it would have been fine by me if they had drenched us instead. During a brief two-minute warm-up I had realised that I would soon be suffering, with the temperature at 37 degrees. If someone had dropped me into the temple grounds from a helicopter and told me to run I would have said 'No way'.

Right from the start we were passing colourful temples. They were clearly the focal point of each village. Along the road were food stalls with seating, and little shops. Dogs lazed everywhere on the hot road. Many villagers had turned on their radios; the music was very loud.

I ran for a while alongside a Thai runner who was keen to practise his English. I was pleased about this because I had not yet had a chance to chat with any local runners. He was curious about marathons in Australia, and told me that running is for old people in Thailand. He translated for me when some onlookers called out to us — apparently they were willing me on to beat my companion, but we were some way from the finish line at this stage. And soon I found that I could not keep up this guy's pace so I had to drop back.

Our supporters, mainly the juniors, were also calling out to us in

English. Things like 'You are beautiful!' — wow, unlikely while running — and 'What's your name?' The older folk just stared.

An hour or so into the race the sun was preparing to leave us for the day. It was a red ball of fire, low in the sky. There was not a breath of wind. We had coconut palms mingled with mango trees, lychees and bananas at our shoulders. There was no sound apart from our footfalls and the occasional bark from one of the resting dogs.

I was finding the running hard. I had aimed to finish about half an hour slower than normal, but by 14 kilometres I realised that this was an unachievable goal. By 30 kilometres I would be shooting for an extra hour, and five kilometres later I would be praying to end the run in less than five hours. Most of us non-Thais ended up running more than an hour slower than we would have managed at home.

To compensate for a slow end result I decided to enjoy myself. I was not prepared to see this race turn into a painful struggle where all I could think of was getting to the finish line. At each drinks station I took a little walk, and as we passed through the villages I had a good look around. This was a rare chance to snoop on the local customs and view a slice of life normally kept away from the prying eyes of tourists.

We had a long out-and-back section between rice paddies — the brightest green of greens — where workers were toiling under their straw hats, and I can still recall the stench of one stretch of road where the villagers must have tossed out a whole load of rotten fish. Remnants were still there, smeared on the ground where we ran.

After sunset our route was lit by a line of glowing balls placed on the country road. The balls gave out little light but enhanced the romantic atmosphere. I could barely see the runners ahead of me, and when a runner passed he disappeared into the gloom almost instantly. There was nobody else about on the road apart from the odd motorbike, but I did worry about tripping over one of the dogs. Our route had been an out-and-back but the return part did not seem familiar, maybe because of the changing light.

As night fell I did not feel as though the air was getting any cooler. The fierce sun's rays were replaced by a sense of steaminess in the thick air. I continued to conjure up images of snowfields and opening the door of my freezer at home. (I have subsequently made use of this experience. While running in very cold conditions I have recalled this Thai marathon and the memories have warmed me up.) There was no breeze, and where our path was lit by candles the flames from the candles barely flickered.

The race was drawing to a close. Greg would have well and truly finished by now. Glenden passed me and I was miffed because I thought I was a better runner. But he had done that training in Bangkok. In the finish chute I saw Richard, a visitor from London. He looked uncomfortable. 'I seemed okay while I was running early on but then I was unable to get my legs to do anything. I didn't know what to do,' he said. 'I just had no power.'

Sadly, this marathon no longer exists. It soon reverted to being an early morning race, as it had initially been. This was a marathon that had been primarily aimed at tourists, meaning that a high proportion of the participants had come along for the novelty value and were not necessarily well-trained. Many of the slower runners had disliked walking and running for hours in the dark night. After another year, and with a morning start, the event was gone from the race calendar.

At the end of 2005 I found myself in Singapore for the country's annual marathon. I was running along in the dark of the early morning with no idea of the ordeal ahead.

The silence was deafening. We were 6000 runners. But there was no sound and no traffic. No birds chirping or insects buzzing. No voices. So strange that nobody was talking. We were all lost in our thoughts.

At six kilometres into the marathon it was still dark, and we had left the central city, with its illuminated office blocks and hotels, to tour the South Marina district of urban parkways. I latched onto a group of runners from Jakarta, Caucasian expatriates visiting for the marathon. 'So what's it like living in Jakarta?' I asked one of them. The runner grunted that it's fine. I then asked him what he did for a crust, at which point he decided he'd had enough of being questioned and told me he did not wish to chat so as to conserve his energy. Another runner, feeling sorry for this idiot woman trying to start up a conversation, informed me that he was from a London running magazine. I asked his name. He told me and then added, 'But I'm just jogging along, you go on ahead and don't mind me.' He was later to collapse from heat exhaustion, and when he wrote his article about his experience he prompted a flurry of letters to the magazine suggesting that marathons like this should not take place.

So it seemed talking was off the agenda. Pretty soon I worked out why.

This climate was completely energy-sapping. During the first hour I felt like a million dollars. I thought I was running the right pace. I went through ten and then 15 kilometres at a satisfactory clip. One of the Jakarta runners caught up and started to chat, almost to taunt me, and almost immediately I found that I couldn't breathe and talk at the same time. The air was so thick it was chewy. Zane, a teacher at the International School in Jakarta, indulged me: 'I came for six months and I'm still there after four years. We have a great running group, and we tour the neighbourhoods together, usually around 4.30am.' He then left me for dead.

Quite suddenly, it was as though the power had been turned off. I was gasping for oxygen. All my strength was gone. The 18-kilometre mark had often been a turning point during my marathons. And here, after 18 kilometres, I was all used up.

Running becomes such a drama in the heat. I had already had a taste of this in Thailand, where it was a new and exciting sensation. Here, I had to tackle the problem of hot-weather running front on.

Sweating — actually, the evaporation of sweat off your skin — is usually enough to cool you down as you run and is the body's most efficient way of dissipating unwanted heat. But when you run in the heat the evaporation of your sweat is not sufficiently cooling; you face a double whammy of the large amounts of heat your muscles are generating as you run, and the hot weather. Your body cannot get rid of your internal heat, and there's the possibility your core temperature will rise above the safe range that allows your major organs to function. Sensing danger, your body calls into play other means of removing the heat from within, including shunting blood to the skin surface to cool it — which unfortunately means that blood is diverted away from your working muscles.

As your liquid loss through sweating will probably exceed the amount of liquid you are drinking, you will also be running with a reduced blood volume. This compels your heart to beat faster to compensate, making you tire quicker.

In a humid climate, as in Singapore, the heat issues are compounded because your sweat cannot evaporate as readily into the damper air. Sweat may be pouring off you (so much so that another guest at my hotel said to me after the marathon, 'How was your swim?'), but this is wasted sweat as it is only the process of evaporation that cools you. You need to drink lots of fluid containing electrolytes, especially sodium, potassium and chloride, to restore the balance of these important chemicals in your body. Electrolytes are lost big time in sweat. Without these electrolytes in balance your body cannot use the fluids you are drinking to stall dehydration.

Once you drink only water and too much of it — something you could do innocently enough while running on a hot day — you face other risks. One of the dangers that had been publicised around the time of my trip to Singapore was hyponatraemia. I had read how this severe and sometimes fatal condition had occasionally affected marathon runners.

So there I was: drinking, drinking, drinking. Then I was worrying about hyponatraemia. I was worrying like this because I had never before drunk so much, both water and sports drinks, on a run. Then again, I had never sweated so much either. I'd never been a huge drinker while running, and it would be unlikely I would drink so much as to overdo it.

My mates from Jakarta would have been heat-adapted, as I came to understand later. Being used to running in these temperatures they would be able to rid themselves of internal heat much more efficiently than I could. They would have a greater blood volume so they could spare blood to be directed to their skin surface for cooling without affecting their working muscles. They would know how much to drink to maintain their blood volume and prevent their heart rate rising. Their sweat would be more diluted so they could maintain electrolyte balance more easily, and they would sweat at a lower temperature so they could get the benefits of evaporative cooling sooner. Oh, to be acclimatised!

I decided to walk a hundred metres through each of the drinks stations, which were every two kilometres, and try to run to the next one. But I couldn't. I faced the prospect of over three hours of walking. And even though it was comforting to see that many of my fellow runners had been reduced to a walk by then as well, I simply could not imagine walking for that long.

I eventually settled into a routine of walking 100 metres and running 400. Sometimes I walked for longer. I tried to make myself run to some landmark I could see ahead, or I allowed myself to walk to a landmark. Kilometre 31 was a big breakthrough: I ran the whole kilometre. I achieved this by counting slowly in my head as I ran. But this didn't happen again. The tasty sweet banana I ate must have kicked in.

I spent the next two kilometres trying to recall the name of my daughter Sophie's school friend who now lived here so that I could look up their phone number and call them — but to no avail. My mind had gone soggy. At least I could remember Sophie's name, and that Sophie had a friend who now lived in Singapore. The marshals seemed amazingly cheerful. But one unfortunate runner's supporter in the crowd berated him for walking: 'You were running last time I saw you, so why are you walking now?'

The Singapore Marathon has had several changes of route over the years. It has started and finished at the holiday venue of Sentosa Island; it has taken runners down bustling Orchard Road, the street with a million shopping centres, in the middle of the day; it has toured suburban housing estates. A friend told me that running down Orchard Road in the middle of the day with cars pouring past was not his idea of an enjoyable marathon. That could be the understatement of the year.

The route has evolved into a journey through parkland, with the intention of giving runners as much shade and time away from traffic as possible. This shows off a side of Singapore which many tourists would probably never see.

After the South Marina loop we left the city centre and crossed the Singapore River. A low mist was hovering. There was a long out-

and-back through the East Coast Parklands. This is Singapore's aquatic playground — beaches, water activities, cafes and tree-lined walkways. But the palm-fringed and rainforest-ed walkways were closed off to the public on marathon day.

It was dark when we left our starting point by the Padang, but we returned in daylight. The sun was shining, despite promises of an overcast day. 'It's been quite cool recently,' an English runner named Chris, who has been living in Singapore for 20 years, told me on the start line. 'I'm about to leave so I thought I should run the marathon again,' she explained. 'I last ran it ten years ago. At least I'm used to the heat, although I've done a lot of my training on the treadmill.' She too left me for dead around the 25-kilometre mark.

I couldn't quite see the finish line but I knew I would get there. Here, past experience helped — a lot. And I did get there in the end: around the bend, and alongside the Padang to finish outside City Hall, in a time that was a good hour longer than I would usually run a marathon. 'Welcome back,' said the race compere over the microphone as he had been saying it thousands of times that morning. Yes, I was relieved to be back. Dripping and hot, but back.

The Padang, in the very heart of colonial Singapore, is a wonderful place to base a marathon. It's a huge open space owned partly by the Singapore Recreational Club, which was founded in 1883, and partly by the Singapore Cricket Club, founded in 1853. Along one side is the grand City Hall where Louis Mountbatten accepted the surrender of the Japanese in 1945, and the finish line is right beside City Hall.

The compere did an excellent job. Almost every runner was announced by name, and as runners came in after five, six, seven and even eight hours he had a bag full of jokes which never emptied. I had never stayed and watched a marathon to the bitter end like this before, and it was unusual for the race organisers to leave everything in place until the last runner finished. At most races the post-race cleanup would be well and truly underway six hours after the race had started.

The sight of these runners pouring in after so many hours was touching to say the least. As Cyril the compere said, 'These are the guys who should be getting the big money.' It was heart-warming to see that virtually every runner ran the hundred metres of the finishing straight even though they might have been walking for hours. This is apart from the guys who were obviously injured — and even they made a valiant effort.

One of the direct outcomes of my marathon in Singapore, the result of a chance meeting with a group of Malaysian race organisers at the race expo, was that the Sarawak Tourism Board invited me to visit Sarawak and join in its first ever marathon, in Kuching. While shorter races had been held before, this was the first year for a full marathon and was also to include a half marathon and a ten-kilometre run. The chief minister had just clocked up 25 years in office and these running races were deemed a suitable celebration.

I located the venue on the north coast of the island of Borneo and grabbed the opportunity. This was a new place to run and somewhere I knew nothing about. It sounded like an exotic location and an event that was breaking new ground. I presumed there would be no need to weave bamboo bridges to ford any rivers or carry spears in case of attack.

Sarawak has an interesting heritage. In 1838 James Brooke from England was travelling the ocean and came across a settlement filled with warring tribes, notionally controlled by the Sultan of Brunei. He managed to get some of the tribes to calm down and live in peace and harmony. Then he and his descendants ran the region as rajahs until the 1940s, when Sarawak came under British colonial rule. It was later declared independent and in 1963 became a Malaysian state.

Sarawak is predominantly jungle, and most of the population outside Kuching live in longhouses, where the whole village shelters under a shared roof. The state has gone to great lengths to shake off its former name — Land of Headhunters — but at the same time the Sarawak Museum in Kuching, which I visited accompanied by my hosts, has extensive displays honouring this past activity. The collection of skulls must be unparalleled. If this isn't gory enough, the museum has exhibits of things like watches and human hair that have been extracted from the stomachs of local crocodiles. The crocodiles here are apparently especially savage. Locals prefer to see their state as the land of hornbills, a jungle bird which has unfortunately been subjected to a great deal of poaching for the ivory in its bill. I felt more comfortable when my hosts took me to the Cat Museum to look at photos of domestic cats and study other feline memorabilia.

The race organisers had invited a clutch of fast Kenyan runners (all had previously won European marathons) to run the marathon, presumably to give the race a creditable winning time. They also invited Vladimir Kotov, who had won the Comrades Marathon in South Africa several times in recent years and had earlier placed fourth in the marathon at the 1980 Moscow Olympics. I went to a lunch with these guys and it was the first time I had met such running luminaries. The Kenyans did not speak any English and seemed very shy, so not much communication happened there. But Kotov was very interested to hear that I had run Comrades and he wanted to know my feelings about it. I wondered why he would be asking me, a runner who travels at little over half his speed. He then told me how his race had been ruined the previous year by the crowds mobbing him as he approached the closing kilometres, forcing him to slow down and let another runner take the lead. He said that he finds it hard to train in South Africa, his adopted home, because he is so widely recognised there.

Unfortunately, the Kuching marathon did not prove to be very exciting. The course was dull. I suspected this was going to be the case when we were taken on a tour of the race route the afternoon before the marathon. As we drove along I kept hoping we would round a bend and see something interesting. As it turned out, both I and my companion, a New Zealander who was hoping to run a fast time, fell fast asleep on the bus. This New Zealander, Gavin, had a team track cycling gold medal from the 1990 Commonwealth Games and had turned to marathon running when his competitive cycling days were over. He had run 35 marathons to date. He started out just like the rest of us: 'I always wanted to run a marathon,' he told me.

So because the scenery was not very engaging, even with tropical vegetation by the roadsides, this turned out to be a difficult marathon. There was very little to take my mind off the effort of running. I got quite bored with long, straight roads, and I was almost going to fall asleep on the course again. To add to the lack of excitement, we had only a small audience in quiet, new-town Kuching, and those that watched us seemed mystified to see Westerners, especially females, in shorts and singlets. Many of the local female runners were dressed in long-sleeved tops and long pants — they must have been baking. My only consolation was a reminder to myself that I was running in a place I had never expected to run a marathon.

There are two faces to Kuching: old and new. The interesting part of town is the original settlement, which developed on the bank of the Kuching River. Local boats, called sampans, tootle up and down the river or cross from one bank to the other. The streets of this old town are narrow — shops clustered close together, cafes and markets everywhere. With a 20-minute drive you would be in the new town, with modern office blocks, an elegant state library and the sparkling new state mosque. It is all spaciously laid out, and long, straight roads connect the various landmarks. I would have preferred to run a marathon in the older part of the town because there would have been so much more going on for entertainment — and, yes, I could have used some entertainment during this marathon. But it would have been totally impractical.

Start time was 6am. The race marquees were set up outside the Bangunan Baituk Makmur, a gigantic government building that completely dwarfed us. It was dark but warm, and things could only get warmer. We started out to the strains of loud music and a lively DJ, but soon the day became a challenge. The air heated up, a light rain started to fall, and when the rain stopped the sun came out to shine brightly. Not perfect running weather at all.

Yet one little novelty of this race kept me alert. We had to run a couple of out-and-back stretches, which an unscrupulous runner could have avoided, thus shortening their race. And to prevent this indiscretion the organisers had said that we would be collecting 'special tokens' at various points along the course. 'Any runner without the complete set of tokens at the finish will be disqualified,' said the instructions. As boredom with the race set in I couldn't wait to see what the tokens would be. They turned out to be thin red and yellow ribbons, which were placed around our neck as we passed specific marshals. It was cute. I have kept my little ribbons as a souvenir.

After my Singapore experience I thought I had learnt how to cope with the heat, and I did quite well until the final 12 kilometres, when I found myself doing a lot of walking. I found, as in Singapore, that the heat sapped my strength in a subtle but devastating way. I made it my goal to finish the race with a run–walk pattern and not give up running entirely. In Singapore I had walked when I had to, whereas in Kuching I walked when I chose to.

I was pleased to be able to get enough to drink during the race — both water and a local electrolyte drink called 100 Plus. This drink came in lots of flavours so there was a surprise waiting at each aid station. Little things can be so exciting when you are under duress. I was probably still becoming dehydrated but I did my best to drink.

In the food tent at the finish there were also some surprises. We were offered cups of soy custard and bowls of congee with some brown puree. I am afraid that, gastronomic adventurer as I am, I found this unappetising straight after a marathon. The servers were so friendly it was a shame not to indulge, but I held out for a meal of vegetables and rice at a café when we got back to the old town and then had dessert at the Malaysian equivalent of Starbucks.

There was only a small female field in this event and I placed 13th overall. For this I received a cash prize of $250, the largest prize I have ever received for running. I even have an ongoing souvenir from this marathon: one of the organisers still sends me a Christmas card every year.

A difficult half century

I should have known better than to run the Phuket Marathon. I could have saved myself a great deal of distress. But if you ask me to relate just one marathon experience out of my hundred, this is the one you will hear.

By the time I went to Thailand in June 2006 I had run several marathons in the heat, and none of them had been easy. However, they had all been memorable so I guess that's why I got on the plane to Phuket when the organisers invited me over.

Three months after running the marathon in Sarawak I went tropical for a fourth time. I might have temporarily forgotten how the heat sucks all your running ability away, but as a factor in my defence I did initially sign up to run the half marathon rather than the full. This wasn't so much a concession to the temperature as a concession to the number of marathons I had run so far that year, the Phuket trip being sandwiched between a marathon in Australia and a marathon in Austria. What's more, having just completed my 49th marathon at Macleay River in New South Wales, I thought it would be nice to have my family with me for my 50th, on holiday in Austria the following weekend.

Phuket is an island off the west coast of Thailand and linked to the mainland by air or by a road bridge. It is the perfect holiday getaway, a land with charming culture and customs, scenery to keep you entranced, and tasty cuisine.

This marathon was held for the first time in June 2006. Phuket already had a well-established annual triathlon, so this was a proven location for a marathon where visitors could combine a holiday with some exercise. Nobody was going to object to running a marathon if they could have traditional Thai dancers, larger-than-life dragons and local bands as entertainment. And fabulous beaches for recovery. The race was held during the wet season as the resorts would be less busy and able to accommodate the hundreds of runners, but outside of the hottest months so as not to impose an undue burden on runners. The burden was enough, as it turned out; believe me.

Altogether, 2000 runners were participating in the races on offer — ten kilometres, half marathon and full marathon — out of which some 500 of us were visiting from overseas. Among the runners I met were a couple from New Zealand who had just run the Everest Marathon in Nepal, an expatriate New Zealander who was living in Bangkok and had been training in the midday heat, and an American couple who had left their two kids with a nanny at the resort while they ran the marathon.

Start time was 5am, when it was still pitch black. The air was already humid as we waited at the Laguna Phuket resort area, with a drum band to entertain us. The resort enclave comprises five top-end hotels spread around a man-made lagoon.

We left the resort area and headed for a tour around the island — up towards the airport with several detours taking us to some of the prettiest beaches. As with the Thailand Temple Run here was a chance to see the real Thailand, not the part that is beautifully groomed for tourists.

In the gloom of the dawn we passed through villages where the locals were opening up their little shops and roadside stalls. We tried to avoid the sight of piles of unrefrigerated raw meat while at the same time enjoying the sight of all the tropical fruits. We made jokes about confusing the villagers' drink stalls with the ample aid stations and inadvertently helping ourselves to a can from their display. The soccer World Cup was into its second week and flags from all nations fluttered gaily, making for a festival atmosphere.

This part of the island had been spared the worst of the 2004 Boxing Day tsunami, but there was plenty of building work in progress. Rather than repairs, this seemed to be fresh development, and there were signs exhorting us to head straight to a real estate agent and purchase our slice of paradise. But as a reminder of the tsunami there were numerous signs along the roads close to beach areas showing escape routes in case of a disaster striking.

At daybreak all the roosters on the island simultaneously found their voice. Lots of scrawny chickens woke up too and took some exercise. Herds of buffalo were moved from one paddock to another — one group of runners had to pause and wait while these beasts crossed the road in front of them. They had sizeable horns and you wouldn't want to find yourself in the middle of a pack.

All the vegetation was bright green as this was the wet season. There were daily afternoon showers — the sort that are very welcome and which clear the air nicely. In between the green paddocks were palm trees, banana plants, groves of rubber trees and patches of sugar cane. It was all very peaceful and most of us ran in silence, at one with our thoughts, as the day unfolded. I was not game to try and talk to other runners as I had in Singapore.

It was cloudy at first, thankfully. I was keeping a slower pace than usual, having worked out beforehand how I would tackle this race. I made sure that I was well-hydrated before the race and that I was well-rested. I intended to walk through the aid stations to give myself a rest and to ensure I had a chance to hydrate properly.

For the first hour and a half I stuck to my race plan. I truly felt I was travelling at a pace I could maintain for the entire race.

On the horizon were hills, but so far our route had been flat. When you fly into Phuket you can't help but notice the hills in every direction. The marathon organisers had tried to make our route as flat as possible but this had been a challenge. The first part was flat, as was the last part along the coastal plain, but in between were moderate undulations. They had a double challenge in trying to keep us away from the busier roads and motorbike traffic, and for the most part they succeeded. I had worried about the motorbikes because I didn't think they would like to share road space with runners. In the early hours the other road users were pedestrians. Later in the day the roads were busier, but we were supposed to be home and hosed by then.

Without any doubt the highlight of the marathon course would be the out-and-back to Nai Yang Beach, near the airport. A strip of blue on the horizon suddenly morphed into a totally divine bay. This area had borne the full force of the tsunami, but the buildings had been mostly rebuilt. An unsealed road was lined with budget hotels and shops, and a long sandy bay was filled with moored long-tail fishing boats — a postcard scene if ever there was one. You can understand why I would have wanted to run here.

The day before the race the organisers took us by minivan over the route and I fell in love with this bay. Then I realised the half marathon did not go here. That's why I switched my race distance. It may sound silly to change my race distance at the last minute. I would never recommend this, except that I had already run a number of marathons that year — the number is eight — so I knew I could manage the full course. Besides, the idea of running a marathon at short notice appealed to my sense of adventure.

In hindsight I wonder if I wasn't just too anxious to get my 50th marathon under my belt.

Right as I was approaching the idyllic Nai Yang Beach my race went to custard. I had passed the 18-kilometre marker when I dramatically slowed down. I felt I could not breathe. There was no way I could run. It was a tremendous shock. Nothing quite like this had ever happened to me before. I had been so keen to run along here, and I couldn't enjoy it properly.

Reluctant to admit to myself that this was serious, I continued on. After a short walk I was determined to run again and to push through the discomfort, but I could not do it. I would set myself a goal of reaching a tree or the next driveway but I never made it. I had to walk, and at a very slow pace. When I came to a downhill stretch I again made an effort to run — I never ever walk downhill because it is such a waste of the benefits of gravity — but the simple challenge reduced me to gasping and shaking. I had to stop completely to recover from this burst of strenuous activity. I had been running with an expatriate from Bangkok, discussing our approach to tackling this race, before taking off ahead of him; now he came flying by. So did many other faces I recognised from earlier stages of the marathon.

I have always regarded myself as a person who finishes things — dull books, detailed embroideries, cleaning out cupboards. Marathons. So there was never a question of pulling out. I thought, in passing, that if I were to pull out I should do it sooner rather than later, so as not to waste any valuable energy on a failed mission, but by the 24-kilometre marker I knew I would see this through to the bitter end. I hoped that my past experiences would get me through.

At 29 kilometres I slowly collapsed by the roadside as I tried to scale an intimidating hill. Remember how I said that this course was mostly flat? It no longer felt flat at all. When I sat up I had cramped both legs.

A race official on a motorbike came past as I sat there and gave me a cursory glance. 'I'm okay,' I said and he left me to it. I should really have been pulled off the course at this point. I am very glad that I was not.

It was going to be a long-drawn-out walk. What made my plight even funnier was that I was wearing a half marathon race bib (the race bibs were colour coded) as I had originally entered for that distance. To the race officials and marshals on the road I was less of a marathon straggler and more of an unbelievably slow half marathoner. But I was well past caring what anyone thought of me. At one aid station I sat down in a dustbin of used drink cups because that looked softer than sitting on the gravel roadside, and it was not so far to bend down.

The day was getting hotter by the minute and there was tremendous glare off the main road that we had to follow for many kilometres. Apart from the cars and bikes, this road was fairly busy with pedestrians going about their daily business and it was hard to pick out other marathoners. But when I turned onto a quieter side road for the final two kilometres parallel with Layan Beach I was delighted to see other race people; and what's more, some of them were also walking. I would have company for the last stretch.

The race director came by on his motorbike while I was in this section. He was presumably out looking for latecomers and anxious to close down his race. I assured him I was going to finish.

The final 700 metres were marked off with signs, hundred by hundred. I tried to run but still couldn't. I collapsed onto a bench at the finish line without even managing to make it out of the finish chute. The marathon had taken me over six hours to complete, and I had been dreaming of this finish for the last four of those.

The race director, having gathered all his stragglers, took me by the hand and led me to the medical tent, where I was bathed in cold towels and nurses poured cold water over me. I found this odd since I wasn't feeling at all hot. A doctor measured the level of oxygen in my blood and pronounced it to be okay — I took comfort from this — although for hours I continued to feel out of breath. My blood pressure was dramatically low. Then my legs and feet started cramping. That was the most unbelievable pain. As soon as the cramp in one leg or foot finished, it would start up in the other one. When I got back to my room I went to bed, and the cramps continued.

In the late afternoon I dragged myself out of bed and walked along the beach to have a meal at one of the little cafes overlooking the ocean. I knew I would get over this, and even by that evening I was well enough to party away at the post-race reception.

I got straight on with the important matter of working out what had befallen me. I texted my daughter Natasha and asked her to do some research. When we met up a few days later she had a sheaf of papers for me. I believe that I had been attacked by my old adversary the heat, and nothing more. I had been running too fast and had been unable to regulate my internal temperature. I had crossed my thermal threshold and been forced to slow down for survival. I had thought I was taking things easy at the beginning of the race but I probably should have run even slower and drunk more. And run the half marathon.

Mr Lebow's good idea

The New York City Marathon is a carnival like no other running event. It stands out from the 'crowd' of marathons in my mind, not only for its size but for the ambience generated by so many runners moving along with a common goal. I tell many people it has been my favourite. I ran the whole way feeling reasonably good. I never went through a bad patch when I felt too sore, or felt like giving up, or questioned why I was doing this. Every marathon is hard, but in New York I finished thinking I had done my job well.

You get an unbeatable high after running a marathon and feeling positive the whole distance. On top of this, I ran my fastest marathon for almost two years when I had not been anticipating any very special result. Between August and September I had barely run at all due to a strained calf muscle. In October I had run the Melbourne Marathon in a disappointing time. Then I went ahead and ran New York 17 minutes faster only three weeks later, and this was a tougher course.

I could spend ages analysing what made this marathon go so well: the tremendous crowd support, the cool temperature on the day, or the thrill of running in this vibrant city. I've experienced all these factors elsewhere without the same result. In the end, I believe I just had a good day.

As I said earlier, the New York City Marathon is the embodiment of the 'people's marathon'. It was the first marathon to attract runners in the thousands, and the first marathon to be held wholly within the heart of a major city. Its legacy lives on in all of us who love running marathons. For those of you who have yet to have a go, it is largely courtesy of the New York City Marathon that you will want to have a go.

I'll explain why with a brief history of marathon running.

Whenever you read about the origins of the marathon it's the Greek foot soldier Pheidippedes whose name comes up. One day in 490 BC, the Greeks were fighting the Persians on the plains of Marathon and beat them soundly. Pheidippedes, a professional runner, reputedly ran 40 kilometres from Marathon to Athens to announce the victory, and dropped dead moments after delivering the news. One reason for the devastating impact of this run — the world's first, albeit unofficial, marathon — could be that he had only just finished zigzagging between Athens and Sparta to ask the Spartans for help against the Persians, before footing it to Marathon to fight. Total distance run over four days: my guess is around 560 kilometres. Training techniques were less advanced in those days and he may not have had a nutrition plan.

Pheidippedes lost out on the opportunity to brag about his achievement but he gave the world an idea for a great sporting competition — even though the marathon he ran was a touch shorter than the current official distance. Even though the marathon he ran very possibly never happened at all. We just don't know.

When the idea of an Olympic Games was revived in Athens in 1896, the organising committee searched for a suitable event to hold as the apex of the games. Something hard? Yes, how about reworking

Pheidippedes's run from Marathon to Athens? His long runs followed by his sudden death had given him a heroic status, and in modern times he has been popularised in a poem by the 19th-century writer Robert Browning. The Olympic Games committee decided to hold a re-enactment of Pheidippedes's 40-kilometre run to provide a link with Athens's past. There was no such event in the original Olympic Games of ancient Greece, where competitors only ran short distances within the stadium.

The marathon from Marathon to Athens at this first modern Olympics turned out to be a success with the crowds, possibly because a Greek runner won. The Greeks had not been performing well at these Olympics, winning no athletics medals at all, so their hopes were pinned on the marathon, the final competition of the games. There were 13 Greek contenders, one of whom was a shepherd named Spiridon Louis. Only five non-Greeks were in the race, including Australian Edwin Flack. Louis managed to win the race and salvage Greek pride after Flack, who led for most of the latter part of the race, pulled out sick in the very late stages.

A running club in Boston observed what a good thing the Greeks were onto and in 1897 decided to hold a marathon. Local runners liked the event and it became an annual race, gaining a reputation throughout the US and overseas. The non-fatal outcome in modern times must have played in its favour. The distance was close to 25 miles — it varied slightly from year to year — and the marathon route was modelled on the route of the Pheidippedes tale, as a point-to-point course from a village outside Boston to the city centre.

The Olympic Games were held in London in 1908 and, naturally, there was a marathon. Its route followed a course from Windsor Palace to White City Stadium. The marathon distance had never been precisely laid down — just keep it really long, chaps — but the few marathons held in those days were usually a bit over 25 miles. The race for the 1908 Olympics had a measured course of 26 miles, which already made it long for a contemporary marathon. Just before race day some bright spark, acting on a request from the Queen, suggested that if the start line could be shifted slightly then the royal family, especially the children, would be able to watch the start of the race without leaving their private quarters. The finish was to remain on the track below the royal box at the stadium. Here is a question: what is so exciting about a marathon start that you want your kids to see it? I always thought the drama came at the end. But maybe this is sour grapes. The effect of altering the start was to make the course longer, not just for that marathon but for virtually every marathon to follow.

Moving the start line made the race distance 26 miles, 385 yards. This distance has come to be the official marathon length, although competitive marathons still varied from 24 to 27 miles until 1921. The official length was set in stone in 1921 by the International Amateur Athletic Federation.

After those 1908 Olympics there was disappointment in Britain with the performance of the British runners in the marathon. A new annual marathon was started up to improve the standard of marathon running in time for the next Olympics. This was the Polytechnic Marathon, held in London from 1909 until 2002 with a brief hiatus in the late 1990s.

As the marathon continued to be a customary feature of the Olympics, regular national championship marathons were held to select team members in all participating nations. Only the cream of each country's runners were involved.

Non-elite runners would have known what a marathon was but few would expect to be able to compete. There were a handful of marathons held worldwide for non-elites, such as a regular marathon in Yonkers

(New York), which has been held almost continuously since 1907; the Kosice Marathon (in present-day Slovakia), which has been held since 1924; and the Polytechnic Marathon. In Australia, the Victorian Marathon Club held an annual marathon from 1953 for almost 40 years. Feilding in New Zealand has held a marathon every year since 1956. Even events like these were primarily for club runners, who trained diligently and took the races seriously. There was no question of the marathon being a personal challenge or a social event. You ran to win or to place for your club.

Running was quite different in those days. Take the Feilding Marathon, for example. Feilding had always been a sporty town and had a cycling and athletics club before it was incorporated as a borough. In 2005 I ran the 50th Feilding Marathon. I spoke to Doug Bond, who had run in the inaugural 1956 marathon at the age of 31: 'I lived for running,' he told me. 'I did cross-country and track; we never ran on the roads. At the age of 40 I was looked on as a freak so I stopped running. It got lonely. If there had been more veterans running I would have kept going.' (No female ran in the Feilding Marathon until the late 1970s.)

In the 1960s a new breeze blew. The land that was bringing us McDonald's was also bringing exercise into our lives. A trio of Americans paved the way for a major change in our attitudes: David Costill, a human performance scientist who pioneered research into fitness; Kenneth Cooper, with his book *Aerobics*; and Jim Fixx, author of *The Complete Book of Running*. It emerged that taking up aerobic exercise, including running, walking, cycling and swimming, was the best thing anybody — male or female — could do for their body. People like me, who have leapt off the couch and felt the endorphin rush only a bout of exercise can bring, are grateful to these guys. I hasten to add that these books were pretty old and dusty by the time I came to hear about them.

Running was no longer to be the sole domain of a handful of gaunt men in ragged singlets. The idea of 'fun runs' was born. But short fun runs, typically ten kilometres, weren't enough. Runners wanted to run further. Marathons sprung up around the world, including at Traralgon in Australia (an annual race since 1968), and anybody could compete in these — in theory, at least; the participants would still have been dedicated runners and entry numbers rarely reached a hundred. Among these small events was an annual marathon held in New York City from 1970 onwards: a multi-lap course held in Central Park.

Little did we know that a new era was just around the corner. Marathon running received a massive shot in the arm in 1976. One single race changed the role that the marathon could play in — I do not think I exaggerate — hundreds of thousands of people's lives. The birth of mass marathon running, the emergence of the people's marathon as we see it today, came with the New York City Marathon of 1976. In 1976, Fred Lebow, the race director since the event's inception, had a wonderful idea: to move the race out of Central Park. He designed a special route for the US bicentennial year. He would link the city's five boroughs on a unique one-way journey. He wanted to close major roads and see thousands of New Yorkers run through all parts of their city to mark this very important anniversary. Nobody had tried before to organise a long run on this scale through a city.

Lebow was a man after my own heart. His 1994 obituary in the *New York Times* relates that he ran 13 marathons in 1970, including his own.

The New York City Marathon of 1976 was brought by the media into homes all around the world. Out of more than 2000 starters, 1500 runners completed the race through the city that never sleeps, as compared with 300 tackling the old Central Park course the year before. This new opportunity motivated slower runners, older folk and women, all of whom had historically been neglected in the sphere of athletics, to give this thing a go. From that day on, every sort of person had permission to run, whether you were big or small, male or female. The only part that mattered was your desire to join in.

By 1979 the New York City Marathon had 10,000 finishers. Lebow had a very good understanding of the direction the people's marathon movement was taking. In a foreword to Sandy Treadwell's *The World of Marathons* he wrote:

> Speaking from my experience as both a race director and a mid-level runner, I feel safe in stressing that it is the people well off the pace who lend that special feeling to a marathon; they are the ones who inspire, motivate, and excite fellow runners, race directors and spectators alike. These people are the true moving force behind any race.

Berlin followed New York's example by moving its marathon from the Grunewald on the city's outskirts into the centre of West Berlin in 1980. The London Marathon, as I've mentioned, was modelled on the New York City event and first held in 1981; this marathon was held in the heart of the city from the very first time onward.

By the mid-1980s runners in numerous other cities around the world had seen the excitement of running a marathon through the very centre of their city. The appeal of such a race remains to this day.

Australians were not missing out on the action. Word got out about how fantastic it was to run a marathon. We all wanted to have this magic experience, but not everyone could get to London or New York. Events like the Canberra Marathon and the South Melbourne Marathon, both started in 1976, were seeing rising entry rates each year. The participants were bitten by the marathon bug and invited their friends along. I've heard that the South Melbourne Marathon had so many runners within a few years that the running club which organised the race decided to hold the marathon twice each year, on successive weekends, so that the club members could run unimpeded by the hordes of non-members.

People got sucked in. One of my regular running buddies, Bruce, was at work in mid-1978 when he noticed a poster on the wall advertising the upcoming inaugural Melbourne Marathon, the first marathon to take runners right into the city heart and open to all comers. He decided to enter, despite being a tennis player and cricketer and not a runner in those days. He explains this quick decision: 'I came from a sporting family and I had always followed the marathon at the Olympics. I knew about the tradition and grabbed the chance to run one.' That same evening he went home and jogged for 50 minutes, his first run. He trained for 12 weeks before the marathon and successfully completed the course between Frankston and the Melbourne Town Hall. 'I had to sit out a club cricket match on the Saturday so that I would be ready for the marathon on Sunday,' he recalls.

In 1960 there were approximately a hundred marathons held around the world, of which the vast majority would have been elite championship events or selection races for national teams. In 2009 there were well over 1500 official marathons held worldwide: annual races that are open to the public and that meet the criteria I outlined in my introduction. Some sources suggest the real number is much higher, and this depends on your definition of an official marathon. You can see that marathon running is a sport in the ascendant.

Certain marathons have a huge participation. There are ballots to get an entry for the London Marathon, Tokyo Marathon and the New York City Marathon to hold the participant level within a manageable range. (There is a point at which a marathon could have too many runners and become unworkable; there could be no starting or finishing area large enough, the roads could not be closed for long enough and the demand for drinks would be impossible to fulfil.) Each of these marathons already has at least three start lines and even then the starts are painfully congested. The 2009 Tokyo Marathon was oversubscribed by a factor of seven to one, and the actual race had over 30,000 participants. New York City is traditionally the largest race, currently allowing almost 40,000 runners, with London and Chicago hot on its heels.

I always wanted to run the New York City Marathon but I was discouraged by the need to enter a ballot to get a place in the marathon, with months of waiting after you apply to find out if you have been successful. When I decide to enter a race I like to get started on my travel plans right away. I don't need to be left hanging, waiting to see if the organisers want me there.

In early 2006 I was browsing the New York City Marathon website and I realised that I had run a marathon in 2005 in a time that would qualify me to bypass the lottery for this marathon in 2006 and get guaranteed entry. It is not widely publicised that both the London and New York marathons have qualifying times which may be within reach of mid-pack runners like me. The qualifying time for New York for my age was 3 hours, 38 minutes, and I had run faster than this in January 2005 in Hobart — a scant seven days inside the qualifying period.

I was in.

I flew to New York and entered into the spirit of the marathon immediately. I toured the city's running stores, buying up running gear as though it were unobtainable in Australia. I spent many hours at the marathon expo in a huge exhibition hall with representatives from every manufacturer who could possibly claim any remote connection with running, plus heaps that couldn't. I got dehydrated and hungry touring the stalls, left to buy a drink and a hotdog, and then toured them all again. It was a shame to get home and realise I had miscalculated the exchange rate so that the merchandise cost rather more than I thought at the time.

What makes New York so special on marathon day is the general mood of excitement. Actually you get an inkling this race is special well before race day. I was amazed to have many strangers stop me in the street and ask if I was visiting for the marathon — New Yorkers aren't known for their friendliness to strangers. I don't think it's just the course that gets everyone so hyped up. It's more the idea of so many people rising to a major challenge in unison. (The organisers make a big deal of the fact that the course goes through the five boroughs — Staten Island, Brooklyn, Queens, the Bronx and Manhattan. But Staten Island's role is small: it has the start line and then shoos you over a bridge into Brooklyn, and you do less than a mile in the Bronx.)

Much of the route is really fairly uninspiring, with long stretches of commercial streets. The visual strong points are the views from the Verrazano-Narrows Bridge in the first mile — the sight of Manhattan in the distance is spectacular — and there are dramatic flashes of Manhattan as you descend the Queensboro Bridge at 16 miles. The final miles in Central Park are great, mainly just because it is Central Park, home to running for New Yorkers.

But the atmosphere is out of this world. Most of the course, once you descend the Verrazano-Narrows Bridge right up until the finish line, is lined by spectators, in many places standing several people deep for long stretches. They're perched on top of signs, on walls, on roofs and anywhere a person can get. Around two million people are estimated to line the course. They stand there while 40,000 runners file by. They're all cheering and having a wonderful time.

The spectators have whistles and clackers and loud voices, and the kids love to high-five the runners. People hand out lollies and even pieces of paper towel so you can wipe your sweat away. The audience has truly got into the spirit of the marathon. They make the marathon what it is.

The organisers require runners to make a very early start for the 10am race by having the official buses take you from downtown Manhattan to Staten Island before 7am. This is so you can eat as much breakfast as possible in the waiting area before starting the race and not need much food at the finish, where, to my surprise, nothing is provided. Well, really, it's so they can close the Verrazano-Narrows Bridge to traffic for the runners. So there you are, standing in a long line waiting to board a bus in the dark in the centre of New York, being handed sachets of Tylenol by enthusiastic girls, just in case the prospect of running a marathon has given you a headache. It is bizarre.

Most years it is very cold at 7am at Fort Wadsworth on Staten Island. The coffee and bagels are most welcome, but I'm surprised that the toilet queues here are as long as at any other marathon. It seems you can't ever have enough toilets at a marathon to result in short queues. I sat around feeling cold and watching kids practising their complex skipping routines. I was not entirely clear why the kids were there.

The walk to the start line seems like a marathon in itself. I had long enough in the starting corral to feel nervous about what lay ahead. When you finally get going, after the 'Stars and Stripes' has been sung and the elite women have been sent on their way, it's almost an anticlimax. You start with a hill up the Verrazano-Narrows Bridge. That's not so easy, but then you have that fabulous view across the water to Manhattan and there are US Navy boats puffing out fountains by the bridge. Runners from the three starting points merge at the eight-mile mark.

All sorts of people run the marathon. Few of them are aiming for a fast time. More on their mind is having a good time. Having come from all over the US and all over the world, they're intent on one thing: completing this marathon. Many runners have their name or at least their nationality printed on their shirt, and the crowd are quick to call out people's names when they can offer specific encouragement. They never tire of telling you that you look good and that you're nearly finished, wherever you may be on the course.

There's much more chatting than you normally get in a marathon. Runners stop to chat to the volunteers at the aid stations. They stop for photos. They stop to talk to their families who have come along to watch. You might not expect to find your family among a two-million-strong audience, but it can be done.

The noise is at all times phenomenal, except on the Queensboro Bridge because the crowds can't get onto it. To make up for this they are waiting on the far side making even more noise than before. And there are numerous bands adding to the hubbub.

In Central Park the already extreme noise level reaches a crescendo. The final miles through the park are fairly tortuous, as the path twists and turns and the finish line stays persistently out of sight. But the yelling puts strength into tired legs. It's also very emotional, and if a marathon finish were ever going to reduce you to tears this would be the one. The only problem is that some participants have simply had too much running by then and they decide to stop. Suddenly. I found the last stretch was a matter of dodging other runners who would abruptly come to a standstill with no warning. I was so astonished to see a runner with a singlet telling me she was from Greenland that I ran headlong into her when she stopped unexpectedly in front of me.

At the finish line the marshals treat everyone like a real hero. It's great. It's like we've all won the race. I've never been congratulated so much. I almost felt like apologising: *No, really, it wasn't so much trouble at all.*

During my week in New York I didn't speak to anyone who didn't know about the marathon. You wouldn't think that people going for a run could have such an impact. It's a big deal to everyone, even in this city where a lot of other stuff goes on too. I asked people how to get to places and they asked me about the marathon.

Two days after the race, when I was standing in line to go inside the Statue of Liberty, one of the security guards pulled me aside. I was worried I had done something wrong because lots of people were being chastised for eating and other unsuitable activities. But no, she said to me, 'Ma'am, what was your time?' I stared back and then the penny dropped. So I told her, proudly. After that I noticed that many people in the queue were wearing a marathon finisher's medal. This is the only time I have actually known runners to wear their marathon medal.

My New York adventure isn't the only occasion I have run a marathon in the footsteps of history.

The Invercargill Marathon on the South Island of New Zealand was first held in 1909. It was the first marathon in the Southern Hemisphere. That year it had 13 starters and seven finishers. The marathon was not held again until 1953, when it had only two runners. Since the 1950s it has been held regularly, but has often had very few participants. Entries peaked in the 1980s and early 1990s, when some years saw over a hundred runners. (The hundredth anniversary marathon in 2009 had a turnout of 266 runners and this would have completely altered the character of the race.)

In 2007 I ran this marathon, a year to the day since I had run in New York. What an incredible contrast in every respect.

That year there were 27 participants in the full marathon. There were no spectators whatsoever, save a few supporters who had deposited their half marathon runners for the accompanying event at the halfway point of our race and happened to be hanging around as we came past.

The current race starts from the sleepy village of Riverton, as it has since the 1970s, and follows a rural highway parallel with the south coast to finish on an oval next to the sports centre in Invercargill. Running a marathon with so few companions requires a different mindset to running in the company of thousands. The road won't be busy, which is a real benefit, but you won't get that lift from feeling that you are somewhere special, doing something special. Rather, you will be wondering why you got out of a warm bed at the crack of dawn when nobody else has.

I would never recommend a marathon like this to a long-distance-running novice. I ran alone for virtually the entire course, except for when a couple of guys passed me near the beginning and when I reached the half marathon field. The half marathon was starting just as I came by, and as I approached their start line I could have been confused for a runner hastening to join that event. Most of the half marathoners took off into the distance, but I caught up with a few of them towards the end.

Most of the runners in both the marathon and the half marathon were local to either Southland or at least the South Island. They were surprised to see someone travel from outside New Zealand for their event. But I had never been to Invercargill during my seven years of living in New Zealand so I was keen to see what it was like. I had intended to do some travelling around, but the weather was so bad I could not go to Stewart Island as I had planned. Both the flights and the ferry were cancelled.

The weather in this Southland region of New Zealand is the butt of many jokes. Basically it is always bad — well, except for the rare occasions when the sun shines. The average high temperature in summer is 18 degrees. It is held to be the cloudiest city in New Zealand. They had had a sunny day a few days before the marathon so it was unlikely we would have good weather on our race day. We had strong wind, but it was a tailwind for most of the course so there wasn't much complaining. We also had some intermittent cold rain, and I wore tights for the whole run — something I have never done for any other marathon, as I expected that my legs would become far too hot and then itchy. But the tights were great for the chilling effects of the wind.

This was to be one of the quietest marathons I've done. Even for a rural run there seemed to be very little going on. Kilometre after kilometre of a long road with many endless straights, and on both sides green paddocks. There were a few sheep — this was New Zealand after all — and little else. I was glad to have brought along some music for company, and I liked breathing in all this fresh, clean air.

I just told myself I had a distance to run and I was going to cover it. I remarked afterwards on the lack of spectators, the quiet. Maybe I was still thinking about New York and the deafening noise from the onlookers. There was activity every inch of the way that day.

The prize-giving ceremony in Invercargill would have befitted a much larger event. There were so few women in the event that we all received prizes.

When the going gets tough

It takes courage to front up for a tough challenge over and over again. I'm making a choice to repeat something that I know will require a great deal of both physical and mental strength. I have been there, suffered and opted to return. Perhaps this makes me an obstinate learner. But I prefer to think it has given me a chance to develop some new skills, especially mental ones.

You may have heard a rumour that marathons are as much a mental challenge as a physical one. Surprised? Most people imagine that the hard part of running a marathon is keeping your legs in motion for a very long time. Yes, running for a long time is testing and you must always train sensibly to be able to run a marathon. But, in addition, an awful lot of what it takes to run a marathon happens inside your head before and during the race. And afterwards, too, as you'll hear later on. Your legs and lungs can only do so much. Unless you are struck down by illness or injury, it is highly likely that your mind will give way before your legs during your training and in the marathon.

Unfortunately, your mind and body do not always work together to get you starting the marathon and through to the finish, and your mind can fight against your body at just the wrong moment. Never more acutely than when you are physically tired.

You need determination to reach a marathon finish line —

both with your training, and when the race is making unreasonable demands on your body. Your persistence is driven by desire — desire to start and finish the marathon. And your successful outcome is aided by self-belief. If you prepare well you can achieve, so long as you believe this.

To stand confidently on the start line you have to have done the physical training. Massive hours of running over a long period of time. During the many months that you prepare for a marathon your desire to train and your desire to run the marathon will vary in intensity. Initially you motivate yourself to run regularly and often because you have decided to do a marathon, and you understand what preparation is required. But this might not be enough motivation. The early excitement of signing up for the race fades. When this happens I find that varying the locations where I run, and running at different times of the day from usual, are ways to help myself. Taking a few days off running also helps, since you will find yourself very anxious to get out and run when you haven't done it for a while. Yes, it's true, taking a few days off will not do any harm. It will not mean you never run again. It will not cause you to put on ten kilos and instantly become unfit.

Knowing that my enthusiasm for running may get weaker during the year, I will usually aim to do more during the first six months. That way it will not worry me if I lose momentum. By July I know that I have come further than I still have to go. Like anyone else, I sometimes lose interest in running. I joke that I should not have this desire to run marathons. Why could I not run 200 metres lots of times instead? When my motivation is low I do less running. By the latter part of the year I know I can run the marathons I have set as my target even if I do not train very much.

Closer to race day, doubts emerge. Have I done enough training?

Have I done the right training? Should I have done another long run? The answer is to be confident, to believe in myself.

I often wonder if I will be able to finish an upcoming marathon. This is not a joke; I can question my ability to run 42.2 kilometres as much as the next person. I remind myself that I have run a marathon before. The odds of my completing the race are overwhelmingly in my favour.

Then I have to watch out for those imaginary illnesses and injuries — common signals of an impending race. I have to be very careful at home during the week before a marathon. If I mention any sort of medical issue I will be soundly laughed at. Any suggestion of pain will be treated with derision. I need a medical certificate in order to elicit sympathy. I have talked about this with a friend who also runs a lot of marathons, and we have concluded that during the days leading up to a marathon we lose the ability to distinguish between real and imaginary discomfort.

And then there's that anguish on the start line, waiting for the gun. Start line nerves are normal. I reassure myself about this before each marathon. There's adrenaline flowing to get you fired up to perform, and some of it is going to manifest itself as nerves. I find the last five minutes before the gun goes off to be the worst part of the day. I cannot talk to anyone. I cannot think straight. And then we are released onto the course and this pain is over. For a while.

Some of what goes on in your head during the marathon can be a real nuisance. It can spoil your day quickly and irrevocably if you let it. Once you spot a problem you need to zap it fast.

Mind games — that's what it's all about. Several varieties of these are needed when the going gets tough.

The issues that are within your control can usually be resolved or at least be made tolerable. You can't do anything about fellow competitors appearing confident, or the fierce wind blowing. But you can control your reaction to the other runners and the weather. You can tell yourself that to them you appear equally confident — after all, you're wearing shoes that appear to have done high mileage — and you can manage your anger at the wind wrecking what should have been a perfect day by reminding yourself that the wind is blowing into everyone's faces.

The thing to realise is that most of the issues that could upset you are under your control.

Visualisation is a technique that can help in advance of race day. Curl up in a comfortable chair and think through the race. Visualising myself winning a marathon in world record time is fun and can liven up a dull afternoon, but this isn't what the technique is really about. What you can do is use visualisation to help you overcome race problems outside of the race environment. You probably won't have four hours to spend doing this, so fast-forward through the early kilometres and head for trouble spots.

From running many marathons, I have identified the points in the race where I am likely to feel bad. I used to always have a low point between 17 and 25 kilometres. Before each marathon I would look where this was on the route map and prepare myself to cope with feeling bad at that stage. I did this by seeing myself run strongly through the pain and come out the other side. Gradually this part of the race has ceased to be a problem.

At some point in the race, usually during the second half, you may decide that you have had enough and you want a break. Or worse, that you want to go home. Now. You may feel discontented, disheartened, bored, outraged, inadequate and downright sick of the whole exercise. You have long ceased to like being here. You cannot understand why running a marathon ever sounded appealing. You are convinced that you are doing a really silly thing in running this huge distance; it's a project that defies reason. You are in a voluntary pursuit of complete exhaustion. Whatever next? When you are physically tired — in this context, from a lot of running — you cease to be able to think straight. All sorts of notions pop into your head, many — no, most — of them counterproductive to the matter at hand, which is to complete the marathon.

If none of this happens, then, believe me, you are having a very good race. My goal, as I embark on every marathon route, is to have a good race.

You do not have to succumb to the negative feelings you get during the race as you tire. The physical tiredness is unavoidable. With the mental fatigue you must take the reins. You do not have to sit down immediately at the 30-kilometre mark when a voice inside is telling you to. Ignore it. You have the power to do so. You are not going to throw away all your preparation by giving up. You do not have to allow yourself to feel that you are a hopeless runner who should not have embarked on this endeavour.

I have learnt that it is essential to keep only positive thoughts in my head during the marathon. This goes beyond feelings about the immediate matter at hand — the race — although thoughts about this should remain positive for the full 42.2 kilometres. If I remember something that has annoyed me, however trivial and whether or not related to running, I toss out the thought. I take great care to banish self-doubt and self-criticism as soon as they rear their heads. I remind myself of my short-term goal, which is to finish the marathon.

A marathon runner from New Zealand who has run hundreds of marathons told me how he was at a low ebb during a recent marathon. He was all set to finish in well over five hours. Then another runner approached him and said, 'Michael, you have been such an inspiration to me with all the marathons you run.' Hearing this, Michael perked up, pleased that he had been a help to this woman, and ran to his usual four-hour finish.

Dissociating mentally during the marathon — thinking about something unrelated — can be a great help when the difficulty of what lies ahead feels too much. The elites are supposed to focus on every footfall, but those of us running for fun can make our lives more enjoyable. Thus, I ponder minor issues, like what I will watch on TV that evening. But I don't try to solve the world's problems. I find a marathon is taxing enough without setting myself other hard tasks. I quiz myself about recent movies I have seen — I can never remember the title or the actors, but trying to do so relieves some race tension and passes the time. My short-term memory goes completely when I have been running for a few hours.

It is always a help to break the marathon up into smaller parts while you are out on the course. I think in one-kilometre sections, or one mile if that is the unit of measurement where I am running. I would never think to myself that I have 15 kilometres to go, because the worry about the effort needed to run 15 kilometres is too draining when I am tired. But I can get my head around the next kilometre. And after that I can cope with the next one.

When the stress gets worse I might find myself focusing on reaching the next lamppost or the next bend in the road and not thinking beyond that. The idea is to break the remaining distance up into manageable chunks (in fact, so manageable that you know you will have no trouble completing them). This doesn't always work for me because a nasty voice in my head will remind me that I know the distance to go is far more than the next bend on the road, so why kid myself? But in Toronto, as I am about to relate, I broke the route up into sections and focused on completing each one. In that way I was able to complete the race. Small goals get you there in the end.

Out on the marathon course I may also try to envisage events after the race finish. I have seen myself walking around the shops or along the beach. This calms me down and also serves as a reminder that the race will at some point be over. Of course, I don't enter a marathon with the sole intention of looking forward to it being over; but this thought can be highly consoling if I am going through a bad patch. Sometimes it is tempting to imagine yourself lying down for a rest after the race but this can backfire and make for sluggish running. There's a similar problem with daydreaming about food — it can make you unbearably hungry.

I generally feel worse from 34 kilometres onward than I have earlier on in the race. So I remind myself as I run that this part of a marathon is always brutal — not just for me, but for everyone. This helps me. I know that the other runners around me are not feeling fresh and sprightly. At the end of the day, the marathon was never intended to be an easy proposition.

The Toronto Waterfront Marathon in September 2007 was my 60th marathon, and provided me with a chance to use all the mental skills at my disposal. This turned out to be the worst marathon experience I have ever had. To this day I don't understand what caused the distress I went through. But it is the benchmark by which I now measure all marathons — I think to myself at least once during every marathon that I feel better now than I did in Toronto.

Toronto is a brash Canadian city dominated by the CN Tower that used to be the tallest freestanding structure in the world. The city centre is a cluster of skyscrapers but not far away are delightful neighbourhoods. I found it a pleasant place to walk around. I especially enjoyed a short trip by ferry to the chain of islands in Lake Ontario. You can take the ferry over to an island, walk across that island to the far lake shore, and then walk along past pebbly beaches to a different ferry terminal for your return trip. The islands would get crowded during the summer months, but marathons are usually held at non-peak times so the island was virtually closed down. I wanted to hire a bike but the hire places were boarded up. I couldn't even get a cup of coffee out there.

Marathon day started badly on a poor night's sleep. I got up regularly all through the night and slept for less than two hours. I cannot normally function on this little sleep, although since that day I have run better marathons on no sleep at all.

I felt like a zombie on the start line. It was warmer than I had anticipated and I was wearing a shirt made of fabric that was too thick. I overheated within a few kilometres and could not hydrate properly. I seemed to be losing energy almost from the start. I promised myself that I could walk a short way when I reached 18 kilometres — this was a reward I was offering myself, a treat, even though walking would make the kilometres go by more slowly.

There is only one answer at a time like this, and that is to slow down. Still feel bad? Then you have to slow down even more. Comfort yourself by saying you didn't have any other plans for the day so it doesn't matter how long you are out there. Put your mind in a special place and create an imaginary fence around yourself so that nothing that is going on outside the fence can interfere. Do not get angry when the rest of the field floods past. Good luck to them if they're in a hurry.

I barely made it to 18 kilometres, and from then on I took short walks every kilometre. I only focused on the immediate next kilometre, often on the immediate next stretch of road. I was really suffering, but in a marathon you do not give up. I had my Phuket memory to fall back on, but the internal struggle was greater here. It was such an uncomfortable day, yet the other runners did not seem to be in strife.

(This proved to be more than a figment of my imagination; when I ran the Boston Marathon in 2008 I met several runners who had qualified for Boston with a fast time in this Toronto race.)

At around 30 kilometres we did the most scenic part of the run, an out-and-back through a nature reserve right by the lake shore. I had been looking forward to this but I barely noticed the water. I was counting my steps.

At the 35-kilometre mark a spectator said to me, 'What are you up to?' I thought she was being facetious and I replied, 'Running a marathon.' I suppose she wanted to know how far along we were. Well, not far enough.

I walked the last two kilometres, mainly under a highway overpass in the midday heat. When I reached the finish line the announcer called out my name, said I was from Australia, and commented this was a long way to travel. In my mentally fragile state I saw this as an accusation of time wasted.

However, after a shower and two jumbo slices of pizza I felt a lot better, and decided that I would be running far more happily in the Chicago Marathon the following weekend. I was not going to let a poor performance worry me for long.

In the Sydney Marathon in 2008 I again had to face the demons of despair inside my head. The circumstances were unlike Toronto, because on this occasion I was physically managing to run, but I had severe difficulty with keeping in a positive frame of mind through the race.

It seemed for many years as though I was doomed never to run the Sydney Marathon, after my initial experience in 2000. I found other running events to do on that same weekend. The first of these was the Traralgon King of the Mountain, a 30-kilometre run from the centre of the Victorian town of Traralgon to the top of Mount Tassie. It was a tough run with the second half almost continually uphill, but along lovely, quiet, tree-lined roads with views over all of surrounding Gippsland.

The first year I ran this I finished second female (it was only a small field) by a very small margin, so I felt I should return the following year and pace myself better. A run up a hill like this is all about the pacing so you don't run out of energy a few kilometres too early and have to walk to the finish. The following year I finished 20 minutes faster in first place. I'm not sure there were any other females that year, but who is asking?

For a couple of years I ran a half marathon at Burnley in Melbourne on the weekend before the Sydney Marathon. It was one of the rare half marathons that I run, and I wanted to run a reasonable time without the pressure of knowing I had to run a full marathon the following weekend. I find half marathons difficult. It's only half of what I usually run — but therein lies the problem. I head out too fast because I think I'm not going very far and I burn out quickly. A half marathon is still a long way to run.

One year on that same weekend I went to Airlie Beach in the Whitsundays in northern Queensland to participate in the first Run the Great Whitsunday Walk event, a race of 24 kilometres on trails through the rainforest. It was exciting to participate in an inaugural race, and we were a privileged group of runners. The volunteers at the aid stations had to be dropped in by helicopter along with their supplies as there was no road access.

Another year I got a lot further down the road to running the Sydney Marathon. I even entered the race. Then a month beforehand I strained my calf muscle, left it a week to heal and promptly strained it again. I had done a 15-kilometre race on hills in Melbourne and I had resumed training too soon after this, with my legs still sore from the race. So I thought it best not to run the marathon as I had things already lined up for later in the year that I did not wish to miss out on.

In 2008 I finally got there. The day before this mid-September marathon was stinking hot at 32 degrees and was the hottest day since the previous summer. Standing in the queue under the blazing sun to get into the registration marquee at midday, I thought this could all be a big mistake.

Fortunately, race day was in the mid-20s. But for someone coming out of the Melbourne winter this was still too warm for relaxed running and I had an inkling this would be a hard day.

This marathon was significant for another reason apart from the fact that I had finally got to the start line. It marked the 100th time that I was running the marathon distance. Not to be confused with running my 100th marathon — I was still some way off that — I was running marathon number 72, having also run 24 ultra marathons ranging from 45 kilometres to 100 kilometres, and four training runs I could remember of more than 42 kilometres. I'm very strict about only calling a race of 42.195 kilometres a marathon, but I liked to acknowledge having run an equivalent distance 100 times.

The highlights of this marathon are the first kilometre where you run over the Sydney Harbour Bridge, and the finish outside the Opera House. You couldn't hope for two more iconic landmarks. In between is all hard slog. Well, that's not quite fair, but it is undoubtedly the case that the start and the finish are what make this marathon special.

The start line is right under the bridge. Running over the Harbour Bridge is a great idea. It probably costs the organisers more in traffic authority fees than any other aspect of the event, but when a marathon has a feature like this the participants are more prepared to pay the relatively high entry charge. It isn't quite as exciting as running across the Auckland Harbour Bridge, which features in that city's marathon, because you can walk or cycle the Sydney version any day you choose, but it's still a real buzz and you aren't made to go on the narrow footpath at the side.

The route took us through central Sydney to the Domain, where we ran past the Art Gallery and Mrs Macquarie's Chair; you could imagine a latter-day Mrs Macquarie sitting there watching us run by. On the way out of the Domain the outdoor Andrew Boy Charlton swimming pool looked inviting even early in the day. We continued up through Darlinghurst — not much activity there apart from a few stragglers on their way home after a big night out.

The next big chunk of the route was through Centennial Park. This is home turf to so many runners. I had started my running habit when I lived in Sydney and I went for my first runs in this park. I did my first ten-kilometre race here — it seemed endless at the time — and I trained for my first half marathon by running a 17-kilometre loop in the park, which was also endless. Maybe remembering the difficulty of those past runs, rather than merely feeling a wave of nostalgia about them, got me into my low mood.

Our route through Centennial Park was complicated — unnecessarily so, it seemed to me at the time. We seemed to twist and turn all over the place and I was already feeling too warm only an hour into the marathon.

Everything was starting to look bleak. We were heading away from the city centre into not-so-interesting suburbs on a wide, straight road. This was close to the halfway mark, and while I was still making reasonable time I was fading fast. I tried to chat to a runner from New Zealand but I found this hard work and decided to reserve my strength. But first I had time to attempt a joke: he asked me what the Melbourne

Marathon is like and I told him that it is very long. He didn't laugh. I guess that was because I had told him this was my 72nd marathon and he must have reckoned that I should have worked out by now how long they are. Anyway, I let him go on ahead.

As we came back into Darlinghurst I felt worse and worse. Amazingly, I told myself that this could be the lowest I had ever been in a marathon. Looking back that can't possibly have been the case, but I felt bad — it was hot, and I'd had a lot going on in my life that past week. Negative thoughts flooded over me. Tears fell.

I continued on through the southern part of the city centre in this frame of mind. I was playing cat and mouse with a youngish guy who also looked to be having a less than perfect marathon. Then I thought to myself: *He hasn't run 71 marathons, and he doesn't know that this will eventually be something in the past that he can laugh about.* This was a great consolation to me — not that he was in strife, but that I had been through this particular type of misery before and emerged on the other side. I romped ahead of him and to some degree the bad patch was over. Dare I say it, this must be one of the benefits of having run so many marathons — knowing that the bad times pass. They certainly don't get any easier and, as I tried to tell my Kiwi friend, they don't get any shorter.

I was definitely feeling better by the time we ran around the edge of Chinatown. I noticed a couple of runners who were having their photo taken by a (presumed) friend; the friend was struggling to get enough ahead of them to take the photos. I joked to the friend that he should be running the marathon, too, and suggested one of the runners could take on the role of photographer next time. It seemed equally challenging.

The second half of the course had many dull parts. Pyrmont and Glebe Island are not generally on the tourist itinerary. Some running events are scenic all the way, but when they aren't it's usually the case that the scenery deteriorates in the second half. I think marathon organisers need to look into the heads of the poor runners and realise that it's when you are struggling that some good scenery can make all the difference. Conversation invariably flags and you jolly well need something to distract you.

The final kilometre as we returned to Circular Quay was good, with harbour views, the bridge and then the Opera House. We ran right by the water on the footpath through the heart of Circular Quay, passing the cafes that were going to be a treat to visit once we were finished with this running caper.

In the last half kilometre I caught up with my Kiwi friend. I tried to out-sprint him to the finish line, but I started too early and I couldn't make it. He passed me and finished a second ahead. That was fun, and I realised I was now in a very good mood.

On the way back to my hotel I met a group of Norwegian runners who had finished the marathon. I wasted no time in finding something to chat about.

I had been to Norway not long before this to run a marathon in the forest on the edge of Oslo, the Nordmarka Skogsmaraton. It had been a spectacular race on hilly trails by a black lake. We ran along the shore of the lake, and spent many hours running through woods more suited to tales of make-believe: a mixture of stately fir trees and deciduous trees newly covered with bright spring foliage. For the first half hour we saw nothing but trees as we climbed gradually but steadily. Just as all this greenery and fresh air began to get monotonous the terrain changed to a morass of streams and smaller lakes. The lakes were uniformly idyllic with calm black waters, and some would have just one or two red timber houses on the shore. Through breaks in the trees we had glimpses of forested hills. The forest was criss-crossed by tracks such as the ones we ran on, with signs indicating place names, although we never seemed to arrive at any named or nameable place, just track junctions. We even had a hailstorm during the marathon and were later treated to a beautiful rainbow.

I told the Norwegians about my experience and one of them said, 'Well done. That's one of the hardest marathons in Norway.' I wished I had been able to recall that day when I was out on the Sydney Marathon course; the positive vibes might just have helped me get out of my slump sooner.

They cancelled the race

Having your marathon cancelled at the last minute would have to be one of a marathon runner's worst nightmares. It would be right up there with spraining your ankle on the way to the race start or waking up with malaria. How about having your plane diverted to an airport on the other side of the country (or the world), because a volcano is spewing ash into your flight path, leaving too little time for you to make it to the race venue? This happened in 2010, when a large number of runners were unable to reach Boston in time for the marathon thanks to the eruption of a volcano in Iceland creating havoc with world aviation schedules. Airlines were still not back on track by the time of the London Marathon that year either, so lots of runners missed that one too. They would have explored all avenues for getting to the race, I assure you.

But straight-out cancellation? Not one person of the couple of thousand on the start line at the Rotorua Marathon in New Zealand in 1999 would have been anything less than furious to hear their event cancelled ten minutes before the start time. Torrential rain the night before the marathon caused the road to subside in places around the back side of the lake. The race organisers clung to a slim hope that the race could go ahead, but the marathon had to be called off. Runners' reactions can only be imagined. They had to bow to the voice of reason, but what an awful shame after all that hard work.

Runners arriving for the 2010 Myrtle Beach Marathon in South Carolina could see that there had been an unexpected dump of snow in town. The first snowstorm in ten years had just hit. They crossed their fingers but on the evening before the race the director announced that he had to cancel the marathon. The course would remain open for vehicles during the race and it was felt that drivers and runners could not safely share a slippery road.

When a race is cancelled at short notice like this there is far more going on than a few thousand disappointed people lamenting dollars wasted on travel. Assembled on the start line are not just folk who like to run, but many thousands of training sessions. Every pair of legs would have been put through a rigorous campaign to ensure they would have the best chance of completing the marathon.

As a runner, you have devoted a proportion of your life to this race. You have spent many long hours working on your running. You made the time to run. Running has been your top priority. You found that your mind became obsessed with the impending marathon, even months before race day. You were thinking about it several times a day. You were starting to make excuses for not attending social functions so you could train, for going to bed early and for not doing chores because you were exhausted after running week in, week out. You realised this tiredness was part of the deal. The family was getting anxious for marathon day to happen so that life could return to normal. You wondered about their attitude, but if you were really taking the marathon seriously you won't have noticed at all. You were already ensconced in your own world. Some of your friends were getting bored, and there's a good chance these were the non-runners. Your marathoner friends understood fully what was consuming you and would fan the flames with their own tales of marathon woe and glory. You lapped up their anecdotes and asked for more.

Race day comes, and then — no race.

In late 2007 the Three Bays Marathon in Portland was cancelled on race morning due to adverse weather. As the race director Peter Reefman explained to me, the decision to cancel was not taken at all lightly:

> The race was cancelled because of a very severe storm that went through Victoria that day. We woke with news of two camping deaths in Lorne that night from a fallen tree, and the wind had gusts up to 120 kilometres an hour. The police met with us at 5am and said it was our call, but they didn't want us to start the race. One of our officials drove around and saw six trees blown over, while the State Emergency Service had been out during the night, clearing roads.
>
> At 5.30am I had a meeting with the committee to see if we wanted to cancel the race, with a 50-50 split. I asked the marathon walkers (who had a scheduled 6am start) what they thought and, while a couple had already pulled out, many wanted to start. So we let them start, but with a proviso that we might pick them up if conditions got worse.
>
> It did get worse: more trees were blowing over out on the course, and the police called me again but said that they couldn't force a cancellation. But we knew that road permits would be in doubt for future races if anyone were to get hurt today, and even if no one was hurt we would still appear irresponsible in the eyes of the police and other officials.
>
> I thought about the relays, especially the kids, and the volunteers. In all there'd be hundreds of people out in what were really pretty dangerous conditions. So at that point I made the call as race director to cancel and we picked up the walkers.
>
> The race was cancelled at about 7am — an hour after the

> marathon walk start, and an hour before the runners were to start. Most people were disappointed but supportive, but a few were very angry with the decision. At the end of the day I think it was the only responsible decision to take, and I am glad I made the call.
>
> By the way, a few people did a rebel run at their own risk. They made it around safely but one said later he almost got hit by a falling tree.

That same year, 2007, had turned on some unusual weather for several of the world's prominent marathons.

The Rotterdam Marathon took place on the warmest April day in the history of the Netherlands. The race started at 11am and by 2.30pm participants still out on the course (which would have been most of the field) were told they should either walk slowly to the finish line or get a ride back in specially arranged minibuses. The announcement was made after over two dozen runners had been taken to hospital with heat-related problems.

The Boston Marathon one week later was almost called off because the weather was diabolical — hailstorms and freezing temperatures — and if things hadn't cleared up rather surprisingly just before the race start it would have been cancelled. As it was, the decision to go ahead was taken only ten minutes before the scheduled start time. Runners were fortunate to have only gusty winds and the cold to contend with.

So what happens when the marathon goes ahead and then partway through the race director decides to cancel it? I was about to find out.

In Chicago in 2007 the summer heat had not yet left by October, and both runners and race organisers at the Chicago Marathon knew that race day could get hot. The average temperature at that time of year was around 12 degrees Celsius. We did not quite expect 35 degrees, 80-percent humidity and the sun blazing down, but that's what we got. Nine thousand out of the 45,000 runners who had registered did not front up for the run, and 11,000 starters did not run the full course. Incidentally, I heard that in my hometown of Melbourne the conditions for the annual marathon, taking place 16 hours earlier, were the best they had been in all the time I've lived there.

It was warm from the moment we set out, partly because of the somewhat late 8am start. The start time sounded late to us, but the 2006 marathon's race day had been cold, with the temperature hovering around zero, and runners would have been glad not to start too early in the day.

The Chicago Marathon is a giant loop passing through the city centre and a whole variety of ethnic neighbourhoods. For many runners the attraction is the dead-flat nature of the course, but it's visually appealing too. We got to run past the zoo, the ball park, schools, a university, famous restaurants, shopping malls and all sorts of other sights.

We started in Grant Park on the shore of Lake Michigan and first took a short tour of central Chicago, crossing the Chicago River three times and passing many of the city's more notable buildings. Chicago is a city of fabulous architecture, much of it centred on Michigan Avenue where the road and river intersect. It was a great start and there was plenty of crowd support here.

Once out of the central city we headed north for Lincoln Park and some elegant suburbs. By the six-mile mark I was feeling warmer than I should have and others were commenting on the temperature, but nobody was yet complaining. There was plenty of water at the aid stations — in fact, so much that volunteers were tipping cups of water over runners who asked for this. This was to prove a mistake for the welfare of runners well behind us, thousands of whom arrived at aid stations to find that they had run out of water. What could be worse for a runner on a hot day than to be turned away at a drinks table? I'll tell you what can be worse. Apparently the few grocery stores that were open along the marathon course also started to run out of drinks. You couldn't buy a drink, even when you were desperate enough to be prepared to queue and pay.

We were taken on a tour around the western suburbs, long streets of terraced brownstone houses. It was the kind of run you might do around your local neighbourhood any Sunday, but with quite a few spectators. Although it was nothing like as noisy as the New York City Marathon and the crowd wasn't several-people-deep on the footpath.

When I reached the 21-mile marker, as we toured some southern neighbourhoods, I realised there was something amiss. Race officials along the course started announcing with loudhailers that the race had been cancelled, but with no clarification as to what that might mean. They simply said, 'The race has been cancelled.'

I was initially mystified and then very perturbed. Did this mean that I was not going to be able to finish this marathon? It might have been uncomfortable running but there was no way I was not going to finish. I had always taken finishing for granted until that moment. Even in the Phuket Marathon, when I could barely walk 20 steps without resting, I expected to finish. Finishing the marathon suddenly became the most important thing in the world to me. Who would travel from Melbourne to Chicago, booking flights and a hotel six months in advance, to run *part* of a marathon? Who would train for six months to run *part* of a marathon? Who would bother starting a marathon if there were no option to finish it? When today's marathon is incomplete you can't just finish the job tomorrow instead.

We continued walking or running forward because there was

nothing else to do, but we had no idea what was going to happen. Would we be forcibly stopped? Would we be taken by bus back to Grant Park? This option seemed unlikely due to the sheer number of us. Then helicopters flew overhead with megaphones telling runners to stop running. Police cars drove slowly up the sides of the course announcing that the race was over.

At the next few aid stations there were marshals telling us to walk. It didn't sound optional, so I took heed. This was the United States, land of TV shows about tough law enforcement. You don't think straight during the late part of a marathon and I was worried I might be removed from the course or worse (although I was hard-pressed to think what could be worse) if I ran and didn't obey instructions.

Runners were collapsing here and there. I've seen the occasional runner have a bit of a stagger or erratic movements or even collapse during a marathon, but not on this scale. Some runners were clearly trying to get as far as possible before they had to give up and almost appeared to be sprinting, but they had little chance of finishing by doing this for four miles in their heat-weakened state.

There were buses parked alongside the marathon route. This looked very odd until I realised that they had the air-conditioning turned on and were for runners to sit inside and cool down. Every subway station that we passed had its platforms crowded with runners who had presumably given up and were going home.

I was lucky because I never had a problem getting drinks, even towards the end. I would have been dehydrated but I was not noticing it at the time.

Since I had run a handful of marathons in hot weather I knew how it felt, and I was reluctant to walk all the way back to Grant Park when I felt I had the ability to run. I knew that it would be essential to take it easy but that running was not impossible. So I began running again, but slowly, and — guess what — nobody arrested me. We all started to pay less attention to the warnings. I ran amongst a group of marathoners who seemed to be travelling fine, and you could tell this because normal conversation was flowing. I was delighted when a runner next to me said we were almost at Grant Park, with just one more turn. I really didn't feel too bad, probably due to all the walking I had done. In hindsight it is amazing to think that I felt so strong and fit in these conditions when I had felt so hopeless during the Toronto Waterfront Marathon only seven days earlier.

There was great confusion at the finish line. It took me some while to work out what was going on. Runners who had not reached the 15-mile mark by 11.30am were not permitted to continue running the marathon route beyond there — the course came very close to the finish line at this point — and had to return to Grant Park. Those runners were allowed to cross the finish line so that they would receive a medal and certificate but they were approaching the finish line from the opposite direction to those of us still in the real race. Finish lines are set up in such a way that you cannot fail to cross and have your time recorded; in other words you can't skip around the back. So these runners who had not finished the full distance were told to cross and then recross the finish line. This meant that there were large numbers of people going in all directions over the finishing mats. It's a tribute to the technology that the mats were able to record all of us, and I suspect some entrants may have received multiple certificates.

We felt rather dazed at the end of it all. Runners were hanging around looking half-dead and sitting on anything that could be sat on. My hotel was close by but I had to rest before I could summon the energy to walk across the road. Most people I spoke to had run a good 40 minutes slower than they had hoped. Stories were already circulating about the number of runners taken to hospital (in excess of 300) and I saw several runners being wheeled about on stretchers. Apparently the available ambulances had long since been used up.

Fortunately, we did receive certificates for finishing, with our times recorded. As a concession to the thousands of runners who had not completed the course there were no age group placings recognised or awards made.

There was quite a bit of controversy after the marathon. Runners claimed that the organisers could have done more. They knew it was going to be a hot day so they could have sent warnings out to the entrants and made sure there were adequate refreshments on the aid tables. Many locals, seeing the drain on the city's medical resources, said that the race should have been cancelled before the start. But then again, this would have been immensely unpopular and very unfair on those runners who were perfectly capable of running in the heat. More experienced runners said that there was a need for entrants to be more aware of what they were getting into when they signed up and that maybe qualifying standards should be introduced. It's not a straightforward issue, and one that is made much more complicated when there are 30,000 or 40,000 participants involved.

At smaller events, race directors have been able to sidestep similar problems by altering the course at short notice. In Wagga Wagga, in New South Wales, the Murrumbidgee River flooded its banks just a week before the annual trail marathon in 2010, giving the race organisers a real headache as the trail on the riverbank levee accounted for much of the race route. Instead of cancelling the race a new course was rapidly devised, to the delight of the participants — hillier and tougher, but at least the marathon could go ahead. Similarly, the Death Valley Marathon course in California has been changed on race day several times when runners would have been at risk running through Titus Canyon, the most attractive stretch of the race — not because of the heat but because of ice and snow. The alternative is a boring slog on a sealed road and there are always complaints.

I managed to squeeze in some sightseeing before leaving Chicago. I strolled along Michigan Avenue, a wide street with pavement dining and many art deco buildings. I walked along the lakefront, too, and I checked out the Art Institute. Then I found two more contemporary edifices, facing each other across the street, Niketown and Borders. It was too hot to be outside so I spent some happy hours among the sports gear, books and CDs.

Bound for Boston

Yes, I have run there. The Boston Marathon has a long and proud tradition. It has an aura that has infected marathon runners the world over. It is regarded as the marathon of all marathons.

Two features have kept the Boston Marathon on a pedestal above other marathons: it is the oldest public marathon in the world, and you need to prove yourself before you can be allowed to participate. In 1976 the race committee took the unusual step of requiring all participants to qualify by running another marathon beforehand within a specified time limit. The time limits were amended in 1980 and again in 2003 in order to control the number of entrants. To qualify to run Boston, you must run a marathon within the 18 months prior to Boston within a time range according to your age. The marathon field still fills its 15,000-runner quota before the application period closes.

Boston is a people's marathon but the entry requirement gives it the status of a more serious race. Running a marathon may be a high point of your running life, but running the Boston Marathon takes things a notch higher. Ask any of the runners who try year after year at local marathons to get a Boston qualifier — a 'BQ'. It's true you can also get an entry into this marathon by guaranteeing a minimum donation to charity, saving you from having to run a qualifying time, but you don't get the satisfaction of running your Boston qualifier along the way.

The Boston Marathon's prestige is also due to the crucial part it has played in the history of women's marathon running.

For female runners, things have not always been plain sailing. Women never participated in the Olympic Games of ancient Greece. They were allowed to join in some track and field events of the revived Olympics for the first time in Amsterdam in 1928. After these Olympics, when three women collapsed during the 800-metre race, female participation in athletics was limited to events not exceeding 200 metres amid fears that women's bodies simply could not handle the rigours of hard running. In the 1960 Olympics women were graciously allowed to compete at distances up to 800 metres, and in 1972 they were allowed to compete at 1500 metres as well.

Between 1896 and 1966, only a handful of women worldwide were recorded as having run a marathon. The Boston Marathon forbade female entrants, as Bobbi Gibb found out in 1966 when she applied to enter the race. She had no idea that women were not permitted to run when she decided to compete in the marathon, and she had done more than adequate training. She had to run unofficially that year (if she wanted to be a participant) and she succeeded in finishing, to the delight of many of the other entrants and the media. In 1967 two females ran the marathon, Gibb and Kathrine Switzer. Switzer obtained a race bib through the normal channels without disclosing her gender (while being aware that women were not allowed to run), and Gibb ran again without a race bib — in other words, unofficially. Gibb was first female home. Switzer's story, involving the race director trying to manhandle her off the course when he spotted a female runner with an official bib in his race, has become part of marathon folklore.

The race director's anti-woman stance at the 1967 race damaged the marathon's image, so from 1968 women were allowed to run at the Boston event. But while they could enter and receive a race bib, their times were not included in the published results (although these results have now been retrospectively adjusted to record females). In 1971 the New York City Marathon decided to hold an official women's division in the marathon and Boston really had no choice but to follow suit at its 1972 event.

Things changed eventually on the world stage. The International Amateur Athletic Federation allowed women to run marathons at athletics world championships from 1983, and in 1984 there was a women's marathon at the Los Angeles Olympic Games.

Women have embraced this pursuit. In Australia the proportion of women at marathons is rising; it sits around 30 percent at the Gold Coast Marathon, and is approaching this level at the Melbourne and Canberra marathons. In the US, the San Diego Marathon and the Portland Marathon had more female runners than male between 2005 and 2009. At the Boston Marathon the days when women were banned are long gone, with around 40 percent of the field being comprised of women for a number of years. Despite its misogynist history, women want to be there as much as men.

Boston doesn't come over as a typical North American city, with few tall buildings in the city centre and the Boston Common, where people stroll past duck ponds and squirrels dart from tree to tree, smack in the middle of the place. It is a charming city for wandering around.

The Freedom Trail celebrates the American Revolution and a walk along it makes for excellent light exercise just before the marathon. This three-mile trail is marked out on the ground in red bricks and leads past 16 buildings and sites that have played a role in the development of Boston and the modern US.

Then you can snack at the pub where the TV series *Cheers* was filmed in the 1980s, and check out the paintings at the Isabella Stewart Gardiner Museum in Ms Gardiner's house, built in 1903. This is an intimate art gallery, with dim lighting to protect the paintings and not all the works are labelled. In 1990 there was a theft of 13 major works from the gallery, but Ms Gardiner had stipulated in her will that nothing was ever to be changed in her house, so the empty frames have been left in situ on the walls. The tour guides may be talking tongue in cheek when they explain the empty frames — I imagine that really they are waiting for the pictures to be returned — but this quirky sight alone makes the gallery worth a visit.

I have had plenty of surprises during my time running marathons, including many courses that turned out quite different from what I expected. Boston was the biggest surprise of all. I had not seen it touted as having an interesting course; it was simply the Boston Marathon, and the name was enough to lure you along. The entire marathon route was endearing, from the start line in the hamlet of Hopkinton situated in the middle of a forest, through quaint New England towns, to a finish in the very centre of Boston. How could so many people have kept so quiet about this aspect of the event?

We were lucky in 2008 to have a wonderful day for the run: wintry but sunny and still with a predicted high in the low 20s. The previous year, as I mentioned, the event had come very close to being called off due to bad storms and hail, which fortunately abated a little during the marathon. The year before that, race day had been unseasonably hot and many runners suffered from heat exhaustion. Boston weather is unpredictable in spring, but the race has always been held on the Patriots Day public holiday in mid-April — a Monday — and there is no chance that the date will be changed in the near future. I had taken along clothes for every weather situation.

At first light we were taken on a fleet of school buses from Boston Common to Hopkinton, 26 miles away. Not a random distance, you will by now appreciate. It was a dull drive, and it encouraged my expectation that this was going to be a dull race. We went along a bleak highway, passing forests of leafless trees, and then we were dropped off at the race headquarters. At first glance there was a few marquees and nothing else.

There was a buzz in the air the likes of which you only find at marathons. But this time it was slightly different. Just about every runner there had run a qualifying marathon beforehand, so we all knew what we were there for. We were composed, ready. Whether we foresaw pain or pleasure, or pleasure with the relentless onset of pain, we were bound by the bond that we had all been through this before. Standing in the toilet queue we could discuss past experiences and goals and fears with panache rather than apprehension. People often pick me for a novice, but this time nobody could say to me, 'Is this your first one?'

For the past few years the marathon has had two starts, half an hour apart, to ease crowding. The race start has also been moved forward from its traditional midday starting time. Thus, runners with a qualifying time under three and a half hours start at 10am, and slower qualifiers start half an hour later. Although slower runners like me might feel sore about being segregated, this is an excellent idea because it allows the spectators along the route to regroup after the first batch has come past and treat those of us in the second batch with renewed enthusiasm. The spectators have had time to rest their voices, have a toilet break and grab a coffee. This might not, however, be the official reason the split start was initiated.

Hopkinton is a postcard-pretty town of colourful timber homes, guest houses and cafes. A lovely place to visit to give marathon runners a send-off. And all the ensuing towns are just as pretty, immaculately maintained and filled with houses out of a TV sitcom. Any marathon runner has heard names like Ashland, Framingham, Natick and Wellesley, and in the flesh these are delightful towns. People have front porches where they can sit to watch runners pass by. The coffee shops have outdoor tables for patrons willing to brace the chilly air. And then there are bits of lake shore. Maybe a train or two passing slowly by.

One of the downsides of the Boston race for serious runners is that the course is basically a downhill run. This sounds as though it makes it easy, but we're talking 26 miles here and an elevation drop of only 425 feet (130 metres). The problem is that a lot of the downhill is in the very early stages, let's say the first four miles, and runners tend to take things far too fast then suffer for a long while afterwards. Accurate pacing was never so important. In the later stages are several notorious uphills, known collectively as the Newton Hills and including one long one called Heartbreak Hill by those in the know, and these hills have caused many a top runner's dreams of glory to fade.

Fortunately, I didn't find the downhills too much of an issue. I took them slowly at the start and warmed up gradually. I had other things on my mind. For my pre-race meal the previous evening I had enjoyed a bowl of chilli and beans, a dish that I am very fond of and have to indulge in often whenever I go to the US. This may sound foolish as a last meal before a marathon, but I have always thought that I have a cast-iron stomach and I have previously had Thai and even Indian curry before a run. My luck was out this time. Even before I had run five kilometres I was on the lookout for a toilet. I saw toilets alright, because the Boston marathon is nothing if not well-planned, but I also found lengthy queues at those toilets. It was awful to have to stand there and watch the marathon field run on by. On my third toilet stop I was redirected by a well-meaning spectator from a toilet with only one person in the queue (himself) to another toilet with a queue of four. I'm sure he can't have realised this, even while it struck me as odd at the time.

One of the major landmarks near the halfway point is Wellesley College, a girls' school. The cheering from the schoolgirls is legendary.

Of course they are mainly cheering for the men in the field and trying to score a kiss from someone en route. But I was running in a field of predominantly women — it was inevitable there would be mainly women in the second wave of starters since all men under the age of 50 have a required qualifying time that puts them in the first wave. I was curious how vociferous the girls would be towards females. I need not have feared; they made a phenomenal din on a day when all the other spectators could hardly be said to be holding back.

Shortly afterwards comes the Newton fire station, where firemen were busy polishing their trucks, and then the start of the hills. There are basically three hills, each one longer than the previous, culminating with a long but steady sweep up Heartbreak. Many runners were reduced to walking by this stage but there was still plenty of cheering to keep us going.

On the far side of the famous hill awaits Boston. The surroundings indicate that you're coming into a city: a subway station, another big cheering school, and lots more buildings. It starts to get even more exciting as the enthusiasm of the crowd builds. Once in the city there are some twists and turns in what has otherwise been a very straightforward course. Most runners were pretty much physically finished upon reaching Fenway Park, home of the Red Sox baseball team, where a match was in full swing (there is always a home match here on the afternoon of Patriots Day), but with a last few turns we were in Boylston Street. Race finish took place outside the Boston Public Library.

Arriving at the finish line of a marathon is always wonderful, but in many of these events in the US the marshals and volunteers really make you feel like a champion. At a small town marathon in Port Angeles in the state of Washington there was a volunteer to assist each and every finisher through the finishing chute. A lovely lady came up to me as I crossed the line, took me by the hand and led me to the recovery area. I hardly knew how to react. I clung onto her hand and felt amazingly grateful for this act of kindness. She did not look like a runner and she may only have had a hazy idea of what I had been though on my 26-mile journey, but she was there for me.

At the Boston finish line you don't get this personal service but you get a foil blanket, drinks, someone to remove the timing chip from your shoe (and if you have been able to remove it yourself they will retie your shoelace without being asked because they are most keen to do something to make your life comfortable), and lots of pats on the back. I enjoy this hero thing. I walked back to my hotel across the Boston Common in a happy daze. I must have appeared completely ridiculous with a foil sheet around my shoulders, my clothes soggy and smeared with the residue of various coloured liquids. But there were hundreds of us in the same boat, and we all had the same thought in our heads: We had run the Boston Marathon.

Outback vibes

One day in late June 2008 I had a serious problem with race beverages. The selection at the aid stations was not to my liking.

I was running the Pichi Richi Marathon for the second time. I ran the Pichi Richi Marathon in 2005 and loved it for its outback vibe, so in 2008 I decided it was time to return.

This South Australian marathon starts on the northern fringes of Port Augusta and ends at the small settlement of Quorn in the southern Flinders Ranges, coincidentally 42 kilometres away. The best section of the route is the Pichi Richi Pass, which starts at roughly kilometre 18 of the marathon route and is a gem of outback scenery. The route is a visual feast of red earth, dry but shimmering flood plains, and in the later stages the stark red cliffs that characterise the Flinders Ranges. There's nowhere else like this. Nowhere else that puts on a marathon, at any rate.

The original Ghan train ran on the single track through the Pichi Richi Pass from 1923 until 1956. One version of the story of how the Ghan got its name is that the sole traveller on the first passenger train through the pass happened to be an Afghan who alighted at Quorn station to say his prayers. The drivers nicknamed the train the Afghan Express for this lone passenger, one of many Afghan cameleers who had settled here. When the Ghan route was altered in the 1950s a spectacular section of track with many bridges, steep cuttings and stone wall embankments was bypassed. A bunch of enthusiasts worked from 1973 onward to reopen the line as the Pichi Richi Railway between Quorn and Stirling North, eight kilometres from Port Augusta. The line had to be completely rebuilt for these last eight kilometres, and after its completion in 2001 a steam train can now take tourists from Port Augusta to Quorn and back.

On marathon day the train operates to a special schedule so runners' supporters can take the train from Port Augusta to Quorn in time for the marathon finish, and runners can return to Port Augusta after their race. You might even get to see the train as you run. In 2005 I was very pleased to see the steam locomotive in all its glory during the marathon, in the distance, and to hear it tooting away.

Port Augusta is an interesting place. It's at the tip of the Spencer Gulf where the Eyre and Stuart Highways meet — the so-called junction of Australia. The Eyre heads to Western Australia and the Stuart to the Northern Territory. There is a road sign near the marathon start with this information, and I have photographed it on every visit. It sounds rather simple, except that the distances are huge.

Approaching the town on a very wet night by bus in mid-2005, I had little idea what to expect. You travel for hours over totally flat land, and then the town pops up on the horizon. Port Augusta is an important commercial centre for the Southern Flinders while tourists head north to towns like Quorn and Hawker.

In daylight I found lots of historic buildings, all of which were nicely polished up. On my 2005 visit I went for an early morning run around the Arid Lands Botanic Garden and didn't see any other runners, but plenty of chirping birds and dry red earth supporting, well, very little. The vegetation was all low and the other main signs of life came from the plentiful geckos.

I was determined to give the town a really thorough working over, so I tried everything on offer. I climbed the water tower for a great view of the region. I toured around the Wadlata Outback Centre, where there are extensive displays covering local Aboriginal history and lore, and the region's mining history is explained in depth. I also strolled along the shore of the Spencer Gulf, observing little beaches and expanses of mangrove. The gulf separates flat Port Augusta from slightly hilly Port Augusta West.

Then I recalled that I was there to run a marathon, and this marathon is certainly a distinctive one on the Australian running calendar. It is not an especially easy marathon as there is a net elevation gain over the route, and there are many hills to be negotiated. Old-timers point out that the final kilometres into Quorn are downhill, but only gradually so.

This has never been a big race, with around 45 marathoners turning up in the early days — the marathon started in 1982 — and numbers dropping to 20 more recently. Many more runners attend the shorter events on offer, a quarter and a half marathon. In 2006 the marathon was organised by the original team for the last time, and it looked for a while as though the event would disappear from the running calendar. Fortunately, the organising was taken over by others in time for the 2007 event.

In 2005 I ran this marathon on a beautiful still day, having heard beforehand that strong winds can play havoc with this event and account for big differences in winning times over the years. This is always a danger with a point-to-point course. But the weather gods smiled on us, with the sun shining, and glorious vistas awaited. The red earth of the outback is always best to see with a backdrop of deep blue sky.

When I returned in 2008 the scenario was quite different. On Saturday afternoon in Port Augusta the winds were strong, with tree branches swaying violently and clumps of leaves being scattered all over the place. The night was noisy from the wind, which did not abate, and we were greeted first thing on Sunday morning with the prospect of a hard run into an unrelenting headwind. We stood on the start line, 28 runners expecting the worst, and we were not to be disappointed.

The route starts with an eight-kilometre stretch through Port Augusta West and then Port Augusta on the shoulder of Highway 1, crossing the Spencer Gulf and using a causeway across a lake which only has water at high tide.

Once we turned off the highway and entered the settlement of Stirling North the wind hit us with full force and was then company for the rest of the marathon. After Stirling North the route is entirely in the outback. There are hills all around with no obvious way out of the bowl, but having run the course in the past I knew in which direction the Pichi Richi Pass lay. It was obvious to me that there was to be a fair bit of climbing.

It didn't take me long to adjust to all this emptiness, even though I live my life in a big city; it is so refreshing once you relax. The landscape is just there, and has been there for a very long time, and a handful of runners aren't going to change anything. So what if there are hills to climb? So what if the wind is howling?

I settled into a rhythm and ran alongside Sally from Adelaide for several kilometres. She had run this course three times. She was originally from England and had lived in Cambridge, where I was born. She told me that her husband had recently left her after many years of marriage and that she had taken up running as part of her recovery from this trauma. Her current partner was supporting her along the way today.

At 17 kilometres the climbing started, firstly with a few rolling hills that made a pleasant change from the long flat stretches we had been running so far. I pulled away from Sally slightly as I was feeling good. The longest hill comes just before the 21-kilometre mark, a steady climb followed by a very pleasant descent. At the end of the descent, Woolshed Flat, the half marathoners have their start line (they finish in Quorn too, having been taken by bus to this point along the road).

You can see the railway line and a small shed marking the Saltia Flat stop nearby. Some of the original bridges are a feature of the run, and in the pass itself the hillsides are close enough to touch.

Unfortunately I did not continue to feel good for long. There were aid stations every five kilometres, which should have been frequent enough on this cool day, but they only had water and no sports drinks. This was a surprise to me as all marathons seem to provide sports drink as well as lollies or fruit these days. Things have changed over the years and we have grown used to the changes. I really needed something more than water and it dawned on me that nothing else was going to be available.

Dehydration has always been a big issue for me in marathons, causing a sharp falling off of performance, although I am usually slow to realise what is going on inside my body. This time I was fully aware, and almost as a psychological reaction as well as a physical one I started to feel weaker.

I would have been sweating, and have lost valuable electrolytes in my sweat; but just as I found on the busway in Brisbane years earlier, by drinking water alone I was not replacing these chemicals. So I was drinking but unable to hydrate.

I knew I would also feel better by consuming some calories, and usually I would do this by eating lollies or sports gels if no sweet drinks were available. I didn't have any food with me, so that idea was of no consolation.

I asked at the next aid station if they had anything other than water and a wise guy told me he had some brandy. No thanks. I started calling out to the few supporters (who stopped from time to time to cheer on their runners who were still behind me) to see if they had anything I could use, but there weren't very many of these people and none of them had any drinks in their baggage. There were no shops along the route. I felt a bit desperate and started to walk for a while every kilometre or so. I knew I was going to finish but I also knew it was going to be a long day. One of the supporters handed me four jelly beans which he said another runner had left behind at a drinks table. They were an odd flavour and I could see why the runner had left them behind, but I appreciated the thought even though this did nothing to alleviate the tiredness I was feeling.

The wind was still merciless. For the odd moment it would appear to stop, but by the time you realised this it was back again as strong as ever. At the 30-kilometre water station I asked again if there were any other drinks available, listing all the possibilities (which by now included tea, coffee and beer) but the marshal laughed. 'It's not funny,' I said sternly.

Salvation was at hand for me, luckily, in the shape of another supporter who materialised by the roadside at about 32 kilometres with a 1.25-litre bottle of sports drink. I could barely believe it! He handed it to me and my temptation was to drink the whole thing down, but he told me to go easy on it; he promised to bring the rest to the next aid station. For the next seven kilometres I was well-looked after, as this well-wisher stood by the roadside every couple of kilometres and passed me the bottle until I had finished it.

By this time I felt great and I ran the last part of the marathon in high spirits. I couldn't make up the time I had lost through walking, but I was pleased to finish feeling strong.

The last part of the course is a gradual downhill, barely perceptible as such and because of the wind it felt like it was still uphill. The route ends on the Quorn oval, bypassing the centre of town. When I ran in

2005 I didn't go into Quorn and I wished afterwards that I had, so I intended to visit the town this year. But by the time I crossed the finish line I knew I wasn't going anywhere that I didn't have to go, and once more I stayed by the oval until it was time to return to Port Augusta.

They had run out of water (and other soft drinks that had been for sale) at the finish line because the half marathon and ten-kilometre runners had all come in before me, so it was clearly to be a day of drink shortages. Throwing morals to the wind, I helped myself to an unattended half-drunk bottle of water.

Sally finished shortly after me and I went over to her. 'I wouldn't have told my partner to hand you that bottle of sports drink if I'd realised the effect it would have on you,' she said jokingly. 'When he told me about you I said to him that we had a spare bottle in the car. I saw you slowing down ahead of me and I knew I was going to catch up with you, then you drank and took off like a bullet. After that I had no chance!' I thanked her profusely. I hadn't realised who the kind man with the drink was. Yet again I was reminded what nice people runners are.

When I returned home I told my tale of how the drinks stations had let me down on this marathon, causing me to have a slower run than I had anticipated. My husband told me that I should go back next year 'and do it properly' — that is, take my own drinks and not rely on the water provided.

So I went back in June 2009. Mostly the same crowd was there, although Sally was not running that year as she had succumbed to injury, and the marathon field was getting back to its 1980s size with almost 50 runners. We had perfect conditions: virtually no wind, a few light showers and slight sunshine. South Australia had been having unusually high rainfall so everything was much greener than I had previously seen. The Flinders Ranges were tinged with green in the distance. There was far more roadside foliage than usual.

But my race did not go according to plan. I had brought enough sports drink to have a half bottle at each aid station from 15 kilometres onward. In hindsight this was too much, because by the 25-kilometre mark I was feeling sick. I didn't drink much water. I went from feeling fine at halfway to feeling awful five kilometres later. I started having to take walking breaks and I could see the clock marching on without me. It was dispiriting but I fought on, knowing that I would eventually finish. And besides, it was still great to be out here in the Flinders outback.

The highlight of this marathon, and indeed one of the highlights of my running life, came when I had to stop at a rail crossing beyond Saltia Flat for the steam train to go past. It had up a full head of steam and was an impressive sight. I had never seen it so up close and personal before and I waved vigorously. I was probably the most enthusiastic waver the driver had ever seen — not only was I excited to see the train, I was also glad to have a 30-second break in my run.

I finished seven minutes slower than in 2008. But who cares? I did achieve one thing I had not managed on my two previous visits: I walked into Quorn after the marathon. Thinking this would quite likely be the last time I do this marathon, I made myself take the one-kilometre walk into town. It seemed wrong to run all the way there only to sit on the oval on the edge of town. I didn't go very far into the town, but I did admire the railway yards, which signs told me are of great historic significance, and I noted a few old pubs. After three marathons here I can properly say that I have been to Quorn.

Through a gorge gently

At the end of 2008 I planned an almost four-month-long rest from marathon running, and scheduled my first marathon for 2009 to be in late March: the Tokyo Marathon. A break between early December and late March may not sound like much, but it represented a major interruption in my marathon pattern. And this break was to give me a chance to address some important post-marathon issues.

Earlier on I tried to paint a picture of the mind–body conflict that makes the marathon more than a physical challenge. Once the race is over there is fresh tension to be resolved between your mind and muscles. You have run your race, got to the finish line, and now feel thrilled with yourself. Or maybe disappointed with your performance. Or just numb from the exertion. In the immediate aftermath of the race you will be happy to lie down, to take it easy for a few days and to have a break from running.

But all too soon — maybe three days, maybe a week after the race — you may have feelings of despondency and sense a gaping hole where your desire to run a marathon used to be. These feelings are created by adrenaline withdrawal, a coming back down to earth after the huge build-up towards the race and the exhilaration of executing your plan. Your previously elevated mood about what you were doing was very helpful in keeping you going on those long training sessions and through the race, but the race is over. Mission accomplished.

Your body is still exhausted by the long run and your energy stores are still depleted, but your mind begins searching for something to fill the emptiness. It's possible that you'll want to go running soon and you will be able to justify this decision in one of two ways. When you've had a successful marathon and met all your goals you'll be feeling great and you might think you are ready straightaway to go and start work on your next challenge. And if you had a bad race where things didn't go to plan you will want to take action to remedy the situation as soon as possible by starting a new training regime. Either way you want to go and run. A voice in your head is asking: 'What's next?'

This is the point at which warning lights should flash. It's not new-training-program time; it's recovery time.

What you are supposed to do is take life really easy and spend some time on alternative interests. But I do not find that my zeal for gardening, knitting or even reading is great after a marathon. Call me single-minded, but after a couple of days I want to go for a run. So, my reaction has been to go straight off and plan another marathon. Over the years I have modified this to the point that when I finish a marathon I always have another one already planned for the near future. This has been great for keeping me happy, and the adrenaline withdrawal is always swiftly followed by a rush of excitement about the next race.

I have risked injury by doing this, as post-race is the easiest time to do damage to traumatised muscles by continuing to train. But over the years I have grown to sense when I seriously have to take a break from training, and if I really want to run three days after a marathon then I allow myself this little luxury.

It's also believed that during the days after a marathon, when your immunity is low because of the stress your body has been under in running that big distance, you are more likely to catch colds, flu and respiratory tract infections. I have only once caught a cold after a marathon, after my 2003 Shepparton Marathon.

Simon Sostaric, the exercise physiologist who did those stress tests on me back in 2003, has left me in no doubt of the risks posed by running marathon after marathon: 'There is potential risk of over-training or over-reaching syndrome, which is characterised by disturbed sleep, mood swings, illness, injuries, inflammation and ultimately performance decrement. Also, the elevation in stress hormones, particularly cortisol, which causes inflammation and fatigue, can play havoc with muscle tissue repair. Being female there is potential for disturbances in hormones, reduction in oestrogen and progesterone, and increased risk of stress fractures and osteoporosis.' I cannot say I was not warned. I am the first to agree that I am carrying residual fatigue from all these marathons, but it does not bother me. I just keep going, and am loving it.

In 2009 I confess I headed for another marathon again before I was supposed to. Early February saw me trolling the internet searching for a marathon to run, and it did not take me long to notice that the Buller Gorge Marathon was on in a couple of weeks. I made arrangements.

I had run the Buller Gorge Marathon before, and I can concur with the organisers that this is New Zealand's most scenic marathon. The race is based at Westport on the west coast of the South Island, and takes place in the gorge of the Buller River, between a restaurant called Berlins at the highest point of the gorge and the centre of Westport. Most of the road is closed to traffic and the undulating marathon course offers magnificent views all the way.

The remote location means that virtually all race participants would be staying in town for race weekend rather than driving over on race morning. Not that the marathon is particularly big; it usually has less than 150 runners. But there is an accompanying half marathon which is one of the best patronised in New Zealand. It follows the second half of the marathon course.

When I started thinking about a motel in Westport I had forgotten about the 2000 half marathon runners who would be staying there. In 2006 I stayed in Westport with three New Zealand friends from Auckland. When they initially tried to book accommodation they had found everywhere already full and had to be waitlisted. This was at least four months before the marathon. Luckily, the race committee are very helpful in persuading local folk to take in lodgers over marathon weekend. We ended up staying at a private home some kilometres out of town and it was satisfactory, but we had an anxious wait before this option turned up for us.

After I had sorted out my flights to Christchurch in February 2009 I had what I thought would just be a preliminary glance over some accommodation websites to see my options. Westport was full to bursting and nobody had any space. This was a blow, and I sent out a lot of emails asking about possible cancellations. One motel did have a cancellation, but by the time I phoned them the room had been taken by someone else. Two days later one motel, and then another, and then a third emailed to say that they had a cancellation and was I still interested? Suddenly I was spoilt for choice.

It takes pretty much all day to get from Christchurch to Westport by bus. There's a mountain range to cross and whichever route you take the journey is scenic. I went via Arthur's Pass, an idyllic small township in the heart of the mountains. Lots of trampers got on or off the bus there. It was cold — surprisingly so, because the South Island was in the midst of a heat wave.

This happened to be the weekend of the Coast to Coast multisport event and the road was very busy, with many cars transporting not only spectators but also kayaks and bicycles between checkpoints. This is New Zealand's premier adventure race, an epic two-day traverse of the South Island between Kumara Beach and Christchurch, where you have running, mountain biking, kayaking and road cycling tasks, and every New Zealander has heard of it. To the uninitiated arriving in the area from overseas it would look most peculiar to see so many vehicles with boats and bikes on their roof racks as if a petrol crisis were imminent.

The Buller Gorge Marathon is a simple run along the Buller River. You start 34 kilometres out of Westport in the Murchison direction, at a parking bay high above the river. This is in the heart of the Buller Gorge. From here you run about eight kilometres upriver to a scenic spot with a restaurant. Then, instead of stopping for coffee and cake, you have to turn around and run all the way back to Westport. You can tolerate the initial long uphill because you know there is a net elevation loss between turning back towards town and the finish line.

For your entry fee you get a morning of peaceful running. Gentle steps accompanied by thoughtful breaths and nature's silence. To your side flows the river — the purest looking water snaking down a wide gravel bed, with intermittent rapids and flanked by lush bush. There are ferns of all shapes and sizes, and everything is the brightest green due to frequent rains in the area. In the distance are green hills and at every bend in the river is a view that makes you question if you could want to be anywhere else.

At times the road is narrow, down to one lane where there are giant rock overhangs. It undulates constantly, only staying flat for a couple of bridges over tributaries flowing into the river.

Since you only come into town — and civilisation — when you cross the Buller Bridge about a kilometre out of town, virtually the entire race is through countryside. There are very few spectators, and probably more cows turn their head to watch the runners than there are humans. One of the landmarks is at the top of a major hill at the 35-kilometre mark, where a man in a kilt traditionally plays the bagpipes. He always has a crowd gathered around him.

In all probability it is going to rain. Barely a day goes by without rain here, and if it does a drought is declared. When I ran the marathon in 2006 light rain started as I reached halfway, and continued until the end of my run with the result that I became very cold and wet. In 2009 the rain already started as I walked to the bus pick-up to take us to Hawkes Crag, the race start, but stopped during the bus ride.

As I ran I waited for the rain to return, but instead the sun came out well before halfway and it remained there shining in a blue sky for the rest of the weekend. (Like many New Zealand marathons, the race is on a Saturday.) This was most unexpected and made the run feel quite different. I noticed things I had not noticed on my earlier trip — distant hills which were no longer inside clouds, and the vegetation around the river in its lower reaches. But mostly the sun kept me warm and I was not complaining about unusual conditions.

Far from complaining, I was running joyfully. This marathon was like a bonus as I had not planned to run one this early in the year. I was pleased to be out doing what I loved. I didn't wear a watch so I had no idea how fast I was running and no pressure to run well. I ran as I pleased, and by chance finished in my fastest time since the previous May. Maybe the couple of months without any marathons had served me well.

I met up with a number of New Zealand runners whom I had got to know over the years and bumped into at many small town marathons. Just as in Australia, there is a hard core of marathon runners here who turn up at most races on the calendar.

The last kilometre is very pleasant as you cross the bridge and come into Westport. Many locals bring garden chairs out onto the footpath, and sit there cheering the runners on to dig deep for every last gram of energy. They are clearly having a whale of a time. This is one of the lovely things about this marathon — the whole town gets behind the runners. The committee members who help you plan your accommodation, the volunteers who check you in at race registration, and the marshals along the course go out of their way to make you feel welcome. This happens at other marathons, too, but here they take friendliness to another level.

We runners don't often pause to consider the demands we are making when descending on a town to run a marathon. Behind the scenes our entry forms have been processed, our race bibs have been prepared and truckloads of equipment have been brought to the race venue. We expect traffic to be diverted, we expect complete strangers to come out early on a weekend morning and hand us cups of drink, and we expect other strangers to stand at road junctions for hours on end repeating the same route directions hundreds of times.

To marathon helpers everywhere — a heartfelt thank you.

European trio

I planned a trip to Europe around the Prague Marathon. This involved running three marathons on three successive weekends. Although a daunting prospect, I recall that I had done this before, and I headed to the airport feeling confident, while muttering, 'Has the time for the Prague Marathon really come?'

With 80 marathons under my belt, my training had changed from the days when I kept myself busy running, cycling, swimming and, in the New Zealand days, kayaking. I had gradually stopped doing triathlons and did not do many running events that were shorter than marathons. I was also cutting back on the ultra marathons. I wanted to save myself for my favourite 42.2-kilometre distance.

Preparing to run multiple marathons in quick succession is undoubtedly quite different from training for your one marathon of the year. If you are training for one marathon and that race is to be the sole focus of your running year then you need to go through the recommended training of base (long distance) work, add in sessions of hill repeats, do precise speed work relevant to marathon running, and put it all together with a strategic plan to bring out your best on race day. There are many training guides available to help any level of runner with this type of training. The usual training programs have a three- to six-month build-up. Those programs are not much help for me. I acknowledge the basics but I want to run a marathon more often than once every three to six months.

If you hope to run lots of marathons all year you have to work out a way of staying physically prepared all year. By early 2008 I had settled into my own method of training. It was simple: I just ran as I pleased.

From time to time I had experimented with doing speed work (repeats of 200 metres to one kilometre) but I seemed to get injured even thinking about it. I've lost count of how many times I tried a three-kilometre tempo run or one-kilometre repeats and upset a muscle that would normally give me no trouble whatsoever. Just going a little bit faster than usual has been my downfall every time. The best advice I was ever given was: 'Don't change a thing.'

With the demands on my body of running marathon after marathon, I have trained myself to run relatively slowly for long periods. My body resists anything else to the point of hurting if I try to trick it. If I were to lapse into jargon I would talk of 'fast twitch' and 'slow twitch' muscle fibres — the fast twitch ones being the ones you use to run fast and the slow twitch ones being the ones you use to run slowly. I would surmise that in my musculature the slow twitch fibres are the only ones still functioning. I don't move fast but I can keep going for at least 42.2 kilometres.

I run a fairly consistent 60 kilometres a week. I stumbled on this weekly distance after many years of running, but I have found that other marathon runners also settle on 60 to 80 kilometres a week for year-round training. A study of 469 non-elite runners in the Melbourne Marathon by exercise physiologist Ian Gillam for Sports Medicine Australia revealed that greater weekly distance can lead to injury before the marathon and less weekly distance may mean you cannot make it through the marathon to completion.

I set myself a target every week of various runs — short runs and longer runs, hilly runs and flat runs. I put in as much variety as I can and try to run at a different time of day from the usual early morning at least once a week. I aim to have two days off running per week. Some weeks I will run five days in a row then have two days off, and other weeks I will have the day before and the day after my long run as rest days. If I am unusually tired or sore I don't run. If the run is going especially well then I may extend it (but that doesn't happen often; like any runner I find it hard to go past my predetermined finish line). And that is how I train.

I tried to explain to someone that I am basically a lazy runner. I do the least training possible to achieve my desired results. Of course it sounds comic for a marathon runner to talk of being lazy, but what I meant was that I do my best never to waste effort.

As you've worked out by now, I am scenery-driven and I get bored easily. Over the years I have developed running routes of all distances so that I have a choice of routes when I feel I want to run for, say, nine kilometres or 17 kilometres. I can head north, south, east or west from my home, and if by chance I have to take one of the kids somewhere that sounds picturesque I will run there.

If I am doing successive marathons with fewer than four weekends off in between, I won't do any runs of longer than two hours. If the break between marathons is greater then I will do one run of up to 25 kilometres. When I am running two marathons on consecutive weekends I fit in minimal running during the week, rarely more than 20 kilometres in total. If I am tired I just try to have at least two short runs (four to five kilometres) to keep my legs loose. Ultimately, my aim is to enjoy my running. If I were to regard it as a chore I would never do it. At times when I can't face running I generally have a break, maybe a week and rarely more. I'm usually keen to hit the road after a few days off.

Training is never quite like the real thing: the race. It is rarely as exciting, and in the case of marathons it is never as hard. I could never push myself in training the way I can during a marathon. Deep down you know it isn't worth it. I don't run that marathon-day gamut of emotions during training either.

Now you've heard my training secrets. But training is a very individual matter and I have merely outlined what suits my personality and goals.

The Prague Marathon fell on Mother's Day in 2009. It was ironic because here I was doing what Mother (this mother) likes best, but I was far away from the people to whom I am mother. It was Mother's Day in the Czech Republic, too.

Prague was a marathon I had always wanted to do. It sounded like such a beautiful city and I had never been there. The marathon had grown rapidly over 15 years and was a firm fixture on the international calendar. I was curious as to why a marathon in a slightly unusual destination had become so well-patronised. It's a spring marathon, early enough in the year for the normally rampant tourism to still be at a trickle, but when the trees are in blossom and the air is balmy. I needed little further excuse to arrange a trip.

Prague as a destination had exploded onto the tourist scene since the country was opened up to foreigners after the fall of the Berlin Wall in 1989 and its repercussions throughout Eastern Europe. The city had apparently become very popular for weekend visits from other points in Europe, especially ones involving binge drinking, so I thought I should go sooner rather than later.

All tourists gravitate towards the Old Town Square. This is an attractive open area, flanked by ornately decorated merchants' houses, a huge fountain in the middle, and is home to a dozen open air cafes. The focal points are the Tyn Church in one corner, with its double towers, dating from the 14th century, and the old town hall in the opposite corner, from the same era. The old town hall has on one side a famous clock, the astronomical clock, and on the hour one of the apostle figurines at the top of the clock comes alive to beat a spoon signalling the time. As the top of the hour approaches the part of the square below, the clock fills with people keen to see this sight, dispersing a minute or two later.

All the lanes leading to the square are narrow, cobbled and lined with souvenir shops or restaurants serving 'genuine Czech food'. There are numerous small churches, and most of these hold twilight concerts; amusingly, they all seem to have the same repertoire of Mozart's *Eine Kleine Nachtmusik*, Brahms's *Hungarian Lullaby*, Bach's *Air on a G string*, and Dvorak's *Largo*. Large groups congregate near every important sight, hanging onto their guide's every word. It is lucky the streets in the old town have mostly been turned into pedestrian zones during the daytime or else they would be impassable for parked tour buses.

This could make Prague sound as though it has been spoilt and I have come here too late. But the city is an absolute treasure. It has such a wealth of amazing architecture. There is something to wonder at around every corner, whether it's a Baroque mansion, a Spanish synagogue, an 18th-century fountain, or a small statue on a gable. After a good three days of walking around I was still finding new surprises — a bell tower, a Gothic church, another shady square.

And that's before even considering Prague's celebrated attraction: the castle. Prague Castle sits high on the hillside on the opposite side of the Vltava River from the Old Town. The castle is a collection of many buildings, of which the grandest is St Vitus Cathedral. This huge edifice sits in a rather too-small square, and the queues to get inside are formidable. The outside is magnificent. Immediately below the castle is the Lesser Town, not as compact as the Old Town but still home to many churches, restaurants and parks. As in many parts of Prague, Starbucks has taken one of the top locations, with a cafe right on Malastranska, the Lesser Town Square. I spent more time than I should have at the various Starbucks — normally I would avoid them like the plague but in Prague the tables at Starbucks always had the best views.

Another of Prague's tourist drawcards is the Charles Bridge over the Vltava. This is a stone arched bridge, built in the 14th century and lined by 30 Baroque statues from the 18th century. It is lovely in an understated way, being only a small, simple pedestrian bridge. Mass tourism detracts from the charm — the entire bridge is a souvenir market, and the crowds passing through make it almost impossible to take in river views as you walk across for fear of tripping over someone or having to barge through a tour group. It is clearly not an option for the marathon to go over the bridge, although that would have been a pleasure.

While I was in Prague there was a temporary exhibition outside the railway station. A hundred signboards, moving year by year, portrayed events from the Communist era of four of the countries — Hungary, Poland, East Germany and Czechoslovakia — that had been under the thumb of the Soviet Union from 1945 until 1989. The purpose of the boards was to educate the region's younger citizens who would never have lived under Communism. The stories were fascinating, hopeful and sad.

Of course, the name of Emil Zatopek came up. Zatopek was a native of Czechoslovakia who came to dominate the world of distance running in the 1950s. His training techniques were legendary, as he pushed his body to cover over 200 kilometres of interval work each week. He routinely trained in his army boots. At the 1952 Olympic

Games in Helsinki he won the 5000 metres, the 10,000 metres and the marathon, all within a seven-day period. This was his debut marathon, but he raced the reigning record holder into the ground.

Some time after the marathon Zatopek is reputed to have said: 'I was unable to walk for a whole week after that, so much did the race take out of me. But it was the most pleasant exhaustion I have ever known.' Yes, I can relate to that.

After the Russians invaded Prague in 1968, Zatopek was punished with hard labour for openly opposing the new hard-line Communist regime. Later, because he spoke numerous languages, he was given the job of translating articles about training techniques from foreign sports publications in order to benefit local athletes; this was described at the time as sports-spying.

I went for a couple of short runs in Prague before the marathon, and in the early morning there were nothing like as many people about as later on in the day. I ran through the Old Town and criss-crossed the river, pleased to see there were numerous bridges so that I could shorten or lengthen my route on a whim. The river has islands with parkland and short dirt trails. Running in the Old Town helped me get used to running on cobblestones in preparation for the marathon. I enjoyed some cobbled stretches right alongside the river too.

I took the opportunity to run through Wenceslas Square during a quiet part of the day. It's more of a boulevard than a square, between the National Museum and new Prague's main shopping area. From the statue of St Wenceslas, the patron saint of Bohemia, at the top of Wenceslas Square is a great view down the boulevard, and people lounge on the steps of the statue all day long.

Race day dawned rather too warm for my liking: 18 degrees at the start, with a forecast for the mid-20s. I set out from my hotel clad only in a crop top and shorts, and was surprised to see many runners in tights and long sleeves. This could have been because the forecast had originally been for very bad weather, and had only been upgraded the previous evening. As it turned out I had made the right clothing decision.

The marathon course started right in the heart of the old city, on the Old Town Square. The race route was a little unusual in that it started and finished with the same ten-kilometre loop. So as we ran the opening part we were passing the kilometre markings for the final stages. This was a loop through the Old Town and across the Vltava River, with the castle looming right above us, and several chances to see the Charles Bridge without actually running across it. We passed such landmarks as the imposing national theatre, the neo-Renaissance Rudolfinum concert hall and other examples of Prague's grander buildings. And we took in newer Prague's main shopping boulevards — Parizska and Narodna.

A substantial part of the running was on cobblestones. And as they are hard on your feet and also make the ground rather uneven, this can be irritating in the later stages of a marathon, when you are getting too tired to concentrate properly. But a surface like this is also a constant reminder that you are in a historic place.

The middle stages were mainly close to the river as we went through suburban areas. We crossed the river several times and I became disoriented, especially as we left central Prague and there was no longer the castle on the horizon to help me get my bearings. This part of the race has become something of a blur in my mind, as I focused on keeping up a good pace and making up for the time I had spent in the toilet queue at the 12-kilometre mark. My five-minute break served me well — I felt quite fresh afterwards, and not only picked up my pace but managed to hold onto it for the rest of the marathon. I had had a similar experience in Boston, so a few minutes' break during a marathon must be a performance trick I can benefit from.

This was definitely a race for foreign visitors. Italians and Germans were plentiful, as well as runners from further-flung places such as Chile and Japan. With 7000 runners (across all events held concurrently), the road was congested pretty much all the way. There were a few bands playing but not many supporters. I had wondered why all the announcements at the start were being made in English, but I could soon see why they were not made in Czech.

The Old Town Square was considerably busier on our return at the end of the marathon. We were protected by barricades through the finish chute, but once we were finished it was a real battle to move through the square with large groups of tourists everywhere. That was the downside of having such a special starting and finishing venue. I looked around desperately for somewhere to sit down but all the seats were taken. I perched on a wall for a while but that was too uncomfortable. From the point of view of the tourists it can't have been too nice having their experience marred by thousands of sweaty runners stumbling along and suddenly sitting down on the ground without warning as their jelly legs gave way.

Prague is in other ways a marathon runner's dream. There are kiosks selling sausages in virtually every open space — and not just your normal hotdog but bratwurst, garlic sausage and other varieties all served in a large roll with onions and mustard. And if there isn't a sausage kiosk there will be a pizza stall selling ten varieties of pizza by the slice. Add that to the high quality of Czech beer and you certainly have much to keep you happy after the race.

This meant I was going to have no problem with my post-race meal.

Eating after a marathon — regardless of whether the marathon has been good, bad or very ugly — is always something to look forward to. It is a symbol that the hard work is all over. It's the moment when the training cycle is complete. It's a signal that you can truly let go and say

'I've done it'. The more junky the food sounds, the more appealing it will be. Pizza is my first choice. There's nothing like burning off thousands of kilojoules to give you a taste for some unhealthy food. At a time like this I can't believe it matters what goes in your mouth, so long as you eat.

Although a shower is a good idea too.

That evening I played at being a tourist and settled into a cafe on the Old Town Square for a couple of beers. There was a brass band concert to celebrate the marathon, but apart from this there was no sign of what had taken place during the daytime. The tour groups had full access to the sights, and the crowds were again able to assemble to watch the astronomical clock chime. It was almost unreal how the marathon could come and go leaving no trace.

Following the Prague Marathon, I spent a few days with family in London and then flew to France for my next race.

The Mont Saint-Michel Marathon is another of those marathons that sound spectacular. I was immediately drawn to it, and delighted that the timing fitted in with this trip. It had previously been an evening race, which was the aspect that had first attracted me, but in 2009 it became a morning event.

The abbey at Mont Saint-Michel is a major tourist attraction and landmark, renowned throughout France. It is perched on a rock on an island in the English Channel (La Manche), connected to the mainland by a two-kilometre causeway. At high tide, access to the rock is only along the road on top of the causeway, but at low tide the rock sits amid a huge expanse of walkable sand. There is more than just an abbey of extreme historic importance on the rock — visitors are also rewarded with a choice of restaurants and a variety of souvenir shops.

The marathon's goal is the rock, but the rock is off one end of a bay and the marathon route follows the curve of the bay to reach the final destination This marathon, my number 82, had the distinction of bearing the longest name of any marathon I have run: Marathon de la Baie du Mont Saint-Michel.

I stayed in the quaint town of Saint-Malo, site of the race headquarters. This is a walled town on the Brittany coast and a gorgeous place to spend a few days. The town was virtually destroyed during World War II, but the walls remained unscathed and the old town within the walls has been rebuilt in the traditional grey stone. Among the enticing features of the town are its many seafood restaurants — I was told there are 150 restaurants in town and most are within the walls. Buckets of mussels are very popular in season, and luckily for me the season had just started when I arrived. Also popular are the oysters from nearby Cancale, where the marathon would start.

On the day before the marathon there was an organised jog around the walls. About 250 runners gathered for a 4.2-kilometre run encompassing the port area and the full length of the walls. The views from the walls are fantastic as this part of the coast is littered with tiny islands and the beaches are long and sandy. Saint-Malo is on a promontory so you can see in all directions from the walls. It was a very nice touch that this run was not intended to be competitive, and we regrouped several times so that the slower runners would not feel left out.

I had only been for one short run since my marathon in Prague, so I was glad about the chance to loosen up and see if I still knew how to run. Sounds silly, but I do still panic about this sometimes.

Race day was forecast to be wet and windy, with a low pressure system hovering over the southern part of England, the Channel and western France. Things did not look good. The race organisers had sent several emails out warning us about adverse weather, and I was not sure

Runners cross the Sydney Harbour Bridge during the Sydney Marathon.

Courtesy of www.marathon-photos.com

The start of the Prague Marathon
in the Old Town Square.
Courtesy of www.marathon-photos.com

Passing one of the many windmills during
Marathon de la Baie du Mont Saint-Michel, 2009.

Courtesy of www.maindru.com

top:
My version of the image that inspired me to do this marathon at Steamboat Springs.

bottom:
The start of the Rotorua Marathon in Government Gardens.
Courtesy of www.marathon-photos.com

top:

The start of the Lake Kawaguchi Marathon, 2009.

Courtesy of www.marathon-photos.com

left:

Denis and I running the Lake Kawaguchi Marathon.

Courtesy of www.marathon-photos.com

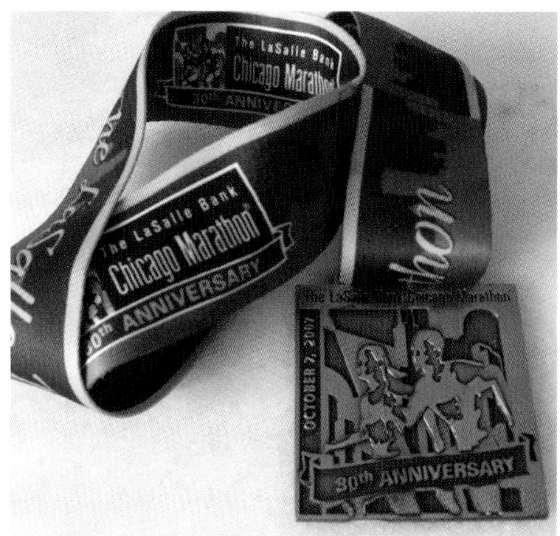

top left:

London Marathon finisher's medal, 2003.

top right:

Chicago Marathon finisher's medal, 2007.

bottom left:

Boston Marathon finisher's medal, 2008.

bottom right:

Los Angeles Marathon finisher's medal, 2010.

top:
My Christmas Island Marathon female winner's trophy.

bottom:
My Melbourne Marathon finisher's medals.

Approaching the finish of my 100th marathon.

Courtesy of www.marathon-photos.com

whether these emails were going to be sent regardless of the weather or whether the forecast was so bad that we had to be informed. At any rate I woke up to the sound of torrential rain.

But by the time I walked to our gathering point for the buses that would take us six kilometres from Saint-Malo to Cancale the rain had slowed to a drizzle, and when we reached Cancale it had stopped altogether. The field where we assembled before the start was muddy, but there was to be no more rain until we were on the bus returning to Saint-Malo five hours later. Phew. There is nothing worse than standing around before a marathon getting wet and cold. Running in the rain is not such a worry; it's the getting soaked before you even start out.

It was ferociously windy. As we stood on the start line I could not tell if this was to be a headwind or a tailwind. When the marathon is all in one direction this factor can make a considerable difference to race-day enjoyment. But as soon as we left Cancale and hit the open road I could see that we would have a fair bit of tailwind, especially as we approached the finish. The grass beside the road was all blowing in that direction.

The idea of being able to see the finish line from the start of a marathon, when the race route is a 42.195-kilometre point-to-point course, is daunting. That was the case today. We had our first glimpses of the abbey during our first kilometre out from Cancale. It was extremely faint and small on the horizon, as though shrouded in mist. It had an almost dreamlike quality, but there it was.

The marathon was a delightful trip through the Breton coastal countryside. We passed through a sequence of villages, each with a long line of stone houses facing the sea, and usually a windmill at one end of the village. The villagers were almost always out in force, cheering us on and leaning from their upstairs balconies. The French certainly know how to support a race.

Between each village were fields of wheat or vegetables. Much of the area is very low-lying. A runner near me became very excited about 'les polders', which I gathered referred to an area where we were running below sea level.

There wasn't a lot of English spoken and it seemed as though all the runners were French. This was surprising as access to this part of France is so easy from England. I really enjoyed the fact that I could understand what runners around me were saying, because often when I run overseas I don't understand the local lingo. My spoken French deteriorates when I run long distances and I wouldn't want to have to think in French, but my understanding is unimpaired. Not that marathon runners say anything of far-reaching importance while running, but I took some amusement from a group who were helping a pair of females through their first marathon — alternating between offering encouragement, saying how little more distance they had yet to achieve (a blatant lie, I'm afraid), and chastising them that 'les enfants' (kiddies) would go faster.

It was even nicer to be able to understand the crowd lining the roadsides. The French are well-known for coming out to support events like the Tour de France, but it was lovely to see and hear them supporting a marathon of 5000 mere amateurs. I had my name printed on my race bib and many onlookers called out my name as I ran by, cheering 'Allez, Julia!' and 'Courage, Julia!'.

At many points, especially in the final kilometres, spectators crowded close onto the road and only left a small channel for us to run through; they were lining the course and leaning in towards the runners just as you see them do on TV to the cyclists every July. They get so close you have no margin for stumbling, and you certainly better not entertain any idea of passing another runner. I was glad the final 200 metres had barricades to protect us from our supporters.

The entire route featured a lot of long straight stretches, followed by a bend in the road and then another straight couple of kilometres. On the one hand this was mentally hard, but the good part was that you could see a long snake of runners along the road ahead and it gave a real feel of being part of something. As the roads were narrow, the impression was of hundreds of runners passing through fields like colourful flowers.

For most of the way the wind was no more than a minor irritation. We would run into it for a while and then have it behind us, and mostly it came across at an angle. But towards the end of the route I was finding the breeze made me cold. I was glad I was wearing my arm warmers so that I could roll them down for a bit of warmth. I had worn them on the start line (noticing that nobody else was wearing them or even gloves) but I had rolled them up almost immediately as they made me too warm. I also became aware of another problem: the insides of my knees were chafing from rubbing together. I've never had this happen before, but running was becoming painful.

It was really quite amazing to watch the mount getting closer — at first misty and distant, then becoming much clearer but still distant across fields, and then finally it was up close. At this point we were still about five kilometres away, but to actually look up and see it looming large was a great feeling after almost four hours of running. At this point, in a moment of irony, we unfortunately turned away and headed inland for a while, but then we were passing under an inflatable arch proclaiming 'La Manche' and we ran directly towards the gleaming spire of the abbey.

I had run with my watch covered up the entire way so I had no idea how I was doing for time, although I was fairly sure the 4-hours-30 pacer was behind me. At the 41-kilometre mark I had a look at my watch, only so I wouldn't be in for too much of a shock at the finish, and saw I had just passed the four-hour mark, but only just. I was pleased, and I ended up running the same time from the gun as I had run last weekend in Prague from the gun. To the second, that is — how's that for coincidence? (Annoyingly, although we were wearing timing chips during this marathon the organisers did not use them to give us an accurate chip race time. They used the chip for our finishing time but all times started from when the gun went off, and I had not moved for several minutes at the start. So my race time printed on my certificate is slower — by around four minutes, I believe — than it actually was.)

We had to run the length of an enormous car park right to the base of the village, as there turned out to be not just an abbey but a whole settlement — I hadn't expected all this development on the island. There were people everywhere, shouting, jostling, and it was with a great sense of accomplishment that I saw the race announcer peer over at my race number and announce my name on the finish line.

It was a slow walk through the finish chute, because I must have finished at a popular time, and I really needed to sit down. But the food tent, when I finally reached it, lifted my spirits considerably: they were handing out packets of chips. Another first, and what a wonderful surprise. The French understand food. Chips are my favourite post-marathon food — well, after pizza — probably because I crave something salty after all the sweet sports drinks.

I didn't have any energy left to tour the mount properly. I walked along a laneway of restaurants and shops and went up one level on the cobblestones towards the abbey, but this was hard work so I came back down again. The view of the abbey from so close was spectacular of course, the ancient grey stone everywhere and the gold spire rising from the jumble of buildings. From the hillside you could make out the villages we had run through; and just as the end had appeared to be a long way from the start, the start was now looking a long way from the finish. But I didn't really need my eyes to tell me this.

There were buses laid on to take us back to Saint-Malo. It rained some of the way and I think I slept. This must have been a reaction to sitting in a warm bus after running on a cold day. Several of the runners had a different reaction to the warm bus, and within minutes of setting off they requested an unscheduled stop. A group of males rushed off the bus and proceeded to stand right next to it to perform their activities; it appeared to be a French custom to forego modesty in such situations.

In the evening, back in Saint-Malo, I had a celebratory Ricard at a pavement cafe, then decided against eating at a restaurant since everything seemed rather quiet and went to the little window that was a fresh seafood takeaway. They had on display mussels, prawns (cooked and uncooked), whelks, oysters (several sizes and grades) and lobster all beautifully arranged. I ordered a dozen Cancale oysters and a few Euros' worth of prawns.

The seafood lady filled the base of a large polystyrene plate with ice, then covered it with seaweed and put the (opened) oysters on top. She placed the cooked prawns around the edge of the plate and added tiny tubs of vinegar and mayonnaise. She then covered the whole platter with cellophane and tied the corners together with a ribbon high above the seafood. It was quite magnificent, and I felt very self-conscious carrying it through the town back to my hotel. I bought a baguette for accompaniment and hey, presto, one of the best meals I have ever had

The next day I continued by train to Germany.

I wasn't initially excited about the Wuerzburg Marathon. It sounded like an interesting city and my older daughter had been there on a school study tour, but I wasn't too convinced about the marathon. The course was a two-lap repeat and this can be hard work, especially if you're finding it a struggle getting around the loop the first time. Also, there was no means of entering from overseas. Marathons that you can't enter online are now virtually unheard of. But I was in Europe and there wasn't very much else available in my line of running that weekend. So I went anyway to Wuerzburg, two hours by train from Frankfurt.

When I got there things didn't look too promising. There was no indication anywhere of an impending marathon, although there seemed to be no shortage of other events being liberally advertised on hoardings — an African music festival, a Mozart festival — but no mention of a marathon, even in the windows of the sports shops.

I was concerned about this, and in my mind I compiled an alternative plan which involved taking the train to another German city, Regensburg, where there was a marathon on the same Sunday. I would have time to take the train from Wuerzburg to Regensburg on marathon morning, run the marathon and then return to Wuerzburg to collect my belongings. I would need to return to Wuerzburg as I already had a train ticket from Wuerzburg to Frankfurt, where I would commence my trip back to Australia. It would not be an efficient way to go about a marathon. But at least I had a fallback plan. Telling this makes it sound ridiculous, but having gone to Europe to run three marathons there was no way I was going to come home having run fewer than three.

After two hours of walking around the sights of Wuerzburg I finally saw my first and only marathon poster. I heaved a large sigh of relief. My lingering doubts were only completely dispelled the following morning when I saw a newspaper article about the marathon.

The other thing that made my arrival here disconcerting was that the streets were deserted when I stepped off the train and walked towards my hotel. I knew that it was a public holiday, but that doesn't usually mean empty streets. When I re-emerged after checking into my hotel the streets in that part of the city were busy, and the cafes seemed especially lively. I asked someone about this afterwards and he said this was a holiday for the city's fathers (not to be confused with Father's Day), and traditionally, locals took it upon themselves to drink as much as possible that day. Presumably, this means they do not waste drinking time walking around the streets by the railway station.

I overcame this slightly odd introduction and found that Wuerzburg is a great city. Although it was almost entirely destroyed by bombs right near the end of World War II, most of the place has been rebuilt and there is plenty to see. The highlight is the Residenz, a Baroque palace designed by one of Europe's most renowned architects of the day for the prince-bishops of Wuerzburg and built between 1720 and 1744. This formidable 400-room building partly escaped destruction with the major bombing of 1945, and its crowning triumph is a ceiling fresco over the main staircase by the 18th-century Venetian artist Tiepolo, believed to be the largest fresco in the world. The other major sight is the Marienberg fortress, high on the hillside above the city and visible from most parts of the city. This fortress was the seat of the prince-bishops for four centuries. It so dominates the city that I could not resist going for a run around the moat one day. The fortress is surrounded by vineyards on the hillside and it was fun to run there.

The city is divided into two parts by the River Main, and in the centre of the city is an old stone arched bridge, not much used by traffic but cobbled and popular with walkers. Another relic of former days is an old crane, something a bit surprising to find listed as a tourist attraction. But there it is, suspended out over the river.

I went to the race expo the day before the marathon — which now confirmed for me once again that the marathon was actually happening. The bigger race expos overseas are exciting because there are vendors from all sorts of stores and manufacturers I have not heard of, and I can collect leaflets for races I did not know about.

At the expo I made a bit of a blunder while purchasing the race shirt. I don't normally buy souvenir race shirts as I have so many running shirts, but I liked the look of this one and I didn't have any others with German writing on them. The shirts were available in an all-over lemon-yellow and in navy with a narrow lemon panel at the side; I opted for the latter as yellow isn't my colour. I was pleasantly surprised at the cheap price. Later that day I got the shirt out to have a proper look at it and immediately realised why it had been so cheap — I had bought the shirt for last year's race. The entirely yellow shirt was the one for this year. I've always thought that wearing a shirt from a race in which I have not run is a real no-no. Clearly I am going to have to rethink this one. The shirt has become one of my favourites and nobody has yet asked me if I actually ran the race.

I had already made another small error in planning for this visit. When it comes to hotels I like to stay as close to the start line of the marathon as I can, even if I am staying at that location for several days beforehand or afterwards. How I feel when I get up on race morning is of the utmost importance, and if I am worried about how I will get to the race start then I know I will not have a pleasant overall experience. I misunderstood the starting instructions on the website (they were only in German) and picked a hotel of my own choice in preference to the recommended race hotel, which I believed to be in a remote location. The race organisers had — surprise! — got it right and their hotel was on the start line. Mine was 30 minutes' walk away.

Contrary to my expectations, the marathon turned out to be a good one. It was a little too warm for my liking, reaching 27 degrees at midday when I was close to finishing, but the course was excellent. The entire course was virtually within the city, and it takes some planning to achieve that without too much repetition. The course was not, as I had been led to believe by the race website, a repeated 21-kilometre loop. It was in fact two distinct 21-kilometre loops, with very little overlap. It seems that the route description in English had not been updated for a couple of years while the course had been changed. The route was fairly complicated but it got us to every corner of the city and completely avoided busy roads and industrial estates. And although I had already been there for several days it brought me to new parts that I had not yet visited.

We headed out from the start for the western edge of the city, crossing the river, and ran through suburbs beneath the vineyards. I noticed a woman from the UK 100 Marathon Club and engaged her in conversation. She was running her 224th marathon, having run 50 last year, which put my exploits well and truly in the shade. She said that she too had come to Wuerzburg because there wasn't much else on that day, but she knew that marathons in Germany were generally good.

There was a samba drumming festival to accompany the marathon and we were treated to this music at many points along the course. It's loud when you run so close that you could beat the drums yourself. We also had smaller rock bands come out to perform, and they gave us good old favourites from the 1980s, which in my limited experience is what gets played at European marathons — except in Vienna, where we ran to the strains of Johann Strauss.

After eight kilometres we crossed the old stone bridge, and in this respect we went one better than the Prague Marathon I had run two weeks previously: the statue-lined Wuerzburg bridge is very similar to the Charles Bridge in Prague, but we had not been able to run across that one.

We then did a pleasant loop around the eastern part of the city, taking in the length of the Residenz and its gardens, several of the city's squares and old churches, and a few hills. We were constantly changing direction so the route never got boring. I was surprised at the number of supporters, but they lined the streets and called out from upstairs windows of apartments. They made a lot of noise, clapping enthusiastically and shaking plastic fans that made a big racket.

We went right through the centre of the city, closely following the tram lines at some points so the trams could not have been operating, and down the main shopping streets. The streets were quiet apart from marathon supporters, this being a Sunday morning and relatively early. The trees were in blossom everywhere, and there was plenty of blossom on the ground like confetti.

After the halfway mark we full marathoners were alone, as the half marathoners went through their finish line. At this point I almost came unstuck. I was following another runner when I suddenly realised she was no longer in the race and was going back to her car. So I hastily backtracked out of the car park, squeezed under a rope and rejoined the marathon.

We headed back across the river and turned to the south to explore another part of the city. We went along the river beneath the Marienberg fortress and its adjacent Baroque cathedral, and followed parkland for many kilometres. Some of the route was on bike trails and some on minor roads, all nicely shaded. I was feeling good along here and passed many runners.

A marshal called out to me that my lips were blue and suggested I drink more water, but I could not possibly have drunk any more. I felt I was well-hydrated with the abundance of water, fizzy apple juice, Coke and electrolyte drinks. They had set up showers over the road also in at least three places, which was handy on a warm day.

We finished with four kilometres back in the city centre. The streets were busier than before but everyone seemed to stop and watch us. We passed the Residenz again, along with the cathedral, the market square and the old bridge, and had a final half kilometre along the river.

The finish area was chaotic and unfortunately not well-signed. I could see runners holding glasses of beer but it took me some while to locate the serving area. Nobody else could find it either. With my halting German and my marathon-fuddled brain I was able to pass on directions to other runners who asked where I had found my pint. Beer tastes so good after a marathon on a hot day. I can also recommend the ice-cream in Wuerzburg — I definitely needed some after running three marathons in three weeks.

Easy on the eyes, hard on the lungs

I have always loved the mountains. When we lived in New Zealand it was a perennial pleasure to be able to go tramping in the Southern Alps. There's nothing to compare with looking up at a panorama of snow-capped mountains, or with struggling up steep slopes to reach a summit.

So, naturally, the idea of running in the mountains appealed to me. But there is a major problem with heading off to run a marathon in the mountains. It's called altitude. Running at altitude is much harder than running at sea level, for reasons I will go into later. Back in 2006 when I went to run the Tirol Speed Marathon in Austria I only thought about the superb scenery I would run through: the Tirolean Alps, the Brenner Pass and stuff like that. We were having a family holiday in Europe and I was allowed to find a race to enter while we were away. Let's all be quite clear on this: I checked with them first that it would be okay for me to do a race during our holiday.

After endlessly searching race listings and getting the atlas on and off the bookshelf so much that I was in danger of wearing out my arm, I plumped for a marathon that met my needs for good scenery, the family's need for an interesting place to stay, and ease of access to the race start to keep me in a cheery mood while waiting for the big day.

The Tirol Speed Marathon has lots going for it. It is held in a truly magic setting, like something out of a child's picture book. The race starts in the late afternoon, so there's no need to wake everyone up when I leave the hotel at the crack of dawn or complain the previous night that I will never be able to get up in time. And the details get better. The marathon has a predominantly downhill course. Who wouldn't want that? It seems only the AIMS (Association of International Marathons and Distance Races) committee, who decide which marathons are eligible for a world-record attempt, are critical of this aspect.

The marathon is based in Innsbruck, Austria, to coincide with the town's midsummer festivities. Innsbruck is a wonderful place — beautiful old buildings, a lively cafe/restaurant scene that spills out onto the streets in the warmer months, enough galleries and churches to keep the most avid culture vulture happy, mountains close enough to reach for a day's hiking, and the fast-flowing Inn River. The old town is a maze of narrow streets; unfortunately, many of these streets have souvenir shops selling signs proclaiming *No kangaroos in Austria*, which is a bit distasteful to us Aussies. The Bergisel ski jump looms over the town. Wherever you look there are peaks on the horizon.

It was a perfect place to hang out before a marathon. We toured the sights without expending too much energy and learnt a great deal about the rule of the Hapsburgs. There was always a cafe to duck into for a strudel or a schnitzel. We even went for a short hike and saw some residual snow from last winter.

I was feeling uncertain before this marathon because the previous week I had run my disastrous Phuket Marathon. Whenever I expressed any concerns, which was roughly once or twice every half hour, Denis reminded me that I had run 49 marathons in a reasonable physical state and only one in a poor state, so the odds were good that I would be okay at the Tirol Speed.

The marathon start was at 4.30pm so we had a leisurely breakfast and went to the railway station to catch the train to Brenner for the start. We went early so my support team wouldn't have to be on a busy train full of runners. For them the train ride was the exciting part of the day — they would see much of the same scenery I would be running through — and they would appreciate being able to get a clear look at it.

I had also acquired for them an invite to the official pre-race meal in Innsbruck on the previous evening. This was a noodle feast, and I had to impress on them that carbo-loading meals are not usually of this calibre.

Some marathons make a point of having a carbo-loading meal the evening before the marathon, which may or may not be included in the race entry price. I have rarely had a decent official pre-race meal. Let's amend that: I have only ever had two good official pre-race meals — one at the Phuket Marathon (a banquet of international dishes) and one here at the Tirol Speed Marathon (a buffet of filled dumplings), only one week later. I'm no longer so sure the meals are bad because of the food. It's the idea of a lot of nervous runners all stuck in one place. At some of these carbo-loading meals it is like eating before an execution. Nobody speaks and we all avoid each other's glances.

They had a good idea at the Warsaw Marathon: you receive a voucher for a pasta meal and you could choose to eat this meal either the evening before the race or have it straight after you finished running. Shame the food really was bad.

The Austrian meal was exciting for us because the noodles (dumplings, to us) were only labelled in German so we did not always know what we were eating. More importantly we did not always know which noodles were sweet and which were savoury, so we sampled combinations like cabbage noodles with custard.

The town of Brenner is almost at the top of the Brenner Pass in the Tirolean Alps and is right on the Austrian–Italian border. It's 'Brenner' in Austria, 'Brennero' in Italy. This is probably the best known alpine pass in this part of Europe. Brenner is a typical border town full of souvenir shops. Except that nobody much goes there nowadays as motorists prefer to bypass the town on the freeway, and with the limited European border-crossing requirements you hardly have to stop there on your way in or out of the two countries.

I had lunch with the family — a hotdog, which in Austria is likely to be a tasty sausage in freshly baked bread. I passed on the ice-cream. They then went back to Innsbruck because they didn't have anything else to do in Brenner. I couldn't blame them — there wasn't anything to do there apart from wait for the marathon start. I sat lethargically — it's called 'conserving energy' — by the organisers' tent and watched runners drift in. Then a good thing happened: a large tray of apple strudel appeared for us to snack on. I do believe I can handle a marathon where strudel is served as an appetiser.

By the time the marathon started I was feeling pleasantly relaxed. It almost seemed an afterthought to be running 42 kilometres back to Innsbruck. It was pretty hot when we set out, but after a few hours the rain started — followed by a thunderstorm. We saw flashes of lightning over the town and it was very dramatic.

The marathon actually started in Italy, with a four-kilometre downhill run on that side of the border before returning back up to Brenner and going into Austria for the bulk of the course. We didn't have to show passports or perform any border formalities.

The marathon course was blissfully scenic. At times it felt like running through the film set of *The Sound of Music*, or a fairy tale, or a travel brochure, except that in real life it all looked prettier. At every turn were timber chalets with pointed roofs, green pastures, cows with cowbells. We ran alongside trickling streams and rushing rivers. People came out of their houses to cheer us on, and at the halfway point in the small town of Matrei they were especially vocal. We had our name printed on our race bibs and it was lovely to be greeted by name; in my case, chants of 'Yu-li-a' followed me wherever I went.

There was a considerable downhill element to the route. The Brenner Pass is at 1370 metres and Innsbruck is at a mere 575 metres. At times we seemed to be spiralling down endlessly for up to two kilometres without a break. I was a bit worried the first time this happened, starting at the seven-kilometre mark, because I thought I might be going too fast. But further towards the end the downhill parts were very welcome. The grade was up to ten percent in places.

Sustained downhill running isn't as easy as it sounds, since you are still making an effort, and after a while you no longer feel as though you are going downhill. Your feet are taking more body weight with each footfall than if you run on the flat, and this gets tiring. Your hamstrings suffer. Many people slowed on the final downhill stretches. I passed runners who had surged past me in the opening kilometres and were now walking. Not that the whole route was downhill; there was also quite a bit of uphill in the middle stages, and flat running which felt like it was uphill.

We entered Innsbruck in the rain and ran down the main street, Maria Theresian Strasse. We came under the Triumphal Arch and into the town centre, which looked different without the traffic that usually filled the streets. They had erected balloon arches and lots of people were watching and urging us on.

My older daughter had been despatched to meet me on the finish line, and she took me back to the rest of the family, who were happily ensconced in a street cafe. If they were disappointed I had finished so soon and was about to interrupt their feasting with tales from the open road, they did not complain. My husband didn't have time to finish his beer before I launched into it. I felt so good, having run well under four hours and vindicated my weak effort in Phuket. As soon as I sat down my legs cramped, but that was a small price to pay — and nothing like the cramp I suffered in Thailand.

This was my first experience of running at altitude, and this was not really altitude to be concerned about. At a thousand metres above sea level running becomes more difficult, but for most people the real challenge only starts when you get up over 1500 metres. When you are at this altitude or higher there is less oxygen in the air than at sea level; your muscles are receiving less oxygen (via your blood) and cannot work at their normal rate. At an elevation of 1500 metres your athletic performance is estimated to be impaired by around ten percent until you acclimatise. The way you acclimatise is to make more red blood cells to transport the oxygen to your muscles; having more red blood cells compensates for the smaller amount of oxygen each cell carries.

A loss in performance is only one side of the coin as you also might experience altitude sickness, and there is no way of predicting if you will be a candidate for this. The studies I've read have been unable to correlate altitude sickness with fitness.

That's my very simplified take on running in the mountains.

In 2007 I went to run at a higher altitude.

I've chosen marathons to run for all sorts of reasons: a fast course (Christchurch), my hometown (Auckland and then Melbourne), my father's place of birth (Warsaw). But I ran the Steamboat Marathon because of a photo in a book. The book was *The Ultimate Guide to Marathons* by Dennis Craythorn and Rich Hanna, and the photo was of the finish line at this marathon. The photo showed the finishing chute with a backdrop of a snowy mountain. I liked the look of that, and in June 2007 I went there.

Steamboat Springs, Colorado, is known as Ski Town USA and offers some of the best skiing on the continent. The town is a mecca for outdoors enthusiasts. In summer, mountain bikers flock there to ride the trails, rafters head there for whitewater rafting, horse riders love it, and there are numerous peaks to climb. In between ski season and summer is a time known as 'Mud Season', when hiking is tricky as there is still some snow about but there is not enough cover for skiing. So to fill in a lull the town holds a marathon. It's great for us as runners because there are few tourists around, accommodation is easy on the wallet, and none of the restaurants are busy. Locals told me that during the ski season you have to make your restaurant bookings before you leave home or you won't be eating out at all.

This marathon advertises itself as having a downhill course, a lure to any runner. Actually, the elevation loss is not extreme, and there is very little time during the run that you feel as though you are really cruising downhill. There are a couple of obvious uphill stretches. In fact, lots of entrants think they should stop calling this a downhill marathon because it makes it sound fast when actually the altitude makes it harder than many flatland races.

The point-to-point route starts at a village called Hahns Peak, one marathon length out of Steamboat, and finishes by the courthouse in downtown Steamboat. No turns. Hahns Peak is a ski resort at an elevation of 9000 feet (2743 metres). Steamboat sits at 6000 feet (1828 metres). The only signs of civilisation along the route are two buildings in the settlement of Clark, and Hayden Airport which services Steamboat.

A bus took us from Steamboat to the race start. I sat with a runner who was the eventual race winner. She was a native of Steamboat but lived in Boston, and had recently run the Boston Marathon. She told me that she had come unstuck the previous year at the stretch by the airport where the road turns flat, and she didn't want a repeat of that uncomfortable experience. She was nervous and explained this was because her family were all going to be there to follow the race.

We watched deer frolicking by a distant lake as we waited on the start line. There wasn't much at Hahns Peak but it was idyllic. It was cold, but not as cold as it had been on the start line three years earlier when it snowed all night before the marathon and half the field pulled out on race day. Those who ran had to contend with a light covering of snow on the road the whole way.

At home I had been anxious about running at altitude as there was no way to practise this beforehand. I had no idea how the altitude would affect me. I went for a few short runs in the days before the marathon and felt fine, so I ceased being too worried about that side of things. Steamboat is situated alongside the Yamba River, and there are bike/walking paths on both banks of the river which make for pleasant and easy running. I also hired a bike and took to some of the trails around the town. I cycled through groves of aspen and found rocky streams. My only altitude-related problem was difficulty with falling asleep, and later on a town resident who had moved there 25 years ago told me that he still had that problem. Curiously, I had my best sleep of the trip the night before the marathon — a night when I would not have expected to sleep well at all.

The marathon turned out to be all that I had anticipated and more. I ran quietly along on my own for most of the way, admiring the spectacular scenery. Green hills and snow-capped peaks were never out of the view, along with tracts of forest. The tumbling Elk River was often in sight. With only a small field of runners, large gaps often opened up and I felt fortunate to have this great place to run through almost alone.

If you want spectators (human ones, since there are plenty of cows about) this is not the marathon to run. It's quiet. You need to bring your own internal cheer squad to keep you going.

In the early kilometres the downhill running was all fairly gradual, so it just felt like running a bit more easily and fluidly than usual. I was concerned for a couple of runners who shot past me; eavesdropping on some conversation, I gathered they were running much faster than their planned pace because it was downhill, with no thought of saving their energy for later. I was to pass several of them later on. In the closing kilometres there was a noticeable number of walkers, energy all used up.

Early on in the race I thought that an organisational hiccup was going to prove my undoing. A water stop was missing and I had to run six miles without a drink. I wasn't feeling especially dehydrated, but I always have to watch my fluid intake because I dehydrate easily and often without realising it is happening. Dehydration is easier at altitude. Luckily it wasn't hot and I didn't suffer too much once I had a drink at the next aid station. The water table team had apparently forgotten to turn up.

The second half of the course was flatter than the early part, and the airport was in a large valley. From here we came into the urban part of Steamboat, where there's a little bit of industry. The riverside bike path comes this far out of town and I was pleased to see the area I had jogged through on other days. Even downtown Steamboat was not busy, with just a few groups of spectators around the finish chute. I spotted a couple of local guys I had met on a mountain bike ride a few days earlier and called out to them (I had told them I was here for the marathon); this made me feel like I really belonged here.

It was fun to run through the centre of Steamboat and finish outside the courthouse. As I approached the finish line I looked up to take in the view I had seen on the photo that started this whole escapade. There it was: the snowy mountain as a background to the main street.

The town had seen a flurry of activity as the marathon runners arrived the day before the race. By the time the marathon had been over for a couple of hours, everyone had left again and the place was dead quiet — almost eerily so. I went to a diner to eat, sat looking out of the window at the fabulous array of mountains only a stone's throw away, and daydreamed about doing this all over again.

When I went to run the Lake Tahoe Marathon in September 2009 I knew I was in for a hard day. My previous marathons in the mountains had been predominantly downhill, or had at least claimed to be, but here was a race with an equal amount of climbing and descending. Starting altitude was 6240 feet (1900 metres), with a highest point of 7000 feet (2130 metres), although I had overlooked these details when deciding to run the marathon. In my naïveté it had not occurred to me that the lake might not be at sea level. I should have read the race description more carefully before signing up. I had picked this race purely on the basis of the scenery, which was considered to be outstanding.

This event gave me a sobering example of how things can go from good to bad very quickly during a marathon. At mile 15 I was feeling really great; actually, even I was surprised how well things were going. I had heard so many alarming tales about this marathon it was almost like I was in a different event. Admittedly I was running a very conservative ten-minutes-per-mile pace, but I felt like there was little chance I would slow down in the foreseeable future.

By mile 16 I was feeling rotten. All my energy had gone and every footfall felt like a major exercise. The reason: a massive hill which was a complete surprise to me. It turned out to be over a mile long and nearly 1000 feet (305 metres) in elevation gain. A sign at the roadside labelled it Purgatory Hill and every hundred feet (30 metres) in elevation gain was indicated by signs. One hundred feet doesn't sound much but I could certainly feel it; this would largely have been due to the whole marathon taking place at altitude, since I was finding any extra burst of energy required took its toll far above what I would have expected.

There were half marathoners skipping past as if they were on oxygen, but many of us were walking. I struggled with running as long as I could but eventually I had to walk. I thought at this time I was near the top, at 6700 feet (2042 metres). But around another bend the climb continued. I jogged a little then resumed walking to the 7000-foot (2130-metre) summit. I was drained.

This was the worst hill in an already hilly race — the terrain had been rolling until that point, with constant gradual ups and downs. After Purgatory Hill came a pleasant descent but the worst was not yet over. We climbed and fell for a couple of miles, but I found the climbing very hard and was often reduced to walking. I tried to not walk for more than 30 seconds at a time to avoid losing momentum.

Then came the climax of the marathon. We descended for half a mile around the rim of Emerald Bay, a superlatively beautiful horseshoe-shaped bay with an island in its centre. Think: deep, blue lake water; green mountains all around; and a fringe of sandy beach. It was drop-dead perfect, and running downhill towards its edge was the icing on the cake, even while we could see the road we would shortly be taking to climb out of the bay on the far side. I was exhausted but I decided that life was good after all.

The marathon, my 90th to date, had started inauspiciously enough in Tahoe City on the western shore of Lake Tahoe, a holiday community of motels, restaurants and boat hire shacks. We were going to run

26.2 miles along the western shore of the lake to Popes Beach. I was expecting a race like the Big Sur Marathon, but by a lake rather than by the ocean. On the bus to the start line my companion had asked me, 'Have you run here yet?' This was a reference to the 6500-foot (1981-metre) altitude at South Lake Tahoe, where most participants stay. Yes, I had tried a few short runs, and yes, it had been difficult. But the main problem I had was sleeping, as had happened at Steamboat Springs.

For the opening miles we ran through small settlements and past pine-forested hills with few sightings of the lake. We switched between running on the road and on a bike path through the pines. We passed colourful cedar holiday homes that would have been worth a fortune as development was clearly not encouraged along the lake. But to be honest I felt short-changed, as if this marathon was not going to live up my expectations; it was supposed to be extremely beautiful, according to reports by past runners. My marathon guidebook, which had previously guided me to such gems as Big Sur and Steamboat, ranked this event highly.

All that was to change by the five-mile mark. We started to follow the lake shore more closely with unobstructed views across the lake. The water was still, the shore punctuated by short pontoons, small fishing boats were moored, and the occasional water skier would pierce the silence. The lake was fringed by pines and backed by mountains, some forested and some fairly bare with craggy peaks. No snow, however, on the peaks as it was too early in the year. Not much in the way of sandy beaches, either; just pebbles or boulders. I apologised mentally to the race organiser for my earlier critical thoughts and settled in for what I now knew would be one of my more enjoyable marathons — at least visually.

I had formulated a plan to run at a ten-minute mile pace (this equates to just slower than six minutes per kilometre), with two minutes of walking every half hour. I wanted to take it easy as I was worried about how I would cope with running at altitude, having only been at altitude for a couple of days. I had originally hoped to finish in around four and a half hours. But after chatting with other runners on the bus to the start line I became concerned and thought this might turn out to be a five-hour job or worse. I decided to listen carefully to my body, especially my breathing.

Within a few minutes of starting I found that, firstly, the running at just faster than ten-minute mile pace was not taxing and, secondly, that I had my iPod playing so loud that I could not hear my breathing to check on it. After half an hour I was not ready for a walk so I kept going. When I had run six miles and should have been going for an hour, I had only been going 57 minutes so I decided to walk until I reached the hour. This then became my race strategy: to run six miles and walk until I made up the time to ten-minute mile pace. This worked well for me and I felt calm and relaxed right up until Purgatory Hill. I thought four and a half hours was realistic rather than overambitious.

After Purgatory Hill my race wasn't the same. I knew I was in for a battle against tired lungs and a mind telling me to walk. I picked up on the downhills but found the flat stretches a problem. This didn't surprise me because I remembered from the downhill running I had done at the Comrades Marathon that running on the flat following prolonged downhill running is very hard. I permitted myself to walk at times if my lungs were burning or I felt I could not take sufficiently deep breaths while running, but clung hopefully to my time goal. I had been through bad patches before, and I knew altitude made things trickier than usual.

We passed the ten-kilometres-to-go marker on the way out of Emerald Bay; US events often show this metric marker as a bit of extra information. A lot of runners were walking, and I was surprised how many racers there were all around. Then I realised we marathoners had been joined by people doing all sorts of other distances between ten kilometres and 20 miles, including relays and walks.

The final two miles were dreary, but only in comparison to what had gone earlier. We followed a bike path through alpine meadows away from the lake. Anywhere else, this would have been great — to be away from traffic and so on — but I was anxious to finish. I calculated I could run 4 hours, 27 minutes, if I really tried, and that would equal (but not exceed) my worst marathon time for the year to date. My thinking was that my other 4 hours, 27 minutes, had been on an easier course (Pichi Richi) so I could be truly pleased to equal that time on this tough course.

I got a welcome second wind in the last mile. Then, as the clock on the finish line came into view, I saw I could just manage 4 hours, 25 minutes, with a sprint. I went all out; for a fleeting moment I noticed walkers three abreast ahead who could foil my plan and I was lucid enough to plot how to get around them. As it transpired, I instead bumped into another finisher who wavered in his stride seconds before the tape, and made it with four seconds to spare. Phew, my 90th marathon finish, and one of the hardest.

Beyond the finishing chute lay Popes Beach, the longest sandy beach on the lake shore. Like many other runners I went straight for a walk in the lake to cool down my legs. The water was actually not very cold, and if I had brought a change of clothes I would have had a swim. I settled for cooling my legs and telling some unsuspecting folk that I had just done my 90th marathon. A couple of girls who had just finished their first ten-kilometre race were gobsmacked, even more so when I said I had another marathon lined up for next weekend — and even that wasn't quite accurate, because I intended to do two.

Double dipping

There is no such thing as an easy marathon. Completing a hundred of them has taught me this. But my St George, Utah, marathon in October 2009 went like a dream, and I had never expected this to happen.

For one thing the event started at altitude, which made it harder. Less oxygen in the air means having to work more for the same result. And I had a different challenge on my plate: I was running two marathons on the same weekend, one on Saturday and another on Sunday, just to see what it was like. Was I nuts? Straight after finishing St George I would drive for almost three hours to Las Vegas and fly to Sacramento, California, in order to run the Cowtown Marathon there the next morning.

I had never done this before. I took on this experiment for no other reason than that it presented a step into the unknown.

I had signed up for the St George Marathon much earlier in the year. The St George event is always held on a Saturday because the town is in a strict Mormon area and activities like running races must not be held on Sundays. The event is always oversubscribed so you have to go in a ballot to gain entry, and once you are successful in the ballot you are committed to running unless you are prepared to forego the substantial entry fee, which is not refundable. I was successful in the ballot. Two weeks before I left home I received a phone call to tell me that my flight home from the US had been cancelled and I would have to stay an extra day over there. So what did I do? I took the opportunity to run an extra marathon.

There is, incidentally, a website that pairs marathons for people who wish to run two in one weekend. Amazingly, there are clowns around who do this kind of thing regularly, or at least like to consider the possibility of doing so. This site paired St George on Saturday with the 'City of Trees' Marathon in Boise, Idaho, on Sunday, but I could not find a simple way of travelling between the two places on the Saturday afternoon. On the other hand, it did not look too difficult to get from St George to Sacramento.

I planned my weekend with great precision. I would run in St George, benefiting from the race's early start so that I would be finished by mid-morning. Then I would drive across the desert to Las Vegas to fly to Sacramento, as there are not many flights out of St George. I would arrive in Sacramento by early evening, gaining an hour from a favourable time difference between California and Utah. The Sacramento event allowed for race number pick-up on the morning of the race, another factor I had to take into account since I could not possibly get there before the race registration and expo closed on Saturday.

When I look back on my race in St George it is as if I skipped along, making my way through the miles as if floating on a cloud. A marathon is usually a titanic battle between your wish to be finished with what you have so boldly started, and the pain of your body which urges you to stop and rest rather than continue to the end. I felt none of this in St George. The result made me supremely satisfied. Such days are rare indeed.

Perhaps my good day was courtesy of my pre-race eating. With takeaway food so readily available in the United States, I have always had a good choice of meals on marathon eve, not all of them healthy.

My pre-race evening meals over the years have been varied. My analysis shows that I have eaten sandwiches before 19 marathons. I have eaten Chinese takeaway before 11 marathons — not so often, but almost every time this has preceded a successful, well-run race; New York and St George stand out in my memory for the good results achieved on a stomach full of Chinese buffet treats. I have eaten fish and chips before 15 marathons; I believe the chips help with my night's sleep. While it is a popular myth that all marathon runners eat pasta the night before their race, I am not greatly fond of eating pasta the night before a marathon — although I have done so at least six times. The last marathon runner I asked about this said that she prefers a steak with mashed potato.

My intention in St George was to run extremely comfortably, so that I would finish the marathon feeling as though I had only arrived at the halfway mark. I really believed I would do this, even though the idea of running a marathon in comfort flies in the face of reality. But, hey, I had run two double marathons (the Comrades Marathon and the Molesworth Run, which is a double marathon in New Zealand) so I knew I could last the distance, especially with a night's sleep in between. This is notwithstanding expert advice that the night in between is the killer because your legs stiffen up and all the race-induced inflammation will manifest itself the next day.

I did indeed set out at a lazy pace and I felt very good. I let the four-hour pace team pass me without feeling any sense of remorse at all. This was not my challenge today. I was just enjoying the experience of being out in the canyon in the darkness. The thought of breaking the four-hour barrier had not entered my head.

After leaving Lake Tahoe the previous weekend I had been almost at sea level in the intervening week, staying in Las Vegas, so my acclimatisation to altitude at Lake Tahoe would have worn off and would be of no help with the thinner air here. But 5000 feet (1524 metres) was not considered to be high altitude and should present little challenge. We were going to drop lower very early on in the race.

We started from a tiny place called Central. A fleet of school buses took us there. What would marathon organisers do without those yellow school buses? It is so handy to have them available for weekend marathons, and it helps remind most of the runners about their childhood, which can't be all bad. After all, running is a fairly childish activity.

The first buses left at 4am, and I boarded as late as possible at 5.15am. At Central the organisers had prepared bonfires so that we could keep warm. At that altitude, there was nothing else there and nothing to do. And it was bitterly cold, too.

This marathon is on a completely closed road and has a net elevation loss of 2500 feet (762 metres). That's more fun to run than a net elevation gain. I did not expect to feel like I was running downhill all the way as I had read about a couple of killer hills along the route.

For the first half hour we ran in the dark through the canyon. It was very quiet, with the runners too sleepy to talk, and no spectators as there was no access for them into the canyon.

I felt good but held myself back. There was a fair bit of downhill in the opening miles and I was aware of the dangers of going too fast — more than anything, hard downhill running would give me tight quads and hamstrings and would spoil my run the next day. They say the worst discomfort is after sustained downhill running because of the braking effect as you try to stop yourself running out of control.

There was a major hill at the small town of Veyo. Luckily, this coincided with one of my predetermined walking breaks so I was able to walk the first third of the hill. Today I had loaded six albums onto my iPod and I had decided to walk the first song from each album. This meant I would be walking roughly once every 50 minutes for four to five minutes. I didn't have to look at my watch; I just listened to the music for cues.

The scenery consisted almost entirely of sparsely vegetated grassland as we passed through a series of canyons. The road would be flanked by rocky outcrops or grassy hillocks or sometimes more dramatic red cliffs. Until we came closer to St George we barely saw a building. The colours at sunrise were exhilarating and the day was completely still.

All this was in great contrast to the conditions for the 2008 marathon, when the day had been windy and it had poured from start to finish. This was yet another instance of the extreme good luck I have had over the years — there have been more instances than I can count of my turn at doing a marathon having had perfect weather when the conditions had been vile in other years, or having good weather on the day I ran but having bad weather the next day or the day before. Thank you, weather gods.

And so the first half of the marathon went by.

The 16th mile was an emotional one for me. The previous Sunday at Lake Tahoe had seen my suffering start during the 16th mile of that marathon. This was not going to be repeated today. Mercifully, this mile was almost all downhill. It was probably at this stage that I had an inkling that this was going to be a good race for me. I just felt strong, and was running comfortably faster than ten-minute mile pace without seeming to exert too much energy.

Spectators had access in a few places in the later miles and were vocal at all opportunities, but we saw very little of them until reaching town, where they lined the streets just as they do at the New York City Marathon but in rather lesser numbers.

We reached the outskirts of St George at the 20-mile mark. I found myself doing some calculations in my head, and I realised that if I continued with my current pace and didn't trip over I might be able to reach the finish line before the clock ticked past four hours.

In my previous 34 marathons I had come close on so many occasions to breaking four hours, but I had ultimately failed each time. Completing a marathon can never, of course, be a failure in any sense of the word, but I had nurtured a secret desire to break four hours just one more time. In 2007, when I broke four hours at Port Angeles, I was hopelessly unaware that this was the last time I was going to achieve this. I did not know that injury was to follow shortly after (a stress fracture in my foot), and that I would make a decision to pick up my rate of entering marathons to such a degree that I would have little chance of running any of them fast. At Invercargill in late 2007 I had run 4 hours, 1 minute; in Luxembourg in 2008 I had run 4 hours, 20 seconds; and later that year I had run 4 hours, 1 minute, at Ross in Tasmania; then in 2009 I had again run 4 hours, 1 minute, at Buller Gorge. On each occasion, except at Buller Gorge where I was oblivious to my pace, I had thought I was capable of beating four hours and had been disappointed.

But I was not going to stress about this. Somewhere along here I forgot to take my walking break as Bruce Springsteen started to sing.

We had a very pleasant downhill trot into town, and this was one of several times during the race that you could see a long string of runners snaking ahead into the distance. This is a beautiful sight, and never more so than when you can also see the road ahead is downhill. I love it when I know gravity is going to do some of the work.

At 23 miles and again at 24 miles I did my calculations. *Try to do it,* I said to myself, *but don't bust a gut; it isn't worth it*. By 25 miles we were twisting and turning through the town. I was starting to go all out. A few hundred metres past the 25-mile mark, I suddenly came upon the four-hour pace team. I had to finish a bit ahead of them to run under four hours myself as they had passed me in the early stages.

Now I went for it. I pushed ahead as fast as I could. I decided that this time it was worth trying to see if I could finally crack the elusive barrier. I reckoned I had ten minutes for the final mile. And the next thing I knew, I had done it. I believed I had finished in 3 hours, 59 minutes, but as it turned out it had taken me longer to get over the start line than I thought and I had run 3:58:50. Finishing a marathon has seldom felt this sweet.

This wasn't the only aspect of the St George Marathon that made it special for me. I had told the race organisers that this was to be my 91st marathon and that I had done more marathons than any other Australian female. The local radio station had heard about me, and asked for an interview so that they could feature me as one of their Marathon Moments during the days before the race. I did the short interview by phone. The interviewer chatted to me lightly before we went to air and told me the sort of questions he was going to ask, presumably so I could mentally prepare quick answers. Then he said we were going live and he proceeded to ask me, on air, a whole different set of questions. I had the responses at my fingertips anyway, saying I had never anticipated aiming for a hundred marathons, that I selected marathons on the basis of good scenery and that my advice to a non-runner was to at least give running a try.

The race committee laid on a lunch for the international runners. This was mainly done because St George has a special link with a Japanese marathon and they like to entertain the Japanese runners, along with the local families who host them. A few other foreigners, like myself, were invited along to help eat up the food — or so I thought.

After a few speeches, and some eating, the announcer said he was going to introduce each runner. He introduced the elite Japanese runners, who did not speak English, and then introduced me. I stood up and was clearly expected to speak. So I said I had done 90 marathons and wanted to be the first Australian female to do a hundred. There was a collective gasp from the room. I felt thrilled. I hardly ever admit my ambitions in public and it was wonderful to have this reaction from around 150 listeners.

The funniest part was that I was sitting next to an Australian woman who was living in Utah and was about to run her first marathon. Before the speeches started we had been talking and she asked if I had done any marathons before. 'Yes,' I said, 'I have done 90.' This did not elicit the reaction I expected, and indeed usually receive when such a large number comes out of my mouth. She just nodded, as if most folk who have run a marathon before have done 90 or so, and she asked which ones I had done in Australia. 'Most of them,' I replied. She asked if I had done Sydney and I gave her an account of the Sydney race, which may have been too detailed for her interest. When I talked to the audience about the number of marathons I had done, the penny must have dropped. My new friend made the loudest gasp of all and said, 'Wow, really?' Then she wanted to know all about them.

The St George Marathon is a popular one for runners wishing to qualify for the Boston Marathon, which I guess indicates that it is considered a faster course than some. It is also good if you can qualify for Boston at this time of year because you get two years in which to run Boston. The qualifying period for Boston in April 2011 started on 1 September 2009, so if you qualified between 1 September 2009 and the date entries closed for the 2010 race you could run either in 2010 or 2011 or both. So a lot of runners come to St George with high hopes and a lot of runners leave this marathon very happy. I shared a ride back to the hotel after the race with a woman who had just qualified for Boston; she was elated and said, 'I am definitely going there next year.'

I showed her I was wearing my Boston 2008 cap and said the event was well worth the effort to get into it.

I had had all sorts of intentions of having an ice bath before I headed out of town and having a substantial lunch, but all I did was have a quick shower and hop into the car for the drive to Las Vegas airport. I stopped to pick up a pizza after half an hour and had a cup of coffee, but I was on such an emotional high it was hard to act sensibly. The next day's marathon felt a million miles away — I just wanted to savour today's achievement.

Everything went like clockwork. I was in Sacramento by 7pm, and at 8pm I was sitting in a small Italian cafe with a plate of spaghetti carbonara and a cold beer. The beer was to celebrate my happy run in St George and the pasta was in preparation for the next day's efforts. Yes — pasta the night before a marathon, despite what I said earlier. I was pleased that my legs were not sore at all.

I went to bed early, thinking more about the day's achievements than the challenge ahead. This was unusual for me — normally, when I have lined up events close together I focus on the upcoming one as soon as the first one is over so that I minimise the tiredness I carry forward. This is a trick for the mind, really; it's like I pretend the first event has not happened so I can persuade myself I am fresh for the second one.

In the morning I had a stroke of luck in getting a lift from my hotel to the Cowtown Marathon start with a couple who were running the half marathon. I had worried about how I would get there since it was not walking distance, and I thought it may be hard to explain to a taxi driver where I needed to go. This couple had done the event last year so they knew exactly where to go and a good place to park. I told them that I had just run another marathon and the girl (whose family lived in Sacramento and were coming to watch the race) said, 'Wow, that is so amazing. That's the first thing I am going to tell my mom when I see her:

that we met you and you were doing two marathons in two days.' I was curious why a local couple had stayed the night at a hotel rather than at their home. It turns out it was the guy's birthday, and his birthday wish had been to stay the night at a hotel before running the half marathon.

At the start area I didn't think much about what I was about to do. I got my race number and walked around a bit.

The gun went off and I got a surprise: my left hamstring was sore. Not really painfully sore, but a bit uncomfortable. I just hoped the discomfort would wear off as I warmed up. I haven't ever run a whole marathon in pain. (The closest I have come is when I ran the Richmond Marathon six days after a hard run at the New York City Marathon — I felt tightness in one calf at the four-mile mark and this stayed with me the rest of the way. I still managed to like that marathon, a very pretty urban sightseeing tour.)

The start was jam-packed with over 4000 runners (mainly in the half marathon) trying to find a spot on the road. This took my mind off the pain and any fears I might have about getting through the marathon. I knew this was going to be a challenge for the mind as much as for the body. We ran through a lovely green park with palm trees and giant fig trees, and then through a residential area that reminded me of Wisteria Lane on *Desperate Housewives* — all the lawns were beautifully manicured and the houses, neat and tidy.

The first mile seemed particularly long, and I realised I was going to have to take this race one mile at a time so as not to feel overwhelmed by the distance I had to run. In an ironic sort of way I think I was mentally the closest I have ever been to how I felt when I ran my first marathon — worrying about the miles ahead and wondering how I would make it to the finish. I decided to go very easy on myself, to have no time goals whatsoever, and to handle the day as it came.

The prettiest part of the route was a long stretch on the bank of the

Sacramento River. It was a still, sunny day, and the river was peaceful. We also took in a couple of quiet suburban roads and a marina. In the full marathon we had to run the half marathon course twice; the event had come in for criticism for being boring because of the repeated loop. But I found the tone of the two laps to be quite different: the first lap was noisy and teeming with the half marathon folk, and I spent my time listening in on other runners' conversations; on the second lap I concentrated on the scenery. On both laps I was aware of the pain in my leg and I kept reminding myself not to think about it.

The theme of the marathon was all about cows. According to the race website: 'Despite being the capital city of California and having a population of nearly one million people, Sacramento has for years been considered no more than the Cow Town that lies between San Francisco and Lake Tahoe.' Some of the marshals were dressed up in cow costumes; there were white balloons with black mottling to imitate cow hide at the relay changeover stations; there were 'cow crossing' signs on paths; and near the end of the course was a sign reading '½ mile to the cowshed'. The start/finish area was dotted with bales of hay to act as seats. The medal for finishers was a cowbell, the nicest cow touch of all.

I intended to do a run-walk routine (alternating 15 minutes of running with three minutes of walking) throughout this race, but once I got going I thought it might be best to run for as long as I could in view of the soreness in my leg. I feared that if I started walking I may not be able to motivate myself to resume running again, and I also thought running was probably going to be less stressful than walking. So I ran the entire first half in 2 hours, 6 minutes.

The second half was a harder story altogether. I started by walking ten seconds after each mile, then 20 and then 30. My running slowed considerably. I focused on reminding myself how pleased I would be when I finished, with having achieved my goal of two marathons in a weekend. Although I had slowed a lot, I was still able to pass many runners on the second lap and this made me feel good. I clearly wasn't doing too badly.

The pain in my leg didn't get any less but nor did it get any worse. This was certainly a long way from being my worst marathon experience, largely because I made sure I was mentally in a good place. There was no way I was going to allow myself to become depressed or mired in self-doubt.

The finish was fantastic. Running through the park for the last mile, I was so pleased. I threw my arms in the air as I crossed the finish line with a time only seconds over four and a half hours. This was a moment to treasure.

After the race something happened that I will always remember. I mentioned earlier that I own a book that describes the best marathons in the USA — *The Ultimate Guide to Marathons* — and I have used its descriptions in deciding which marathons to run. The book was co-written by Rich Hanna, who happens to be the race director of the Cowtown Marathon. After I finished his marathon I went straight over to say hi to him and to mention what an inspiration his book has been for me. I also thought I might as well tell him that I had come to his race from St George (a marathon I had vowed to one day experience, based on the book's write up). Rich immediately called out to the race announcer and said he should chat to me. I explained to the announcer what I had been up to, and this guy got on the loudspeaker and gave me the best wrap ever:

> Now, Julia Thorn has just finished the marathon. Yesterday she ran a marathon in St George, Utah. She ran a personal record there [I meant it was a personal best since 2007, but that's just a detail]. Then she came and ran a marathon here. I don't want to hear anyone in

> the Cowtown Marathon ever again say they are feeling tired. This woman has run a marathon, got on a plane and gone through all the fuss at the airports, and then run another one the next day. Most people would only run two marathons in a whole year, if not in their lifetime, and this woman has done this in a weekend. Can you imagine the conversation on the plane: *What did you do today? Ran a marathon. And what are you doing tomorrow? Running a marathon.* This is the most incredible thing I've heard today; actually, it's the most amazing thing I've heard in the five years of this marathon.

I had the biggest smile on my face. It was a good day. It was a good weekend.

My hometown marathon

Travel is great, particularly when there's a marathon to run on the trip. I thrive on the excitement of being in a new place to run, whether it's Toowoomba or New York. Variety is something I never tire of. There are only a few marathons I have run more than twice — I run the race once for the new experience, a second time in case the weather is different or if the course is changed, and then I like to head elsewhere.

But for the marathon in Melbourne, my hometown, I am prepared to make an exception.

I see that it can enhance my race day to have the home comforts: my own bed the night before the race, my husband Denis to drive me to the start line, my own couch to relax on afterwards, my own fridge to raid. Denis runs the half marathon and we spend a happy afternoon comparing notes.

The whole idea of running a marathon close to home becomes something of a novelty. After a year of casual running on streets very close to the marathon course I am running a long race here. Even though it is near home it still presents all the drama of completing an arduous challenge. As with any marathon you never know what the day will throw at you, but the hometown race has distinctive features.

First of all, I drive to the start. On the old marathon course, this meant that I drove two-thirds of the course before running the race as I lived near the 30-kilometre mark of the marathon. It always struck me what a long way we were driving. Was I dumb? I knew beforehand that the marathon was going to be 42 kilometres long. But in the car on race morning this has seemed a colossal distance.

Then, much as I am used to the fickle nature of Melbourne weather, I don't know what the weather will be like on race morning. We can have a pleasant cool spring day on the Saturday and wake up to a warm and humid morning for the marathon. Melbourne's weather uncertainties, which include unpredictability about the wind direction, have meant that you never truly know what sort of day you are going to have for the marathon. Tailwind, headwind — it could be either and I have experienced the two, both unexpectedly and forecast.

The best thing about running at home is that people I know are watching along the course. I will hear my name and it won't just be because my name appears on my race bib. What's more, I can share my race with several of these people afterwards when we get together for our post-race gathering.

At home, breakfast is simple. There's no hunting around for a takeaway place to get coffee from at 6am, or having to go into a hotel buffet breakfast and just eat toast. I hate seeing all that food and having to behave as though I am on a fast. My breakfast desires on race morning are uncomplicated. I have a muesli bar or two slices of toast or two bananas, plus coffee. I don't savour the food; this is pure fuelling up. Sometimes when travelling I have not been able to get hold of a cup of coffee before the race (at the marathon in Richmond, Virginia, I put my coffee money in a charity box when I found I had too little to cover the cost of a takeaway coffee in the hotel lobby), but by the time the starting gun goes off I have usually forgotten this — the adrenaline in me acts as enough of a stimulant to get me moving.

I will have trained on the course, which is a mixed blessing. I will know the marathon route intimately — where the hills are (although in Melbourne these are far from severe), where we have to make turns, where to look at the view. But if I feel low during the race I will also know just how much further I have to suffer, without having any surprises to take my mind off this.

Melbourne's marathon is flat and usually fast, unless adverse weather impedes that. There are spectators but not in huge numbers. Most onlookers would be watching out for a runner they know rather than having ventured out for the sheer spectacle of thousands of runners in the streets. This is not yet a marathon on the scale of New York or Chicago. Non-runners can still remain blissfully unaware that it is happening unless their driving plans are affected by road closures. But the marathon seems set to grow. In 2009 the size of the field was threatening the Australian record set in Melbourne in 1983, when the marathon had over 6000 entrants and 4798 finishers.

(I have always been curious why the number of marathon finishers is often so much lower than the number of starters, especially in less recent races. It appears that this is partly because in the past there were rarely shorter races accompanying the marathon, so a runner who wished to run only a shorter distance — but under race conditions — had to join in the marathon and pull out when his mission was accomplished. The way half marathon popularity has ballooned in the past decade tells me that there are loads of people, and there may always have been, who want to compete over a course longer than ten kilometres — a prevalent 'fun run' distance — but do not wish to run a full marathon.)

Between 2001, the first time I ran this marathon, and 2006, the marathon route did not change much. The race started in Frankston and took us, in the first few years, to Albert Park, and in the later years to the Arts Centre on St Kilda Road. So we never made it right into the city centre but we took in the attractive Port Phillip Bay coastline. We followed the direct coast road from Frankston, through Mordialloc to Brighton and on through St Kilda. For the Albert Park finish we turned away from the beach in Middle Park, and for the Arts Centre finish we headed inland down Fitzroy Street and then St Kilda Road.

I can plot the progress of my marathon running career through my attempts at the Melbourne Marathon. I first ran this race as part of my sequence of marathons in every Australian state, when I was a relative novice. My times improved for a few years as I trained more seriously. Then tiredness crept in and I was unable to maintain the momentum — for me this is an inherent problem with the Melbourne Marathon as it is held in October, late in the year. Finally, I came to regard this as a marathon I would always run but I would no longer expect to run a fast time, and consequently I would focus on enjoying the experience of running on home turf to the exclusion of all other race ambitions.

In 2001 we had a tailwind for the first half. The race announcer mentioned something about the possibility of a course record that day in view of the tailwind. I shot off like a bull at a gate, and paid the price for the rest of the morning. I was surprised to find so many runners reduced to a walk through St Kilda, but I have noticed this each year I have run this marathon, whatever speed I have run. I see from the race results that my friend Jane, who is another prolific marathoner, was the next runner to cross the line behind me, but in those days I was yet to meet her.

I remember standing on the starting line and overhearing a conversation between two runners in front of me. One asked the other how many marathons he had run that year, and the reply was '15'. I was taken aback, and immediately butted into their conversation with: 'This is my fifth for the year and I thought that was an awful lot. How can you do 15?' I was told that there is not so much difference between running five in a year and running 15. I took this message to heart. In 2005 when

I ran 14 marathons I realised this was right; it wasn't so different. The bigger leap is from one to five.

I didn't know many people in Melbourne back in those days and it was extra special when onlookers called out to me. I was chuffed to be recognised. I was also a lot less familiar with the course than I have become over the years, so it was still moderately exciting.

In 2002 we had bad headwinds all the way. Again I went out too fast. I ended up running exactly the same time as the previous year, give or take a few seconds. This was disappointing because I thought I was becoming a better runner. I blamed a sore hamstring I had been suffering for several weeks before the marathon.

For 2003 the conditions were pretty near perfect until the wind came up along Beaconsfield Parade near the end — it was a horrific headwind. I felt dreadful for the last ten kilometres, but this was genuine fatigue as I had been trying extra hard; I had done a personal best at the Shepparton Marathon two months earlier and I wanted to keep this trend up.

I didn't prepare differently for the 2003 Melbourne event than I had for the earlier ones, but I was paying attention to drinking more and that could well have made the difference to my finishing time, which was 12 minutes faster than the previous year. This has remained my fastest Melbourne Marathon.

In Melbourne in 2004 it was very hot on marathon day. I felt bad the entire distance, save the first kilometre when I was still well-hydrated. The last 41 kilometres of a marathon can be very taxing. This marathon came near the end of a long year of running a great many ultras and marathons, the first year that I had dared give myself such a hectic schedule. Most of my results were good but I could not keep this improvement up indefinitely. I was just thankful I was still fit and healthy by October. At the finish I wandered around Albert Park in a daze; it was almost like a desert with the glare of the sun and the brown grass.

In 2005 it was wet and windy as we huddled outside a gym in Frankston, seeking shelter from two heavy squalls and gale-force winds before the marathon started. The rain stopped before gun was fired but things never warmed up, and the wind threatened to put paid to plans for running a fast time.

But running marathons is all about overcoming the odds. What's a bit of bad weather between friends? And friends I found aplenty among the field of marathon runners. I had started out with one of my regular running partners, Annette, and she was amused at the way I interviewed — as she put it — other runners as we drew level with them. I was feeling very chatty and exchanged comments with many runners along the way.

The number of ten-year and 20-year Melbourne Marathon runners astounds me every year. What an admirable quality to have the strength to come back year after year. And as for the guys whose singlets proclaim they have done the lot — well, they just blow me away. I asked one of these stalwarts which had been his best race. I fully expected him to say his first, because the first marathon usually is the one you remember the most fondly, having ventured into the unknown, having run a personal best without really trying. But he said it was the time he went under three hours, his eighth attempt, 'when I was only a boy'. I know I should have been able to do the sums and work out what year that was, but after only ten kilometres out on the road my brain was of little use.

I saw a runner with a singlet proclaiming he had run a hundred marathons. This got me excited. So I didn't beat about the bush, I straight out asked him his name. It turned out he was from England. How many marathons had he done? I thought he was telling me his race number not his number of races: 342. I could understand and believe him but this was a hard fact to take on board, so I was reassured when he added, 'But just now I feel as though I've never done one before.'

I made a new friend from New Zealand, from the Hawke's Bay Running Club. He was on a mission to join the New Zealand 100 Marathon Club, but he had some way to go, having run only 67 marathons. This year he had run Prague and recommended it. Next year Paris was on the agenda.

Other runners were holding conversations too. This was so much more sociable than running along in silence. I would catch snippets. Sometimes I longed to ask 'Why did you do that?' or 'And did she agree?'

As we approached Brighton and my home training territory I was feeling comfortable. Not that I have always felt too good here. The first year I ran this marathon I saw some friends standing at the 28-kilometre point and I told them I wasn't feeling very happy. In a way this was a self-fulfilling prophecy because I deteriorated rapidly after that. I vowed not to say that sort of thing to a supporter who had waited patiently for a fleeting, or maybe not so fleeting, chat. (I've observed that some runners are glad to pause and hold a whole conversation with their mates on the sidelines.) I think it's important to stay positive during a marathon however hard it gets. As a runner, you chose to suffer this.

Leaving Brighton this year I still felt okay. Actually, I had never felt better at the North Road far boundary in Brighton in five years of running the marathon. I had some energy for a surge. Two years previously Annette met me along here and tried to convince me that this part of the route is downhill, to help me out. I didn't fall for that one; this year she was running the marathon too, and I wondered if she remembered her comments. Some of the members of my regular running group were out on the footpath to cheers us on. That gave me a real lift. One of these guys asked me that afternoon if the support helps. Of course it does. It makes me very happy to be running in my hometown.

I was looking forward to turning off at Fitzroy Street, because I had never run the marathon on this course that goes to the Arts Centre. Denis had run the half marathon that morning, and he said that it was nice to run along Fitzroy Street and see the cafes with people eating breakfast. They're a distraction, and at the same time they're oblivious to the pain we're going through — or if they *are* aware of it they're not letting on, with their gay chatter.

And then it was down to the serious business of the final four kilometres along St Kilda Road. This was a great experience on the world-famous boulevard, despite buffeting from the wind at various intersections. Not much time for interviews here. Just one foot on the ground followed by the other one. It was nice to be able to see the finish line from some distance away. At the finish I caught up with a runner, Richard, from London, whom I had met at the Thailand Temple Run earlier in the year. We both laughed at what a completely different race this one had been.

The marathon in 2006 was an odd one for me. I ran a very strange race where I behaved as though I was in much faster shape than I was and by halfway I realised I was not running with my brain.

Over the winter I had strained my calf muscle repeatedly by not letting it heal properly after each strain, and I had pulled out of the Sydney Marathon in September. I would have pulled out of the Melbourne Marathon too had it not been my hometown race, as I wanted to be truly fit for running in New York only three weeks after the Melbourne event. Maybe I didn't satisfy my expectations here, but the race served me well as a warm-up for the New York City Marathon.

I set out with two runners from my Sunday running group, but very soon decided that I would go on ahead. I can't imagine why I did this as they are both faster runners than I am, but I guess I fell for that old mistake of feeling good at the start of the race and ignoring a more sensible approach. After 15 kilometres I drew even with another runner from this same group and we ran together for an hour or so. He was running his first marathon, to be followed by the 210-kilometre Round the Bay in a Day bike ride the following weekend, a circuit of Port Phillip Bay using the ferry between Sorrento and Queenscliff.

Somewhere beyond halfway I had to slow down, and I continued alone. Meanwhile my earlier running companions had become separated and in these late kilometres one of them passed me. I was feeling demoralised and low. I persevered, but without enthusiasm, and eventually reached the finish. I sprinted to break four hours and just made it. Right next to me, I was surprised to see, was one of the friends I had started out with.

In 2007 the Melbourne Marathon course was completely changed. I didn't do the marathon that year, deciding instead to go to Chicago (the Melbourne and Chicago marathons regularly fall on the same day). Denis laughed at me, saying it was obvious I liked travelling more than I liked running, because why else would I travel halfway across the world to run a marathon when I could run one at home? In the northern hemisphere this is one of the busiest marathon weekends in the year.

The new course was used again in 2008. That year I ran on a warm, windy day, on no sleep the previous night. I was still jet-lagged after coming home from a funeral in England.

We started close to the Melbourne Cricket Ground, ran along the edge of the central city area, crossed Albert Park and followed the shoreline from Port Melbourne to Hampton before turning back. Rather frustratingly, the organisers had decided that anyone who could not complete the marathon within 3 hours, 45 minutes, would have to take an alternative route to the finish, and our final kilometres were a tedious zigzag through the parkland around the MCG. The faster runners had been allowed to run along Flinders Street, which sounded much more fun.

This was my fourth marathon in four weekends and I think I put in a commendable performance. It turned out to be the fastest of the four. As I came up St Kilda Road with about six kilometres to go my legs were crying out for me to stop moving, or at least slow to a walk, and I managed to ignore their pleas. Even when I caught up to and then passed a friend, I did not slow to chat with him but continued on. It was a pure case of mind over matter, of silencing the devilish voices in my head.

In 2009 I found myself going one better by attempting in Melbourne my fourth marathon in three weekends. Over the preceding two weekends I had run three marathons in the United States, and when you take the travelling into account and the loss of an entire day as I crossed the International Date Line coming home to Australia, this meant I was running four marathons in fourteen days. After the first marathon at Lake Tahoe I think I kept myself on an emotional high for the next two weeks, as I did not foresee much pain in this challenge.

I am not a real believer in so-called runner's high. The expression is sometimes used to suggest that when you run you become so happy that you cease to notice the difficulty of what you are doing. My own experience says this is not the case. But I do know that there are very good feelings to come from running, especially the longer distances. After a marathon these good feelings can persist for several days, but they are usually followed within a week by a sharp bump down to earth, as I described earlier. I suddenly start to question what exactly I have achieved by running all these marathons, whether I should really be doing this, and — the most evil self-doubting question of the lot — *why do I bother to do this when I am so slow?* This time around I did not have the low after the first three marathons, leaving me in a positive frame of mind for Melbourne.

Marathon day was something of a family affair, with Denis running the half marathon and my son Dominic running the ten-kilometre race.

On race day I felt more capable than I had when I fronted up to the 2008 marathon. This was just as well as I had promised to run with one of my running partners, Phil, who had not run a marathon for the past 24 years. I thought he had trained well for this marathon and I was looking forward to running with a friend rather than alone.

Phil had run four Melbourne Marathons by 1985 but knee problems were getting the better of him. 'I couldn't even walk upstairs because my knees gave me so much trouble,' he told me. 'I couldn't keep up the level of training I had to do to run another marathon.' He continued to run shorter races, up to half marathon, and then in 2009 he decided to give the marathon another crack. 'I was running all week with people who were training for the Melbourne Marathon, which meant I was running more than I had been, and I thought that if I was doing their training I should be able to run the marathon. My knees had settled down and I felt I was ready to run a slow marathon.'

I didn't see Phil at the start line and I started out running alone. I fell into step with a Spartan (ten-years-plus Melbourne Marathon runner) and we chatted. I told him it was my eighth Melbourne Marathon and he took this to mean it was my eighth marathon, which is a fair misunderstanding; I did not have the heart to set him right straightaway. He said, speaking as a Spartan, that the eighth is probably the hardest because you are so close to ten but still have some very hard work to do to get to ten.

Around the five-kilometre mark I saw Phil and ran with him from thereon. We chatted a bit and ran in silence, and things went well. We looked out for mutual friends along the course, both runners and spectators. I remembered again what I love about the Melbourne Marathon — knowing other runners and having onlookers call out to me — and this is the real reason I run in Melbourne every year while I get bored of repeating other marathons.

This was a very comfortable marathon for me. I had some tightness in my left hamstring but it was less severe than the pain I had in Sacramento the weekend before. Early on in the marathon I suddenly had sharp shooting pains down my left leg, which I worried about, but these stopped after a few minutes.

Almost all the rest of our running group had come out to support us, and they had given us a detailed itinerary beforehand so we knew exactly where to expect them. Some of them were supporting on bikes — an excellent idea as it meant they could move from point to point rapidly and be with us in more places.

We had trained a lot on the course. What we did not realise at the time of this training was that we had been making one slight detour off the course around 35 kilometres; outside of race day there was a section of the marathon route we could not run for traffic reasons. This is one of the risks of training on the marathon route: you may think you are training on the course but you are not, and the different route directions during the race might throw you. On race day, a marshal situated at this very point directed us in what we thought at the time was the wrong direction, but naturally we did as we were told, along with hundreds of others. I made a snap judgement that the marshal probably knew the course. This surprise coincided with Phil feeling he was going to have to walk for a bit. He urged me to go on ahead. He assured me that he was going to finish, so I went on. I picked up the pace a little but basically I just wanted to enjoy the final kilometres. I wasn't going to break any records today, for slowness or speed.

By this stage in a marathon, getting close to the finish and having been on the road for over four hours, there are so many runners who are really struggling. The good thing is that you know you are going to finish, even though moving forward is tough. You know that running onto the MCG, through the tunnel that was used in the Commonwealth Games marathon in 2006, is going to be a big buzz, but when you are so completely worn out even that prospect does not fully sink in. The final metres around the outside of the stadium are endless, however frisky you may be feeling.

Right in the finish chute I caught up with a Taiwanese friend, Ching-te, whom I had met at many marathons this year. I said, 'Ching-te, I have just run 42 kilometres to see you!' I do a lot of marathons, but he manages to outnumber me with ease. We drank a cup of water together to toast another achievement.

Running in Japan

Tokyo streets are mad crazy with people all day long. It's fun to be a part of the action. You have to focus your eyes on the spaces between people and aim for those spaces. You can maintain a good speed doing this although it does mean that you walk much further than if you were to go where you need to go in a straight line.

Walking the streets without bumping into anyone is good practice for running a marathon with 28,000 participants. This marathon had the busiest feel of any I have ever done.

I had been to Tokyo in 1983 and it had not been a very successful trip, partly because the value of the yen was so high that everything was phenomenally expensive, and partly because it was so hard to understand anything or be understood. But in 2009, from the moment I stepped off the subway in central Tokyo into the hustle and bustle, I realised this was going to be a wonderful trip.

My impressions were confirmed when I arrived at the marathon registration and saw that all female participants were being handed a bunch of flowers. A novel touch. This bunch of freesias made a great improvement to the appearance and scent of my hotel room during my week in Tokyo.

Entry was by ballot many months before the event. It was apparently oversubscribed by a factor of almost seven — 210,000 applicants for

35,000 places (including the ten-kilometre race) — so I was pleased to get accepted. I was less pleased when, having secured my berth, the credit card company rejected my payment, possibly because I had experienced some recent fraud on this card when it was illegally used in Japan. After a tense week, made tenser since I had already paid for flights and hotel, this was sorted out.

The marathon was well-thought-out and gave us a good tourist itinerary around central Tokyo. I was quite surprised how the organisers were able to arrange closing off such major streets to all traffic. We went through the busiest parts of Tokyo. In the New York City Marathon you do not run down Fifth Avenue and in the London Marathon you do not run through Oxford Circus.

So the route of the marathon was definitely memorable. But what will also stay in my mind are the crowds along the route cheering constantly and cheerfully. I had always thought of the Japanese as being reserved but there was no way you could call their enthusiasm for us reserved. Spectators high-fived and called out some words that meant *keep going* and smiled all the time. The runners responded in like fashion. Even though I couldn't chat to more than the very occasional runner, I felt a great sense of belonging. There were very few non-Japanese runners but I felt quite at home.

The other thing that marked this marathon out from many others was the food. I'm not talking about the sustenance from the aid stations, which was flawless in its ready availability and quantity, but the food provided by the spectators. For most of the course there were spectators handing out lollies, wrapped chocolates, fruit (bananas, strawberries and orange slices), cookies and slices of cake. And then they handed out balls of rice with sauce or fish mixed in, small bowls of miso soup, and even tiny cups of ice-cream with a spoon. It was a veritable feast. And after every episode of food there would be someone 50 metres down the road with a plastic bag for the rubbish. And sometimes even someone with tissues to allow us to clean up after the meal. No wonder I ran a relatively slow time — I was too busy eating.

The race started in Shinjuku by the twin towers of the Metropolitan Government Buildings. There's a great observation tower at the top of each of these buildings, from where you can see Tokyo stretch to the horizon. It was, of course, very congested for the early kilometres as we ran along wide streets flanked by tower blocks of offices.

Early on I enjoyed running alongside the Imperial Palace Gardens. It's a huge park surrounding the relatively modern Imperial Palace, with a moat between us and the gardens, and several old stone bridges across the moat. After passing the gardens we reached Hibiya Park and the turn-off point for the accompanying ten-kilometre race, so the running mob thinned out a little. I took a little peek into the park, Tokyo's first Western-style park as opposed to the more formal Japanese gardens.

It was a complicated route. We headed south towards several tourist sights: the Tokyo Tower, which might have been created in imitation of the Eiffel Tower, and then the Zozo-ji Temple, which originally dated from the 14th century but was mostly destroyed in World War II. Then we got a glimpse of the Rainbow Bridge at the top end of faraway Tokyo Bay. Most of what you see in Tokyo seems fairly new.

The many bands and other forms of entertainment along the route kept our spirits up. We were treated to military bands, groups of cheerleaders, traditional dancers and performances by school students. It was all done with great enthusiasm. The runners were enjoying the support and the entertainers were enjoying the entertaining.

We returned to Hibiya Park and headed north through the Ginza district. This is the foremost shopping area in Tokyo and is always throbbing with people. The main shopping street was cordoned off just for us but you could see that the surrounding streets were very full.

Sunday is especially popular for shopping because many of the streets are closed to traffic on that day. I was amazed that we could get priority to run down this main shopping street on what would usually be its busiest day of the week.

We continued on for several kilometres parallel to the Sumidagawa River, right to the Kaminarimon Gate. This is the entrance to Tokyo's best-known temple, Senso-ji Temple in the district of Asakusa, rebuilt in the mid-20th century. All tourists go there and it is like a little town unto itself. It wouldn't be practical to run through the temple grounds, so we were routed in another direction. Meanwhile, the elite runners were coming past us on their way back to Ginza. We too returned to central Ginza, passing dozens of small shops and restaurants and watching the tail of runners travelling in the opposite direction. If you didn't realise already from the persistently crowded route, seeing all these runners emphasised the sheer volume of us out there that morning.

The weather was deteriorating with short intervals of light rain, and this section had been windy, with strong gusts. The gusts seemed to come between the buildings, so the weather was probably a lot worse than it appeared, and we had protection thanks to the continuous high-rises around us. We had been expecting a cool, cloudy day but the sun had come out briefly in the early kilometres. Now it seemed to disappear for good.

As we turned south for the final seven kilometres out to the Tokyo Big Sight exhibition centre on an island in Tokyo Bay, the weather worsened. The rain became heavier and the wind strengthened. I was not so worried about running in the rain but I was concerned about how cold I would get once I stopped running because I did not have any clothes to change into. I hadn't been able to get through the crowds to the baggage vans at the start since I arrived quite late at the start line, so I had ditched the old clothes I wore on top of my running gear.

This area had a different feel about it, more industrial and also newer, as much of this land has been reclaimed from the bay in recent times. These last kilometres were hilly, which we had been anticipating, but even forewarned this is a bad time in a marathon to hit hills. We were still jam-packed even at this late stage.

We crossed a number of canal bridges, some slippery, and ploughed through puddles until finally reaching the Big Sight. There were meant to be dance performances and displays of acrobatics happening around the finish line but it appeared the rain had put a damper on all this.

But on the finish line there were, for the first time, announcements in English. In fact, most of the talking was in English, in contrast with the start of the marathon when nothing at all was in English. I heard no English, saw no English. (At the start of the marathon there had been great excitement when the participants around me noticed a certain runner standing near them who must have been a celebrity. They all took photos of him and he smiled charmingly. Nobody could explain to me who he was and I never worked this one out.)

It was slow progress getting through the finish chute, into the exhibition centre and out the other side to the train station, and the long ride back to central Tokyo. We were each handed a souvenir towel in the finishing chute and I wrapped this around me to compensate for the lack of dry clothes. I sat on the train with it draped over my legs, feeling rather stupid, but aware that I could have been a great deal colder without it. I guess the red face with blue lips made me appear an oddity anyway.

The journey back to Shinjuku took almost two hours. When I stepped out into the teeming streets the frenetic activity and noise greeted me like a security blanket. I wanted to be a part of it. Instead of resting after the marathon I walked around the streets, investigated the shops, and stopped for sushi at a little café, to savour my last evening in this vibrant city.

記録証 CERTIFICATE

2009年3月22日／March 22, 2009

東京マラソン2009

TOKYO MARATHON 2009

兼第12回世界陸上競技選手権大会男子代表選手選考競技会

ナンバー NUMBER CARD	50811
氏名 NAME	JULIA THORN
所属 NATIONALITY	AUS
種目名 EVENT	マラソン女子
順位 PLACE	1243 位 ／ 6320 人中
記録 TIME	4:22:35

通過点	通過タイム	スプリットタイム
5km	0:35:17	
10km	1:05:32	0:30:15
15km	1:35:24	0:29:52
20km	2:05:02	0:29:38
中間点	2:11:45	
25km	2:35:41	0:30:39
30km	3:06:29	0:30:48
35km	3:37:51	0:31:22
40km	4:09:32	0:31:41
FINISH	4:22:35	0:13:03

ネットタイム（参考） NET TIME	4:17:54
年代別順位（ネット） PLACE BY AGE GROUPS	マラソン女子50～54歳 96位 ／ 451人中
男女総合順位（グロス） OVERALL PLACE(GROSS)	9589位 ／ 29109人中
男女総合順位（ネット） OVERALL PLACE(NET)	9835位 ／ 29109人中

Shintaro Ishihara
大会会長　東京都知事
Chairman, Tokyo Marathon 2009
Governor of Tokyo

Yohei Kono
組織委員会会長　日本陸上競技連盟会長
President, Tokyo Marathon Organizing Committee
President, Japan Association of Athletics Federations

Finisher's certificate from the Tokyo Marathon.

❖

I was sad to leave Japan and I talked about it so much at home that by the end of the year Denis was ready to go back there with me. We needed a reason to go, and as a good wife I found a marathon for both of us to run. The Lake Kawaguchi Marathon in late November fitted the bill perfectly.

This was described as a scenic marathon, with thousands of runners enjoying the unsurpassed views of Mount Fuji while twice circling a lake beneath the mountain. Kawaguchi-ko — Lake Kawaguchi — is a smallish town on the shores of one of the Fuji Five Lakes which dot the base of Mount Fuji. It is under two hours' drive from Tokyo and a popular Japanese tourist spot. In summer, hikers use the town as their base for walking up Mount Fuji. About 200,000 hikers make the trek each summer. Mount Fuji is the highest mountain in Japan, at 3776 metres, and it is an active volcano although it has not erupted since 1707. We were there well outside the hiking months of July and August, but we were able to benefit from the good infrastructure that was in place to help hikers and visitors, namely hotels with English-speaking staff and signposts with English writing.

I had two goals for this trip: firstly, to see Mount Fuji (more on that later); and secondly, to have us both run the marathon in comfort. Mentally, I was done with running for the year. I had no more challenges to set myself, as I had already run 18 marathons since February. I had run a two-year personal best in September and I had been to many fabulous places during the year. This would be marathon number 95, and on completing it I would have run a fifth of my lifetime's marathons in just one year.

In an effort to show that I do know how to train for a marathon even though I refuse to follow the rigidity of a program myself, I aimed to coach Denis to run a personal best at his third marathon, and to enjoy his running experience.

My job was to have him complete the marathon in less than four and a half hours. He had run the Melbourne Half Marathon in mid-October so I planned his training to build on that.

We had previously run two marathons together. The first time was on the Gold Coast in 2007, at which time I was running my 58th marathon as Denis ran his first. 'There was a lot of talk about marathon running in the house. I wanted to see what it was like to run a marathon,' he told me. I had left him to his own devices regarding training, since he was already proficient at the half marathon distance, but we ran the marathon side by side. He started the Gold Coast Marathon with a minor leg injury which was to get much worse during the morning and drastically impeded his forward movement.

Eighteen months later we both ran the Honolulu Marathon in 2008. Denis was suffering leg cramps by halfway and was reduced to walking by the 30-kilometre point. This was a shame because race conditions that day were unusually benign for Honolulu: we had light rain and a cool temperature instead of the usual heat and sunshine that make this one of the harder marathons on the international circuit. At this marathon, as at the Gold Coast, we made slow progress to the finish. Denis had not been able to enjoy either marathon experience because of pain, and to me this fact was worse than our disappointing finishing time.

I felt partly responsible; I knew so much about marathon running but I had not succeeded in passing my knowledge on. I suppose I had expected him to absorb it by living with me. I knew he had done a slew of two-hour runs, but we saw in hindsight that this was not sufficient.

It only trained him to run for two hours. His physical training had not been adequate, but he also needed a better appreciation of the mental demands of completing a marathon. Many of the mental tricks of the trade have become second nature to me, but that's come about after dozens of marathons.

When Denis decided to run the Kawaguchi Marathon — 'This time I am going to run the whole marathon,' he announced — I gave him a training program with strict instructions to follow it to the letter. I felt it was important to emphasise this. He was not to juggle the days' runs and do the short ones when he felt like it several days in a row, or finish the long run a kilometre from home and walk the last part. What you do in training is what your legs will want you to do on race day, so it's not sensible to actually train yourself to finish the route early and walk the last bit, even when you have a sound reason for doing this. In Denis's case the reason for doing this was to finish at the local shop to buy a drink and the Sunday paper, but as a hard taskmaster I decreed that he must run home first and then visit the shop.

The sting in the tail was a 40-kilometre run he was to do three weeks before the marathon. I would not normally advocate this, and usually a 30-kilometre run is quite enough as a long training run before a marathon, but in my husband's case he needed to know that he could run this far without walking. This turned out to be an even harder mission on the day as the temperature climbed over 30 degrees before he had finished that run. I felt I was verging on cruelty here. But the following day I got a surprise taste of my own medicine when I went to Marysville to run a marathon in remembrance of the Black Friday 2009 bushfire victims. The day heated up to the mid-30s and this was the hottest marathon I have run in Australia.

This was Denis's training program:

Weeks to go	Mon (km)	Tues (km)	Wed (km)	Thur (km)	Fri (km)	Sat (km)	Sun (km)	Total (km)
7	rest	5	rest	5	10	5	25	50
6	rest	5	rest	5	6	12	32	60
5	rest	5	rest	5	rest	15	15	40
4	rest	5	rest	5	rest	12	40	62
3	rest	5	rest	10	rest	15	30	60
2	rest	5	rest	5	rest	10 km race	14	34
1	rest	6	rest	6	rest	4	Marathon	58

Then I set him some reading in order to help him understand the mental issues that always lie in wait to disrupt the marathon, even when you have trained perfectly.

I said that I was prepared to run the marathon alongside him if he would run at my pace. What I meant was that I was going to hold him back until I was confident he could finish the race without crashing and burning. On our previous attempts he had gone out too fast, with me in tow, at his two-hour run pace, and I was not about to watch this happen again. I warned him that if he succumbed to walking at the 30-kilometre mark I would probably not choose to walk to the finish with him.

Almost everything about this marathon turned out to be challenging. Until we actually crossed the start line I wasn't sure we were going to be participating. The physical task of running 42 kilometres paled in comparison with the logistical dramas. We needed a race entry each, a hotel room and bus tickets from Tokyo to Lake Kawaguchi. To an experienced traveller this should have been easy.

The race entry was straightforward and done online, except that the race website did not like two entrants sharing one email address and rejected the second entry form. This we resolved easily by using a second email address. Then the credit card company did not like two identical payments on the same credit card and held up the payments.

A hotel was suggested on the race website, and I gathered from reading about the marathon on various running forums that it would be best to stay at the recommended hotel as the staff could speak English. This hotel offered a shuttle bus to the race start — an added bonus. We duly booked the hotel when entering the race and were told an invoice would come by return email. Months passed and the invoice did not arrive. Meanwhile the race website posted a note saying the hotel was full. My research online established that every hotel and backpackers' hostel in the town was full. At this point we did not know if we had a hotel room booked or not.

I eventually phoned the race organiser to enquire about our hotel invoice; he was surprised to hear from me and said he was emailing the invoices very soon. The next day our invoice arrived. This was either pure coincidence or I had jogged his memory about sending them out. So I paid the invoice by bank transfer, as instructed, expecting some form of confirmation from either the hotel or the race organiser. Emails requesting confirmation that the race office had received the funds were met by silence. Two months passed and then the confirmation arrived a week before the race.

The final challenge had been to get bus tickets for the ride out of Tokyo. The bus company website was only in Japanese and, on translation, we found there was no way to book the tickets from Australia. I envisaged thousands of runners vying for a handful of bus seats, not realising that there is a bus every half hour between Tokyo and Lake Kawaguchi. We went along to the bus station. Actually, we had to find it first. The bus station is beside Tokyo's Shinjuku railway station, a vast place filled with scurrying commuters, confusing shopping arcades and signs seemingly written in code. Once we found the correct bus station, since there were several bus companies and each had its own depot, and then the room selling tickets for today's travel, we had to be directed to the room selling tickets for future travel (tucked away upstairs — behind an unmarked door, of course).

Nobody else on the bus looked like a runner, and there were no other runners at the hotel when we got there. But as the race start line was being set up on the lake shore when we first arrived, we knew it would all work out in the end. The next day we saw runners trickling into town, and the hotel explained its shuttle bus arrangements. They said they would be ferrying runners to the start as required and didn't see the need for a timetable. This was in line with the vagueness of all the other information we had been receiving, so we crossed our fingers.

Our arrival at Lake Kawaguchi was on a beautiful afternoon two days before the marathon. Mount Fuji was resplendent, towering over the town with a lovely cap of snow. The next day the sky was blue once more and we took a short boat cruise on the lake to get the best view of the mountain. Clouds were already appearing by late morning, and by the afternoon the mountain was gone. Unfortunately, we had seen the last of it for our visit. We were pleased to have seen the whole mountain. In 1983 Denis and I had hiked up Mount Fuji without seeing the summit or view from the summit at all. The idea is to hike part of the way up, spend the night at a hostel almost at the summit, and hike to the summit to watch the sunrise the next day. We spent a miserable cold night, saw nothing at the summit, and came home with a collection of photos of ourselves standing in fog.

On race day there were further obstacles. At the hotel lobby we saw dozens of runners milling about and no van in sight. Our spirits fell. But to our considerable delight we soon noticed that there was a queuing system in place, with each of us receiving a numbered ticket to show our place in the queue, and the shuttle van materialised to do an excellent job of getting us into town. Race morning was also cold, and we wore tracksuits to the start. We could not find anywhere to officially deposit our clothes while we ran. But we did notice that there were bags of clothes scattered all over the place — under trees, on picnic tables, leant against buildings. At some of the bigger races you are encouraged to leave any warm-up clothes at the race start to be donated to charity, but these bags and packages did not look as though they had been abandoned; we thought the bags had an air of expecting to be reunited with their owners after the race. So we followed suit and left our gear under a picnic table.

We had difficulty getting into the starting chute. Although this has been a marathon with a cast of thousands for many years, it was being operated as a small-town event and seemed to have outgrown its boots. The expo had been just a few tents in the lakeside car park, and the starting area — in the same car park — was woefully small for so many people. We waited at the side and joined the running throng after the gun had been fired — scrambling through hydrangeas, clambering over a barrier and dodging rubbish bins on the way — as hundreds of other runners were doing. This was quite entertaining.

This Kawaguchi Marathon showed us that, despite its quirks, a marathon overseas is very similar to a marathon in Australia, and you can bluff your way through. Were it much different we would have been completely sunk in Japan; but since we knew the ropes back home we could work out what was going on here, even when there was no explanation that we could discern or comprehend.

A marathon running friend recently asked me what it is like to run a marathon overseas. I have done so many overseas marathons that I felt I ought to be able to find an answer. Well, the people standing around you are speaking in a different language and the marshals will utter incomprehensible words as you run past, and some of the foods will appear strange. The differences that I notice tend to be little local customs which are unique to one or two countries — such as the timing chip deposit in Germany and Austria, which is refunded after the marathon if you remember to queue up for your refund; and the need for a medical certificate before the French will allow you to participate in any of their races. In Japan, nicely turned-out ladies stand by the roadside offering runners home-cooked treats served off pretty crockery.

The marathon comprised a ten-kilometre trip through the town followed by a tour twice around the lake. It was a very pleasant course for a marathon, with nothing boring at all, and was fairly flat. On a clear day you would have seen Mount Fuji for about half the time. But there was plenty more to see along the lake shore and inland. Mount Fuji is just one of many mountains in the area, although by far the highest. We could see mountain ranges in all directions as we ran. The autumn foliage was superb, with orange or golden leaves in abundance on the mountainsides and along the roadside. There were a few boats out on the lake, a couple of water skiers, and the lake's surface was very still. It was cold, the temperature never rising above three degrees.

The route was crammed with runners the entire way. Not only were we almost eight thousand in the marathon, there were a 27-kilometre race and an 11-kilometre race happening simultaneously. We let other runners flood past us for the early kilometres as I was confident we would be passing them later on. But we still ended up doing a lot of dodging and weaving. This is tiring and wastes energy but can't be helped in such a big event, especially when the road is narrow. In the later kilometres, when we were passing hundreds of runners, we got a false sense of running faster than we actually were.

My intention was to go out easily and get to the start of the second lap of the lake feeling fresh. I must have taken it too easily because our ten-kilometre time was very slow and Denis was having trouble running at my leisurely pace. We picked up speed when I noticed the 5-hours-30 marathon pacer nearby — this gave me a shock, but I realised later we were never running at that pace.

Things went well for the first half, which we went through in 2 hours, 19 minutes. This was much slower than the first half of Denis's previous marathons, and I waited for the payoff. As we started on the second lap of the lake he stopped for a toilet break and told me to go on ahead. I was feeling good and I ran along at my own speed knowing I could maintain this to the finish. I looked back from time to time to see if Denis was approaching but I never saw him, and I decided to leave him to do his own thing.

I enjoyed the second lap around the lake and noticed all sorts of attractions I had missed before — little bays and inlets, colourful trees, runners in fancy dress. I don't know if this was an illusion, but I felt that many of the female spectators were singling me out for smiles and words of encouragement. I also observed from across the lake that the second part of the lap was almost all downhill and I looked forward to that. Denis caught up with me at 35 kilometres; he had been gradually making up time. He was still running well and I believed he could finish strongly. We separated again in the next two kilometres as we came back into the town. I was running mechanically, and after one drinks table I looked around and he was no longer there.

Even on a run like this, when I was mentally very relaxed and I harboured no time goal, I was tiring by the last half hour. I could sense my legs would cramp if I stopped for too long at the drinks tables. So I grabbed drinks quickly, took a handful of the unusual bland, spongy, white lollies, and moved on. I wanted to be finished and tucking into some delicious Japanese food. Across the road from our hotel was a supermarket that sold the most beautifully presented takeaway food: sushi, yakitori skewers, crumbed chicken cutlets, tempura vegetables and prawns, and other stuff I couldn't identify. I couldn't wait to get back there.

I came across the finish mat in 4 hours, 26 minutes. As I was removing the timing chip from my shoe I watched Denis cross the line a minute behind me. He was very pleased, and said later: 'I felt in control much more than before. I felt confident. I was never in doubt that I would be able to run the whole way. I had set myself a realistic finishing goal, whereas the previous times I think I was too ambitious.' This was almost a 30-minute personal best for him so we were both happy.

Looking at our kilometre splits — as I had succeeded in committing them to memory during the marathon — I saw that we had run the first half of the race at between 6.8 and 6.4 minutes per kilometre, and then run the entire second half in exactly 6-minute kilometres. I rest my case (from Chapter 7) about negative splitting for a good result.

Best of all, our clothes were still under the picnic table where we had left them.

Two sides of Los Angeles

Halfway into the Catalina Island Marathon in California, I was experiencing a sensation which might sound all too familiar to any long-distance runner. I was wondering why I could not run any faster. But this was not mere tiredness. I felt good in myself and had power in my legs, yet I was battling.

This trail marathon is reputedly hard, with long hills. The mid-section was not hilly, though; it looked flat, hence my dismay at my slow pace. After the initial miles I had been feeling that I was going to have a good day and run faster than expected, as I had weathered the early hills well and I knew I had crept up through the field.

And then at the 18-mile mark all was explained. I came to a junction that was unexpectedly at the top of a cliff. My road joined up with Airport Road, although I could not for the life of me imagine there being an airport here, where there was just a lot of nothing. (I subsequently learned that it's called the Airport in the Sky and has been there since 1946.) I could see our finishing point, the town of Avalon, far below. Our track had been climbing slowly but surely for the past five miles to reach this point at 1600 feet (487 metres). Silly me — I had thought I was running on the flat. This is what sometimes happens when you run in the dark: you can't tell if you are running on the flat or on a hill. Here, I had no point of reference to tell me that I was climbing.

The view down onto Avalon, a speck on the distant shoreline, was one of the most beautiful sights I have ever seen while out running. It was made all the more heart-warming by the calculation that I needed to do a lot of downhill running to get there.

This was altogether a superb marathon. I had stumbled into it by chance, looking for a second race to combine with my trip to the Los Angeles Marathon. Here was another marathon in the Los Angeles area only eight days earlier. A veritable gift. The best part was that I had not anticipated how enjoyable my run on Catalina Island was going to be.

Catalina Island is 22 miles (35 kilometres) off the coast of Los Angeles, and is easily reached in an hour by catamaran — leaving San Pedro I saw dolphins frolicking beside the boat. Catalina is a mountainous island, 21 miles by 8 miles, and there is very little inhabitable land. It has been used as a holiday destination since the 1880s. In the past, silver has been mined on the island and it has featured as a backdrop in numerous movies, which is not a big surprise when you consider how close it is to the capital of the movie industry. The town of Avalon is the only real settlement and everything there is crammed into the little usable land. The architecture ranges from Spanish-style public buildings, to workmen's cottages, to rundown 1970s accommodation houses. Most of the island beyond the town is now owned by the Catalina Island Conservancy and it is only used by hikers and bikers.

People get around in golf buggies; there is a ten-year waiting list to get a permit to keep a car on the island.

In summer the island throbs with visitors, but I went there at a very quiet time as the marathon is held well outside the tourist season. I was the only person staying at my bed and breakfast — even the owner was off the premises.

I had an extremely relaxing day on the island before the marathon, as there was absolutely nothing to do apart from read and stroll. Many of the shops and cafes were closed, the Catalina Casino (an historic circular building that dominates the sea front, housing a ballroom and museum) was undergoing renovations, and it was too cold to sit on the beach. I put a lot of thought into my meals for the day, and after checking out all options I decided the best way to use the available resources would be to have morning tea at the diner, lunch at the Chinese restaurant, and pizza for dinner.

The marathon was a one-way trip between Two Harbors, a tiny bay on the north coast of the island, and Avalon. Our route was a sort of zigzag, taking us southwards to Little Harbor and then eastwards to Avalon.

For those of us staying on the island we had to be on a ferry bound for Two Harbors and the marathon start by 5am. This was going to be painful. But looking back on it I cannot say just how painful it was; I know I grabbed a takeaway coffee and made it onto the ferry but I have no recollection of how I did it. The sea was calm and this was a good sign for the day's running: no wind to contend with.

When we arrived at Two Harbors our disembarkation was delayed. Another ferry had brought runners over from Los Angeles, and after tipping them onto the island it had found that its anchoring rope was jammed and could not be released. There was only one landing pontoon. For almost an hour we sat on our ferry while the other boat tried to sort itself out. Finally their skipper agreed to cut the rope (we were told he was reluctant to do this because of the expense of purchasing a new rope), and we were relieved that we would not have to sit on our boat for the rest of our lives. There were a lot of jokes about swimming to shore.

This was a blessing in disguise as it saved us having to hang around cooling our heels for an hour before the race got underway — 'cooling' being an apt description as the air was far from warm — while on the boat we had heaters and coffee. The race was only five minutes late in starting and, fortunately for the organisers, nobody threatened to sue.

The marathon route started almost immediately with a climb of a couple of miles on a dirt trail. Two Harbors was soon below us, and we were treated to the sort of vistas that would be with us for the entire run: mountain peaks and unspoilt coastline. Such an amazing contrast to the huge city only a short distance away. It was truly spectacular and I could see why runners return to this marathon year after year. The field spread out very quickly and I found myself running alone for most of the morning. The speedy runners raced off into the distance and the slower folk, who made up the bulk of the participants, held back. I held back too, but I did not walk at all.

We had ups and downs all the way to Little Harbor; our path was never flat for a moment. Little Harbor turned out to be one of the world's most exquisite bays. There was nothing there save a small hut. Watching the waves crashing into the bay and seeing large rocks scattered all around, it's hard to imagine many vessels like to harbour there.

From here we had to cross the island, and we had a better formed dirt road to run on. I could see runners heading uphill towards the horizon, but that didn't faze me since I was having a good day. I had not run a marathon for six weeks, and I felt that had I had a flat road marathon to run that day I would have achieved a fast time. As it was, I intended to do well on the island trails. I loved the solitude and the wonderful sea views. We looked southward, away from Los Angeles, much of the way.

By the time I reached Airport Road most of the participants I could see ahead were walking. One runner heard me coming up behind him and valiantly attempted to keep on running. But at the finish line he told me that as soon as I passed him he had started walking. I had not experienced this *last person still running* phenomenon since the Comrades Marathon five years earlier.

Not that we were yet at the top. There were another two miles of brutal climbing to go. Before I made it to the top I did something I do not usually bother to do — I looked very closely at another runner's T-shirt. Then I thanked the runner for allowing me to do this. He was confused, no doubt thought he had misheard me, and ignored me. The reason was that he was wearing the race T-shirt from a previous year, and on his back was a profile of the course. I was grateful to see that we were nearly at the highest point, and I planned on using all my efforts to get there. I was confident about the descent that would follow.

I've always thought that a souvenir race T-shirt with a map on it was daft. If it's on your back you can't make use of it to navigate, and why do other people need to see a map of where you've been? But at that moment I judged it the best thing I had ever come across.

I loved the descent. It was effortless and long. Three miles, to be precise. We lost a thousand feet (305 metres) in a mile, and then continued gradually down the next thousand feet to the finish line in the town centre. On the way down I passed a chap I had been talking to on the ferry over to Two Harbors. This was his first marathon, and from his comments I deduced that he expected to run a much faster time than I was aiming for. He was hating the downhill. I commiserated, without much heart in my voice, and continued on my way.

We came into town via the Botanic Gardens, and the final half mile was on a paved road. An announcer was calling names as we finished. As I crossed the line he said, 'Julia Thorn from Brighton. Now where is that? Can you come to the mike and tell me?' I went over to see him and filled him in on the details, also letting him know this was my 97th marathon. He was suitably impressed and told the spectators this during a lull in proceedings. But later in the day, when he handed over my second place age group award, he referred to me as 'Julia Thorn from Brighton, Canada' without batting an eyelid.

I went back to Los Angeles the next day. The catamaran was packed with folk wearing identical T-shirts — each one with a map on the back, by the way — and many of these folk seemed to have difficulty walking. It only takes eight hours in bed after a marathon for you to stiffen up and find walking a major ordeal.

After a week in Los Angeles I was ready to toe another marathon start line. This race was going to be completely different but it promised to be an exciting urban adventure.

I had been for a couple of short runs near Hollywood, where I was staying. I ran through a maze of narrow roads up from Hollywood Boulevard to Mulholland Drive, where my reward was a great view of the Hollywood sign, and another day I ran into the Hollywood Hills for a view down over the whole Los Angeles basin.

During this week I was dealt a blow I had not been expecting. In the months before the 2010 Canberra Marathon, scheduled for April, there was doubt as to whether the race was going ahead, as it was the subject of a legal dispute. To me this wasn't to be just another marathon; it was going to be my hundredth. I had scheduled this into my program back in September when I was about to run my 90th. I felt personally peeved that a dispute should threaten an event as important to me as my hundredth marathon, although, of course, the uncertainty was keeping a large number of runners on tenterhooks. I had no choice other than waiting to see what happened. When I left home for Los Angeles I had believed the marathon in Canberra would still take place.

While in Los Angeles I heard that it had been definitely cancelled.

I had to push the disappointment to the back of my mind, and I delayed making a decision about where to run instead until I came home.

The Los Angeles Marathon course was new for 2010. The organisers had decided we were to pass as many famous landmarks as we could, and our run turned out to be a tourist's dream. We saw virtually everything that has made the city famous, and we didn't just glimpse these sights from a distance.

From the start line outside Dodger Stadium we would make a loop around the stadium, tour Echo Park and its lake, and then head through downtown Los Angeles, noticing the Chinatown gate and the old Spanish-style buildings of the original settlement on the way. In the city we were to cruise past City Hall and the Art Deco concert hall before hitting Hollywood. We would spy the Hollywood sign on the hillside high above us, and run along the Walk of Fame, past Pantages Theater and Grauman's Chinese Theater, then past the Hotel Marmont and on through West Hollywood to Beverly Hills. Following a jaunt down Rodeo Drive we would move towards Westwood, Century City and the war veterans' administration. As a last fling we were to follow Santa Monica Boulevard towards the coast and run our final mile alongside the ocean to Santa Monica Pier.

The route was to have us run streets whose names are known worldwide, like Sunset Boulevard, Hollywood Boulevard, Wilshire Boulevard and Rodeo Drive. Entertainment was promised all along the course: cheer squads, rock bands, drummers. The only thing the organisers could not guarantee was that our favourite film stars would be among the spectators. Shame; the men's defending champion had said at a press conference that he hoped some film or TV stars would come and say hi to him as he ran.

It was one of the best-thought-out marathon routes I have seen, and it lived up to its promises. Many of the larger marathons I have run in the US have tried to give a flavour of the city by touring all sorts of diverse neighbourhoods. This has been extremely successful and has made for some great marathons, especially in New York and Chicago. But here in Los Angeles the neighbourhoods were not so much on the agenda as the tourist sights, and this was a great coup.

When I had told other runners on Catalina Island that I was off to run the Los Angeles Marathon I got a mixed reaction. This was not only for my attempting another marathon so soon. Many marathon runners fall into one of two camps: their passion is for small, rural races away from the cities, or they like the big city marathons. Some of those I spoke to who had chosen Catalina as their choice of marathon for the year could not imagine enjoying a run through Los Angeles with 25,000 other runners. 'I can't stand the crowds,' said one guy. 'You can't run properly; you can't get to the drinks tables. It takes ages to get started and to get into your rhythm. You can't run a decent time.'

I couldn't disagree. There are facets of these mega marathons that do not appeal. The entry price is always high, and once you need to stay in a city centre the accommodation costs are bound to skyrocket. The course is going to be crammed full, and the first few kilometres are always more of a walk than a run.

But what a joy to be able to run through the heart of a city with only runners for company. To be surrounded by others, thousands of others, who share a common pleasure in the simple act of running. To be able to see sights without the noise of traffic in the background and your views obscured by buses, trucks and cars. It's a luxury I am all too happy to pay for. The confusion at the start can be irritating but it gives you a good chance to warm up properly before you really have to get going. I don't mind if my finishing time is slower than elsewhere.

I loved the isolation of Catalina Island, and I wondered if it may have been the most exhilarating marathon I have run. Yet this did not stop me being happy to be running a marathon in Los Angeles only a week later. The race was well-hyped on TV during the week leading up to it. But there wasn't quite the same impression of lots of runners converging in one place, a feeling I had so strongly in New York, Boston and Chicago.

Even before we could get started we were treated to Los Angeles hospitality: a traffic jam. I guess most of the 25,000 runners wanted to have a lie in and get to the race as late as possible, as it was going to be pretty bleak hanging around Dodger Stadium first thing in the morning. I was on a special bus laid on for marathon runners. Around me runners were calling their mates who were stuck in cars or other buses, and the outlook for getting to the race start on time was grim. Traffic was barely moving on the freeway and the ramp off the freeway into Dodger Stadium was at a standstill.

Some runners decided to hop off the bus and get to the start line under their own steam. We could see runners already jogging along the emergency lane of the freeway. This was still over a mile away from the stadium and it wasn't my idea of a good beginning to a race. It seemed very likely that the traffic jam was being caused by runners trying to get to the race, in which case there would be so many people arriving late that our late arrival would not matter.

I'm glad I took this view, since it wasn't long before someone on the bus heard on the phone from a friend on the start line that the start had been delayed. This decision seemed to be enough to settle the traffic and we actually made it to the parking lot only a minute or so after the original start time. With the later start time up my sleeve I was able to get a cup of coffee before heading into the starting corral.

This was far from an easy marathon. The course that had been used until this year was faster, and runners who had done this event many times before had not expected this. Most of the major city marathons are flat or fairly flat because this makes them more appealing. There is more of an illusion with flat marathons that anyone can give it a go, and novices are comfortable tackling such courses.

We started on a hilltop, which boded well for some downhill running later, but much of the early route was uphill. It was especially pleasant in Hollywood to note that we were running along a ridge, still quite high up, so we would have to descend at some point. The final sweeping descent to the coast was fun, and it came in an appropriate stage in the race, when we were tired.

The journey past most of the city's most famous sights — they had to omit Disneyland as it was too far away — was fantastic. The roads were wide enough to accommodate us all. It would have been fun to linger on the course and take photos and listen to the music and cheer squads. But this was race day. I've often noticed places along a marathon course where it would have been pleasant on any other day to stop for a while and soak up the scenery; sometimes I resolve to return there the next day, but I have rarely done this. At least in Los Angeles I had done a week's worth of sightseeing before marathon day so I had already been to many of the landmarks we were passing. I had been to a couple of recording studios for show tapings; I had done the Walk of Fame; I had taken the public bus through Beverly Hills where you can get an idea of the amazing mansions; I had strolled along the beach in Santa Monica. This is a very vibrant part of the coast as, apart from the permanent fairground on the pier, you'll always stumble across some form of free entertainment and see colourful characters going about their daily lives.

So we moved along in unison down the wide avenues, taking strength from each other's company and keeping going.

We were all taken aback by the fog along the coast. Suddenly, when there should have been ocean before our eyes there was blankness.

We turned left at the foot of Santa Monica Boulevard for a mile of beachfront running — sans view. Never mind; we were nearly done with the hard part of the day. It was cold at the sea front and I was shivering by the finish, even though the sun had been shining most of the morning. The organisers had promised a finish line party by Santa Monica Pier, but that was a good half a mile from the finish and I was gong to be too cold to go down there. I had a brief look at the view, once I could see it, and found a bus back to my hotel.

The following Saturday I ran my 99th marathon in what I am rudely going to call the middle of nowhere. At first sight you could not possibly imagine why there was a marathon to be held here, at the small town of Ellensburg, three hours' drive from Seattle. I arrived in the evening, having driven over the still snow-laden Snoqualmie Pass with fabulous mountain vistas, and all I could see were motels and fast-food joints lining the highway into town. There was no indication of an impending marathon but at least the staff at my motel had heard about it — the start line was to be right outside the motel's entrance.

I had arrived for the Yakima River Canyon Marathon, and it turned out to be the perfect run for those haters of city marathons. I had to go only a short way out of town to discover the reason for this choice of venue. The Yakima River flowed close to the town, initially through fields and barren land, before entering a canyon: steep-sided and with a sparse covering of fir trees. The setting was sublime. For me it was a chance to enjoy a complete change of environment from the previous weekend. The marathon course started at the edge of Ellensburg and followed the Yakima River for — let's see now — 26 miles and 385 yards, to end in a parking bay by the side of the canyon road. It was a carefully contrived course and much appreciated by a small group of around 500 runners.

I can recall only small parts of this run. Perhaps I was excited to be running my 99th marathon; perhaps it was because the marathon course simply followed a winding river and didn't hit any landmarks. I remember one bend in the river, where we were suddenly enclosed within a narrow gorge — high rocky cliffs to our left and a good view down below. There were glimpses of snow-clad peaks in the distance, the Cascades range.

Mostly I was too busy chatting to look around, even when one of my new friends was constantly saying, 'Look at this, look there, isn't that great?' This was a fellow nicknamed 'Rev' and president of an American running club called the Marathon Maniacs. Maniacs these folk are, indeed. Members are encouraged to run strings of marathons, like running four in four successive weekends, or 13 in six months, or marathons in 20 different countries within one year. The total number of lifetime completed marathons is of less significance. At the opening bronze level, you have to complete two marathons within 16 days or three marathons in three months. To attain the platinum (eight stars) level you must run 45 marathons in a year or 28 marathons in 183 days. Among the members are runners who have run over 400 marathons ... 400 marathons; can you believe that?

We chatted as only two marathon-obsessed runners can. A fly on the road would have found our conversation ridiculous in the extreme. We listed marathons run the way you might list the clothes waiting in your laundry pile. We spoke of marathons to be run the way other people might be deciding on a dinner choice. We then moved on to chat about our families and how we find time to run, and came back to comparing marathons run.

He too had found that running marathons frequently was

possible even though none of the training guides on the bookshelves acknowledge this. He had run the New York City Marathon a week after the Marine Corps Marathon during his first year of running, and from then on it was all downhill — to becoming a fully-fledged Maniac.

It is obviously very much harder to climb through the Maniac ranks when you are based in Australia. There are so few marathons on the running calendar here that you can't easily manage the sequences like 13 marathons in 79 days for seven stars, or 52 marathons in 365 days for ten stars. With no more than 30 annual marathons, mostly held in the winter months when there might be three of those 30 marathons on the same Sunday, it takes careful planning and many years to amass a portfolio of completed strings of marathons.

As well as the Maniacs having a good presence here, this marathon was a reunion marathon for the North American 100 Marathon Club. The race director was the co-founder of that club. While the Maniacs are concerned — or should I be saying 'obsessed' — with 26-mile marathons, the 100 Marathon Club accepts all races of marathon length or longer. Some members have not run any standard marathons but have notched up over a hundred ultra marathons. (That does not mean that a double marathon counts as two marathons. A hundred-mile race, of which there are many held annually in the US, still counts as one marathon, as opposed to four, for the club's purposes.) I qualified to join this club when I completed the Honolulu Marathon in December 2008, my 76th marathon, as I had also run 24 ultras by that time. I would not have decided to enter the Yakima River Canyon Marathon had it not been for this chance to meet other members of a club I would never have imagined I could one day join.

The Australian 100 Marathon Club and the New Zealand 100 Marathon Club only allow you to join when you have run a hundred standard marathons, an important distinction. Neither of these clubs holds an annual reunion, but in Australia the Macleay River Marathon in June is one that many members make an effort to attend, and in New Zealand their chosen event is the Feilding Marathon in November. Needless to point out, these are not large clubs.

At the official meeting of the North American 100 Marathon Club I was completely blown away by the wealth of running experience contained within one small room. There were folk who had run hundreds of marathons and spoke of their experiences in a matter-of-fact way, as though we are all out there doing this. Which, on this occasion, we were. There was a guy planning a marathon on the ice in northern Canada. There was a man who walks marathon after marathon carrying a full-size US flag, walking the marathons in upwards of seven hours in honour of fallen servicemen and 9/11 victims; there were runners who have run a marathon in every US state and Canadian province — twice.

It was a great pleasure for me to meet so many likeminded individuals. I had been curious to see what they would be like and most of them were people just like me, with running dreams and a lot of races under their belt. I've always had that problem I alluded to in Chapter 2 of finding it hard to cope with the naysayers who pour cold water on my aspirations, saying that surely all this running must be bad for me. But here was a room full of new friends who made me ask myself quite the opposite: whether I was running enough; that in fact I could be out doing far more marathons. And what I also observed was that every one of these guys looked a picture of health.

I reminded myself that to join my own country's 100 Marathon Club I still had one more marathon to run.

One hundred marathons

The marathon bug bit me and spread a good poison through my body.

I have had many occasions of great happiness in my life: the day my mother bought me a pink dress I very much wanted; the day I was accepted to study at Oxford University; the day I fell in love; the day each of my children was born. The moment I realised I had just run my hundredth marathon is right up there.

My journey to fulfilling this dream was, by my reckoning, successful. I have never been injured during a marathon, vomited during a marathon or failed to complete a marathon. I have been in physical discomfort and I have been in mental discomfort but I have always pulled through.

I have not smashed speed records or run where nobody has run before, but I have done something truly fulfilling. I can't say I have adored every minute but I have enjoyed most of it.

When the Canberra Marathon was cancelled I was faced with the task of finding an alternative race to be my hundredth marathon. I was keen to pick one of the larger events and for Denis to be able to join me there. I settled on the Rotorua Marathon.

There were two compelling reasons for this choice. This was the next major marathon on the calendar in Australia or New Zealand after the cancelled Canberra race, and I could see the symbolism in running my first and hundredth marathons at the same venue. I had been back to run the Rotorua race only one other time in between, in 2005.

I had worried about how I would feel in the weeks leading up to this hundredth marathon. When I had picked the Canberra Marathon as my hundredth I had been pleased that there would not be much of a gap between number 99 and number 100 — just two weeks — during which time I could recover from the jet lag of returning from the US. But I had an additional three weeks to wait for the Rotorua Marathon. Sensible folk would consider this to be good — an extra three weeks to get over the earlier race and to prepare for the next one — but to me this was a burdensome additional three weeks of keeping my fingers crossed that nothing would happen to stop me reaching my milestone. I have rarely been injured and more than ever I needed to avoid injury now.

I fully expected to be plagued by all sorts of imaginary aches and pains, but these did not eventuate. Not until four days before the marathon. Then I came down with an ache the full length of my left side, and a calf muscle which spasmed through the day. I couldn't do much apart from hoping for the best, and true to form these injuries proved to be illusory and disappeared.

Marathon day dawned. The day that I was once more to run the iconic lap around the lake. It was a perfect day for a run. In the night it rained, and the forecast was for a wet day, but a light drizzle soon cleared and sunshine appeared to be on the agenda. It was pleasantly cool — and, gee, this was a treat after months of running in a warm Melbourne autumn — with a slight breeze.

Denis deposited me at the start line and I successfully located my friend Chris in the starting corral. This was no mean feat among almost 2000 runners. Chris lives in Auckland and I first met her in the lobby of our hotel after I finished the Rotorua Marathon in 2005. We got into the lift at the same time and it was evident by our slow movement that we had both just run the marathon. That was her second ever marathon, after a break of many years, and she had run a personal best by two hours so she was ecstatic. I, on the other hand, was disappointed with my run and was complaining. Since that time we had run several events together, including the Buller Gorge Marathon in 2006.

Chris's first words on seeing me (wired up to my iPod) were: 'Well, you won't be needing that. We're going to talk.' And talk we did. We made our way out of Rotorua's Government Gardens (and it didn't even cross my mind that on my return to the gardens I would be about to finish my hundredth marathon) and headed west towards Mount Ngongotaha. We had a lot of catching up to do — verbal catching up, that is — and we barely paused for breath. I didn't notice the scenery at all. We were running a relaxed pace and I was feeling calmer than I had anticipated.

I had asked my older daughter Natasha to paint two cloth signs for me announcing that this was my hundredth marathon, and I wore one on my chest and one on my back. Nobody was going to be in any doubt as to how special this marathon was — and still is — for me. Lots of runners said something nice as they came past us, and any spectators who did not notice me were made aware of what I was doing through Chris calling out to them: 'Hundredth marathon. It's her hundredth marathon!' Many spectators and marshals gave me an extra clap, and I couldn't deny that this was just fantastic!

When I ran here in 2005 I went too fast on the early hills and my race was spoilt by the time I reached the lake. But this time I was pacing the route well and it was a great pleasure to have our first glimpses of the lake. It looked still and chilly, with a little autumn foliage on the trees.

We came upon the early low hills before we reached the lake, and then the main climbs came after we moved slightly away from the lake around the 18-kilometre mark. Chris considered walking up the first hill, but I wanted to run so I waited for her at the top. The second hill, the one we call Heartbreak Hill, soon followed, and I was feeling strong so I decided to go on ahead. I then ran alone for the next ten kilometres. (We had an agreement that either of us could do this.) Finishing time was not important to me that day, and I was running a pace that seemed sustainable and stress-free. I did not care when I finished so long as I finished feeling good. This was not a day for yearning for the run to be over or for collapsing on the finish line.

I started to feel an endorphin rush. The enormity of the occasion was making itself felt for the first time that day. Then I knew why I was running there. This wasn't only about running a hundred marathons, or about being the first Australian female to do this — although both these things are extremely important to me — it was more than that. It was about doing something I love.

I had come a long way since starting my first marathon on this very same course. Almost 4220 kilometres, to be precise, in marathons alone. But that statistic does not tell the full story by any means. Every marathon has required effort. Every marathon has taught me something. Every marathon has left me with an indelible memory. Where I ran into unknown territory in 1997, I now ran with knowledge, focus and confidence. I had run fast marathons and slow ones. On the road I had been happy and I had been sad. I had found out what a runner needs to do to get through a marathon. I had discovered what I needed to do to enjoy a marathon. I feel blessed to have been taught these lessons, and they are the best lessons I have ever learnt.

During these ten kilometres I barely noticed what was going on around me. I had glanced across the lake at the outline of Rotorua on the far side and it did not seem so distant. I would get there. Mostly, I was lost in thought. Cameos flooded my mind: I am being handed a cup of water by a girl dressed as a fairy in a tutu during the Fox Cities

Marathon in Wisconsin. I am bending down to pick up a discarded glove off the ground in the Hogeye Marathon in Arkansas so that I can keep one hand warm on this freezing-cold day. I am staring back at a crowd of kangaroos who are staring at me from their paddock during the Canberra Bush Capital Marathon. A man doing the race on stilts passes me during a marathon in Luxembourg. I dreamt on and on.

Once, I was brought back to reality when I heard an aid station volunteer telling another volunteer: 'She is running her hundredth marathon.' Then I heard this statement pass down the line of volunteers at that aid table. I was rapt. I wished I could continue to stand there and watch them talking about me. I had always thought of myself as an underachiever, and here I found people awed at what I had done.

I continued on, past the airport. This was a stretch of the marathon I had been dreading. When I ran this marathon in 1997 it seemed to take a long time to get past this airport. When I ran here in 2005 the airport had grown considerably, it seemed to me, and I believed I would never reach the end of it. But today I was steaming past it. One reason was that a plane had just landed and there was a strong smell of jet fuel, which I was anxious to get away from; I had the strength to put in a surge. When you run the Rotorua Marathon it is usually the smell of sulphur that runners worry about, but I had not smelt anything of the local scent.

At the 35-kilometre marker I noticed my friend Jane, from Melbourne, standing by the roadside. I wondered to myself why she was standing there. I knew she was running the marathon — this was her 60th marathon, no less, and a special day — but I didn't know why she was *standing* there. Then I saw she was talking to someone. Initially I couldn't work out who it was. Why was my brain not functioning? And then I realised it was Denis. Denis had run the accompanying ten-kilometre race (a new innovation at this marathon since my 1997 visit has been the introduction of a couple of shorter races to keep the support crews entertained). He had come to the marathon course to see me. Jane had spotted him, told him I was not far behind, and waited for me. I was delighted to have her company for the final kilometres.

Denis handed me three balloons, as part of our pre-arranged plan, and I carried these to the marathon finish. They kept bobbing around and I was constantly fiddling with them. A runner asked, 'Do the balloons help?' I thought to myself that they did — they kept me in a deliriously happy frame of mind. Jane and I chatted, and the remaining kilometres passed. As we reached the outskirts of the town I told her about the fellow in the football socks whom I followed along here in the 1997 race. I could see him ahead of me. But this time I could also see the finish line, and I could not see that during the 1997 race — back then I had not yet experienced a marathon finish line.

I knew that very soon we would make a turn into Te Ngae Road, and from there into the Government Gardens, and from there to the finish line, where my life would be changed forever.

As we turned into the Government Gardens I spied Chris's husband, Tom, who had already finished the marathon. He greeted me. At that point I had just been remembering that episode at school when I lied about running a mile around the playing fields; this little memory entering my consciousness coincided with Bryn Terfel singing the emotion-filled line 'I am dreaming of the mountains of my home' on my iPod, and the tears started to fall. I blurted out to Tom, 'I'm the girl who couldn't finish the mile at school,' but I was sure he could not have understood what I said. There was no need to worry about that now; I was concentrating on the new milestone I was about to reach.

And here was the finishing chute. The moment that I had played and re-played in my head so many times was about to become real. My tears had dried (thankfully, as I didn't want them on my finisher's photo) and I had a surge of extreme happiness as I reached the finish line. I felt the full force of my achievement and savoured the glorious sensation. I had run my hundredth marathon.

I left the finish chute and found Denis behind the barrier. I could only whisper: 'I have done it!'

And then time stood still. I was seeing my earlier visit here. I was hobbling back to the hotel in Rotorua after my first marathon, Denis supporting me because my ankles kept giving way beneath me. I remembered how it felt that afternoon to have run a marathon. I could still hear the teasing about my over-large breakfast the next morning.

I made the right decision to come back here.

Once upon a time I did not know what a marathon was. Then I found out, and I ran one. Before I ran my first marathon it would never have crossed my mind that people run a hundred, or hundreds, of them. I thought that running one marathon was quite enough of a challenge for a person to undertake. I knew barely anyone who had done this. After I succeeded in finishing one marathon I would never have imagined a lifetime was long enough to run a hundred of them.

So I just went on running in my own little way.

I'm not sure when I first decided to aim for a hundred marathons. In Rotorua in 1997 I was overjoyed to finish one marathon. At the Alice Springs Marathon in 2002 I only focused on finishing my tour of the Australian states and territories, and never thought of that as my 13th marathon. My Christchurch marathon in 2004 was a milestone for giving me my personal best rather than for being my 20th marathon. By the time I ran my 30th marathon in Canberra in 2005 I knew I had run a lot of marathons and I would not often meet runners who had completed as many, but I had no idea how many more I would run.

Maybe I tentatively considered the possibility of running a hundred after running my 40th marathon in Feilding, New Zealand. This was where I first met a whole group of runners who had each run over a hundred marathons. But it was a long time before I could see myself getting near to achieving this. With my disastrous run at the Phuket Marathon in 2006 I clocked up 50 marathons and I felt that I might, given sufficient time and low temperatures, be able to do 50 more. It may have been a goal but it was surely still not a realistic one. I never voiced it to anyone. Even at home it was only an unspoken dream of mine.

And then by late 2008, 76 marathons under my belt, it seemed like I could be able to get there. Since completing the Honolulu Marathon in December 2008, a day would not have gone by without me daydreaming about this hundredth marathon — while doing the dishes or unpacking the groceries or sitting in traffic. I envisaged the scene on virtually every training run. I just hoped that nothing would go wrong.

When I was bored I would count the marathons I had yet to run. I had to check and re-check that I was really going to get to a hundred. I would play guessing games with the ones already run, like *Which was number 32? Which was the coldest? How many have I run in hail? Which one had the best aid stations? Which one had the best expo?* I would try to recall what I wore, what I ate afterwards, what I did afterwards. I would make lists of races: how many marathons I have run in cities and how many in the countryside; how many have been a point-to-point course and how many have been one big loop. I would challenge myself to name the marathon I would run if I were only allowed to run one more, and to name the marathon I would be least likely ever to run again. My running has afforded me countless hours of entertainment, even aside from the times when I have raised a sweat.

One day, when I was out on the road participating in my 90th marathon — Lake Tahoe — I had a revelation. I suddenly understood that I was not going to stop at running a hundred of these things. I would want to keep doing it. I told this exciting news to my family. I phoned them specially. 'We always knew that,' they said in unison; 'How can you pretend you have only just realised?'

This marathon in Rotorua was not an ending.

For the first time in six years I did not have another marathon already scheduled. That was a pact I made with myself before this one, so as not to overshadow the occasion. But I knew there would be more marathons — many more. I enjoy this too much to stop. When I'm asked why I run marathons I tell the truth: I love it. And that's a strong enough feeling to ensure I will not be stopping any time soon.

Appendix

My 100 marathons

	Date	Marathon and Location	Finish Time	No. of Finishers
1	3 May 1997	Rotorua Marathon, New Zealand	3:51:38	2,197
2	7 March 1998	New Plymouth Marathon, New Zealand	3:59:08	164
3	24 October 1999	Auckland Marathon, New Zealand	4:07:49	513
4	30 April 2000	Host City Marathon, Sydney, New South Wales, Australia	3:54:35	4,796
5	29 October 2000	Auckland Marathon, New Zealand	3:59:32	934
6	8 April 2001	Canberra Marathon, Australian Capital Territory, Australia	3:36:59	510
7	29 April 2001	Lest We Forget Marathon, Brisbane, Queensland	4:10:15	143
8	8 July 2001	San Francisco Marathon, California, USA	3:51:01	2,249
9	26 August 2001	Adelaide Marathon, South Australia, Australia	3:40:09	226

10	14 October 2001	Melbourne Marathon, Victoria, Australia	3:48:22	1,286
11	6 January 2002	Hobart Marathon, Tasmania, Australia	3:54:29	38
12	14 July 2002	Perth Marathon, Western Australia, Australia	3:50:50	229
13	18 August 2002	Alice Springs Marathon, Northern Territory, Australia	3:45:04	17
14	13 October 2002	Melbourne Marathon, Victoria, Australia	3:48:27	1,487
15	13 April 2003	London Marathon, UK	3:46:51	32,167
16	31 August 2003	Shepparton Marathon, Victoria, Australia	3:31:33	37
17	12 October 2003	Melbourne Marathon, Victoria, Australia	3:36:16	1,534
18	2 November 2003	Portland Marathon, Victoria, Australia	3:36:04	50
19	25 April 2004	Big Sur International Marathon, California, USA	3:34:46	2,858
20	6 June 2004	Christchurch Marathon, New Zealand	3:28:43	310
21	13 June 2004	Traralgon Marathon, Victoria, Australia	3:30:29	54
22	4 July 2004	Gold Coast Marathon, Queensland, Australia	3:41:30	1,841
23	1 August 2004	Townsville Marathon, Queensland, Australia	3:38:25	67
24	22 August 2004	Mudgee Marathon, New South Wales, Australia	3:35:45	39
25	4 September 2004	Christmas Island Marathon, Australian Indian Ocean Territories	3:57:30	3

26	10 October 2004	Melbourne Marathon, Victoria, Australia	3:52:56	1,482
27	17 October 2004	Toowoomba Marathon, Queensland, Australia	3:50:45	23
28	9 January 2005	Hobart Marathon, Tasmania, Australia	3:35:54	49
29	19 March 2005	Thailand Temple Run, Bangkok, Thailand	4:39:39	284
30	10 April 2005	Canberra Marathon, Australian Capital Territory, Australia	3:59:57	785
31	24 April 2005	Brisbane Marathon, Queensland, Australia	3:54:40	118
32	7 May 2005	Rotorua Marathon, New Zealand	3:55:15	1,678
33	4 June 2005	Stockholm Marathon, Sweden	3:47:21	12,701
34	10 July 2005	Pichi Richi Marathon, South Australia, Australia	4:03:09	24
35	21 August 2005	Noumea Marathon, New Caledonia	4:03:00	98
36	28 August 2005	Adelaide Marathon, South Australia, Australia	4:10:44	176
37	11 September 2005	Dunedin Marathon, New Zealand	3:49:45	92
38	9 October 2005	Melbourne Marathon, Victoria, Australia	3:46:16	1,561
39	30 October 2005	Auckland Marathon, New Zealand	3:47:38	1,016
40	12 November 2005	Feilding Marathon, New Zealand	3:48:20	45
41	6 December 2005	Singapore Marathon	4:47:33	5,095

42	11 February 2006	Buller Gorge Marathon, New Zealand	3:52:17	117
43	26 March 2006	Kuching Marathon, Sarawak, Malaysia	4:49:20	80
44	1 April 2006	Queenstown Marathon, New Zealand	3:58:05	78
45	8 April 2006	Canberra Marathon, Australian Capital Territory, Australia	3:55:33	864
46	30 April 2006	Brisbane Marathon, Queensland, Australia	3:52:06	165
47	21 May 2006	Bunbury Marathon, Western Australia, Australia	4:10:23	89
48	28 May 2006	Williamstown Marathon, Victoria, Australia	4:09:57	86
49	11 June 2006	Macleay River Marathon, New South Wales, Australia	4:15:48	61
50	18 June 2006	Phuket Marathon, Thailand	6:13:27	511
51	25 June 2006	Tirol Speed Marathon, Innsbruck, Austria	3:51:26	469
52	30 July 2006	Cities Marathon, Sydney, New South Wales, Australia	3:49:59	95
53	8 October 2006	Melbourne Marathon, Victoria, Australia	3:59:08	1,712
54	5 November 2006	New York City Marathon, New York, USA	3:42:02	37,936
55	11 November 2006	Richmond Marathon, Virginia, USA	3:59:15	2,917
56	3 June 2007	Steamboat Marathon, Colorado, USA	3:58:51	358

57	10 June 2007	North Olympic Discovery Marathon, Washington, USA	3:59:48	405
58	1 July 2007	Gold Coast Marathon, Queensland, Australia	4:47:44	2,628
59	23 September 2007	Fox Cities Marathon, Wisconsin, USA	4:13:24	853
60	30 September 2007	Toronto Waterfront Marathon, Canada	4:39:24	2,040
61	7 October 2007	Chicago Marathon, Illinois, USA	4:42:41	28,815
62	4 November 2007	Riverton to Invercargill Marathon, New Zealand	4:01:31	27
63	5 April 2008	Great Forest Marathon, Levin, New Zealand	4:13:49	74
64	21 April 2008	Boston Marathon, Massachusetts, USA	4:07:22	21,963
65	27 April 2008	Vienna Marathon, Austria	4:07:15	6,204
66	3 May 2008	Europe-Marathon, Luxembourg	4:00:20	1,338
67	25 May 2008	Williamstown Marathon, Victoria, Australia	4:03:51	68
68	14 June 2008	Nordmarka Skogsmaraton, Oslo, Norway	4:13:23	367
69	29 June 2008	Pichi Richi Marathon, South Australia, Australia	4:20:57	30
70	22 August 2008	Wagga Wagga Trail Marathon, New South Wales, Australia	4:03:41	49
71	7 September 2008	Ross Marathon, Tasmania, Australia	4:01:18	15
72	21 September 2008	Sydney Marathon, New South Wales, Australia	4:15:35	1,923

73	28 September 2008	Warsaw Marathon, Poland	4:21:05	2,638
74	5 October 2008	Marathon Provence Luberon, France	4:22:35	339
75	12 October 2008	Melbourne Marathon, Victoria, Australia	4:11:35	3,326
76	14 December 2008	Honolulu Marathon, Hawaii, USA	4:50:59	20,058
77	14 February 2009	Buller Gorge Marathon, New Zealand	4:01:05	161
78	22 March 2009	Tokyo Marathon, Japan	4:17:54	29,108
79	5 April 2009	Hogeye Marathon, Arkansas, USA	4:06:52	130
80	12 April 2009	Canberra Marathon, Australian Capital Territory, Australia	4:13:30	1,167
81	10 May 2009	Prague Marathon, Czech Republic	4:08:41	3,976
82	17 May 2009	Marathon de la Baie du Mont Saint-Michel, France	4:12:03	4,928
83	24 May 2009	Wuerzburg Marathon, Germany	4:11:54	902
84	14 June 2009	Traralgon Marathon, Victoria, Australia	4:04:15	37
85	28 June 2009	Pichi Richi Marathon, South Australia, Australia	4:27:35	49
86	5 July 2009	Perth Marathon, Western Australia, Australia	4:10:55	430
87	25 July 2009	Bush Capital Bush Marathon, Canberra, Australian Capital Territory, Australia	4:21:51	35
88	30 August 2009	Shepparton Marathon, Victoria, Australia	4:03:55	41

89	6 September 2009	Ross Marathon, Tasmania, Australia	4:15:17	20
90	27 September 2009	Lake Tahoe Marathon, California, USA	4:25:56	398
91	3 October 2009	St George Marathon, Utah, USA	3:58:50	5,618
92	4 October 2009	Sacramento Cowtown Marathon, California, USA	4:30:07	326
93	11 October 2009	Melbourne Marathon, Victoria, Australia	4:35:31	3,706
94	8 November 2009	Marysville Marathon, Victoria, Australia	4:45:19	87
95	29 November 2009	Lake Kawaguchi Marathon, Japan	4:26:27	7,374
96	24 January 2010	Carlsbad Marathon, California, USA	4:28:30	1,194
97	13 March 2010	Catalina Island Marathon, California, USA	4:35:48	564
98	21 March 2010	Los Angeles Marathon, California, USA	4:19:11	22,403
99	27 March 2010	Yakima River Canyon Marathon, Washington, USA	4:15:53	530
100	1 May 2010	Rotorua Marathon, New Zealand	4:31:07	1,702

The details regarding the number of finishers has been taken from information supplied by race organisers, from various internet and hard-copy sources, and from my own records. They are accurate to the best of my knowledge.

Index